No Dancin' in Anson

No Dancin' in Anson

An American Story
of Race and Social Change

Ricardo C. Ainslie, Ph.D.

JASON ARONSON INC.
Northvale, New Jersey
London

This book was set in 10 pt. New Century Schoolbook by Alpha Graphics of Pittsfield, New Hampshire and printed and bound by Book-mart of North Bergen, New Jersey.

Library of Congress Cataloging-in-Publication Data

Ainslie, Ricardo.
No dancin' in Anson : an American story of race and social change / by Ricardo C. Ainslie.
p.cm.
Includes bibliographical references (p.) and index.
ISBN 1-56821-585-1 (acid-free paper)
1. Ethnology–Texas–Anson. 2. Racism–Texas–Anson. 3. Race discrimination–Texas–Anson. 4. Anson (Tex.)–Ethnic relations.
5. Anson (Tex.)–Social conditions. I. Title.
F394.A56A56 1995
305.8'009764'733–dc20   95-18805

Manufactured in the United States of America. Jason Aronson Inc. offers books and cassettes. For information and catalog write to Jason Aronson Inc., 230 Livingston Street, Northvale, New Jersey 07647.

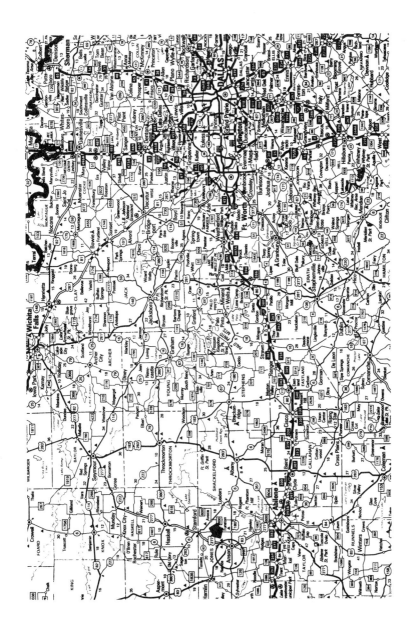

o VERONICA
GARCIA

o MIDDLEBROOK'S

ANSON, TEXAS

TO GARCIA'S →

COUNTY JAIL

OPERA HOUSE

JONES COUNTY COURT HOUSE

FEED STORE

o TORRES

ANSON CITY HALL

o DOMINO HALL

BEA's CAFE'

ANSON HIGH SCHOOL

TO RAMOSVILLE 3 MI. ←

ANSON CHURCH OF CHRIST ✝

✝ FIRST BAPTIST CHURCH OF ANSON

HATAHOE DRIVE IN

o OLD PIONEER HALL

OKLAHOMA 175 MI.

N

BROWNING'S
o

ANSON'S CATHOLIC CHURCH ✝

DALLAS FT. WORTH 295 MI. →

W —◇— E

EL PASO 360 MI.

S

AUSTIN 258 MI.

ABILENE 23 MI.

TO TRUBY CHURCH OF CHRIST 7 MILES ←

In memory of
Nancy Ozee Croxdale:
always a West Texas girl at heart
who took good care of me
during my years in exile

Contents

Part III–A Hollow Victory

Preface

Throughout the writing of this book I experienced a recurring image: the scene is early morning in a primeval landscape. The terrain is hilly, and the hills are skirted with a light fog creating a feeling of inchoate mystery. A cluster of people, walking through the only geography known to them, reaches a ridge, where, across a small valley, they encounter for the first time a mirror of themselves. Off in the distance is another clan whose search for food has brought them into unknown territory. The two clans face one another. Prior to this fateful encounter, each clan's experience of itself has been governed by that ubiquitous egocentric penchant for viewing one's group as the only genuine representation of humanity—"The People" or "The Race" as anthropologists have so often observed. Now, as the clan gazes across the foggy expanse, it is equally governed by that other ubiquitous human penchant, namely, to view the Other as a source of anxiety, as threat, as evil, as danger.

Like every living organism, the clan's first and foremost interest is its own survival. Thus, two primitive instincts infuse the experience of the moment: territoriality and the question of who has access to, and control of, scarce resources needed if one's group was to endure; and, secondly, the question of sexuality—who might destabilize the delicate alchemy of reproduction, thereby threatening the continued existence of the group.

This presumed encounter contains, in derivative form, many of the elements with which we continue to struggle in today's

tortured world of ethnic difference—a world all too often characterized by hatreds, deep mistrust, and anxiety. It is evident
that prejudice is as universal as it is destructive and dehumanizing. Powerful psychological processes, which complicate human relations immeasurably, are at work in the arena of ethnic and cultural difference. Perhaps most important among
these is the pull of known worlds (psychological worlds, cultural
worlds) that complicates the ways we engage people whom we
experience as different, as Other. We want to stay within the
familiar, and we often experience anxiety when our links to it
are threatened. These links are deep, organizing psychological
forces for all human beings. The processes that make the familiar so essential to our psychological well-being thus play a pivotal role in our engagement of the Other, whose very existence
may represent a threat to our self-cohesion. Ethnic prejudice
plays on these fears, utilizes them, and is constructed from them.
This book is best conceived as a series of meditations on the
problematic nature of otherness in our lives.

    In the spring of 1987, the little town of Anson, a small farm-
ing and ranching community in West Texas, experienced a major
upheaval. A group of parents petitioned the Anson city council
to repeal a city ordinance that made public dances within the
city limits illegal. The parents had but one concern in mind: they
wanted their teenagers to have a safe, chaperoned prom for their
graduation at the high school. The idea of a prom dance, which
in most American communities would have been absolutely
ordinary, stirred the deepest passions in Anson, dividing church
congregations, neighbors, and even families. My first visit to
Anson occurred just as the battle between the pro- and anti-
dancing forces had reached full pitch. It had not been my intention to study this conflict; indeed I had been totally unaware
of it prior to my arrival, but I quickly understood that it represented considerably more than a difference of opinion as to
whether dancing constituted a sin, as some of its opponents

believed. The conflict was a piece of symbolic action representing immense underlying tensions within this community. Further, it provided a natural channel of expression for these tensions.

Prior to 1964, when Congress passed the Civil Rights Act,
Anson, like the rest of the South, was a community strictly segregated along racial lines under Texas's Jim Crow laws. This
circumstance changed quickly following the passage of the Civil
Rights Act. When I first arrived in Anson, little more than two
decades after the demise of the Jim Crow laws, Anson was
roughly 35 percent non-white. Every local who was old enough
could readily remember the "Whites Only" signs in the windows
of local restaurants and the segregated seating in the now defunct picture show. Although change had been in the air in
Anson for over two decades, Anson's dance fight seemed as root-
less as it did spontaneous. It felt to many in the community that
the events had suddenly come upon them with little warning.
In actuality, the points of tension had been steadily gathering
momentum for decades, and the resulting conflagration cut to
the very heart of the community.

In the first portion of this book, the story of Anson's dance
fight as a community event reveals a more latent meaning,
namely, a community's struggle with social and economic
change, ethnic difference, and prejudice. In the remainder of the
book, Anson's dance fight becomes a vehicle for an exploration
of more personal, individual encounters with the questions of
ethnic difference, prejudice, and social change. I will show the
psychological mechanisms at work in our encounters with otherness through the lives of individuals who have been the object of prejudice, individuals who have had to come to terms with
the meaning of their own prejudiced feelings, and the fate of individuals who have taken it upon themselves to change their
community. I believe that the complex psychodynamics of ethnic difference reflected in the Anson life-stories are illustrative
of more universal challenges. Indeed, I argue that the mechanisms at work in prejudice are alive in each of us.

This last may be considered a bold and unsettling statement. Worse, it may suggest to some that I am diluting the perniciousness of prejudice by normalizing it. That is not my intent. On the contrary, the book illustrates the deeply destructive nature of prejudice as well as the difficulty with which such feelings are relinquished.

Clifford Geertz (1973), the cultural anthropologist, notes that small facts speak to large issues. It is through the flow of human behavior, or social actions, that cultural forms find articulation. The conflict that erupted in Anson, a small community seemingly far removed from the main crossroads of American culture, mirrors the struggles that the rest of America faces over the questions of ethnicity and cultural diversity.* In this book I explore some of the forces that make cultural change difficult for all of us, as well as examine the psychological processes at work in ethnic and other forms of prejudice. I view these two topics as intertwined. That is, cultural forms define those who occupy the position of Other in every social group. Therefore, cultural transformation typically has implications for how the Other is constructed. The same is true in its reciprocal; efforts to redefine the nature of otherness have implications for culture itself.

My approach will make some readers uncomfortable. Some of the individuals whose lives I describe, dyed-in-the-wool rac-

---

*Recently, in a series of exchanges in the *American Psychologist* (1995), numerous contributors made clear the confusion within the social sciences about the concept of race. This confusion is reflected in the awkwardness of the vocabulary available to describe different members of the human species, a vocabulary that variously uses "skin color (black, red, yellow, white), continental origin (African, Asian), anthropological designation (Caucasian), or colonial history (Latino)" (Dole 1995) as points of reference. Similarly, in an article that set off this exchange (Yee et al. 1993), the authors point to the lack of a consensus among scientists as to what constitutes appropriate definitions of racial categories. For the most part, I use the terms *race* and *ethnicity* interchangeably in this book, although, following Montagu and others, I have a preference for *ethnicity* because of its cultural implications as opposed to the biological, genetic connotations of *race*.

ists for example, turn out to be people whose humanity is nevertheless discernible. I will show that cultural change is often difficult and painful, even for those who seem to be moving closer to the elusive American Dream. In short, my portrayal of this charged subject matter veers away from the ideological in the direction of what I hope is a more three-dimensional examination of the complex relations among individuals who differ from one another in terms of ethnicity, class, and, at times, language.

My exploration of the diverse issues addressed in this book is suggestive, rather than comprehensive or exhaustive. My intent has been to engage the reader in a reflection upon issues that I believe affect all of us, and within a medium that brings these issues to life—namely, the story of Anson's dance fight and the life-narratives that focus on individuals and families within this community.

A few words about method. Geertz (1973) notes that "man is an animal suspended in webs of significance he himself has spun" (p. 5). The webs are cultural structures that give our lives meaning. The exploration of these webs, the effort to understand them, requires an intimate engagement with the events and actions that carry their meaning. This is what Geertz, citing Ryle, calls "thick description." As a method, it presupposes a kind of detailed or extensive immersion: the exploration of cultural gestures.

Thick description is what we make of what we see. However, methodologically, it is derived from the principles that guide ethnographic field work in anthropology. Within ethnography, the requirement of simultaneous immersion in one's subject matter while maintaining a degree of detachment and the requirement of empathic, sensitive attunement side by side with healthy, constructive skepticism and critical reflection are commonplace. The tensions produced by this methodological imperative are also quite familiar to psychoanalysts. The settings differ—such as Geertz's study of Balinese cockfighting versus the analytic couch–but at its best (that is, when not formulaic or reductionist) psychoanalytic understanding, like ethnographic thick description, comes from the richness of intimate observation. Both rely on narrative to give coherence and to build understanding.

For this reason, I have approached the subject of this book with a methodology approach that relies on an amalgam of ethnographic and psychoanalytic method. In addition to the work of Clifford Geertz, I draw heavily from memories of George Rosenwald's seminars at the University of Michigan and what he terms life-history research. The work of Robert Coles has also been an important model for me, as has that of Oscar Lewis (who is really the inspiration for the notion of psychological ethnography, despite the problems he encountered with it). Ultimately, this work rests with those traditions in which narrative is the centerpiece of method. The book relies heavily on the story of social conflict within a struggling community, as well as the individual portraits of those people who struggled with the issue of social change and ethnic prejudice.

Because it is what I know best, the vocabulary from which I draw is primarily that of psychoanalysis, a language of the interplay between conscious and unconscious conflicts, a language of desire, anxiety, and defense. However, there are broader issues that escape intrapsychic formulation in the traditional sense and veer into social and cultural spheres within which psychoanalysis has all too often dissolved into truncated voice, reification, or reduction. I have tried to avoid such pitfalls, knowing, however, that any effort to explain, to articulate, quickly finds its object to be all the more elusive, like the wakened dreamer who attempts to capture with words the powerful, suggestive, nuanced contents of a dream, only to end with a partial rendering, an approximation that falls short of the thing itself. I know that my account is incomplete, or, as Geertz says is characteristic of all ethnographic accounts: "essentially contestable." Thus, while this work is perhaps best characterized as an example of applied psychoanalysis, that is, the application of psychoanalytic concepts and, to some extent, psychoanalytic methods outside of the clinical situation, it is a project that is truly interdisciplinary in spirit.

Most important, however, this book is simple story-telling. I have a great deal of faith in narrative as method, and the heart of this book lies in the narratives that the people I interviewed were willing to create with me. My greatest challenge was the structuring of the stories–trying to figure out how to bring these individual lives into some kind of coherence in a narrative that reflected my subjects' humanity while also conveying my understanding of what I saw and heard.

I made nine trips to Anson between the spring of 1987 and the winter of 1992. Over the course of these trips I tape recorded formal interviews with more than sixty people. Many of these subjects I interviewed extensively; others I interviewed only once. I chose many of my subjects because they had played a part in the events that were unfolding within their community, or because they had a distinct perspective on Anson's dancing controversy or related issues. I chose to interview some people simply because I found them interesting, or because I was referred to them by other people in the community. I interviewed people whom I initially met at Bea's Steak House, the Hatahoe Diner, the cotton gin, the domino hall, or elsewhere in Anson. The interviews do not constitute a random selection, by any stretch of the imagination.

I know that my presence shaped this project, which, in a postmodern world, is stating the obvious. In addition to this now-common understanding of the interactive and subjective nature of all interpretation, I am also thinking about this in a specifically psychoanalytic sense. In psychoanalysis transference refers to the psychological processes by which patients transfer onto their analysts feelings—hopes, fears, desires—that are important and meaningful to the understanding of their lives. In this sense, patients "use" their analysts who become, usually transiently, props on the patients' psychological landscape.

At times, I felt a similar process at work in Anson. Once, an elderly woman opened her door when I arrived unannounced to interview her. "You must be *that* man," was how she greeted me. It was clear that she had heard an earful about me already. Similarly, a rumor of unknown origin made the rounds to the effect that my study was funded by Harvard University. (When I first heard it I wondered if this was a compliment or the kiss of death.) On more than one occasion I received later calls from people I had interviewed in Anson: "Ricardo, my wife and I have been talking about your visit and there's something we've decided you really need to know. . . . "

In other words, Ricardo Ainslie became a peculiar presence in this community, with people bringing varied personal motivations, interests, or, as one would say clinically, transference-based fantasies about me and my project, to our interviews. At times, these considerations emerged in the guise of normal human vanity, like Janet Malcolm's commentary regarding the dynamics at work in journalistic interviews. ("I don't flatter myself to think that you might use this, but you might keep it among your notes," read one letter, appended to a photograph of the person in question, which had been sent along with some material that he thought–correctly–might be of interest to me). At other times, there were people who were anxious that they might reveal too much, or that I might misuse their interviews.

People in the community talked about me. They shared stories about their interviews with one another and wondered what I was about and what my intentions were. It became clear to me that there were individuals in Anson who wanted their story to be told, and I was the vehicle for those wishes. More than that, there were instances where it was evident that for some people I was serving an interest, I was part of an agenda. Admittedly, I could not always discern that this was the case, though I always tried to be cognizant of this as a possible motive in what people said to me. In short, my book is embedded in the stories people told me—stories about themselves, stories about each other—that had all sorts of personal motivations behind them. Some might view this as a source of distortion or error. I view it as human nature.

There is another way in which I have shaped this project. The impetus for my work in West Texas was personal. I grew up, the son of a Mexican father and an American mother, speaking English in a Mexican world, speaking Spanish in an American world. As a child I had a keen sense for the border; I must have crossed it one hundred times as we flew or drove to visit my mother's family in Texas. The contrast between these two worlds is obvious, but for me there was something almost palpable in the crossing. All of those things we so loosely cluster under the term *culture* impinged directly upon my senses. I always carried two passports, each a kind of magic key to enter its corresponding world. And, always, the feeling I had as I entered one or the other country was of a bit of disingenuousness—hiding one part of my identity from the official examining the documents that certified the other.

I found the interviews in Anson to be a complex psychological experience. I often felt torn–allied, if in different ways, with many of the people I interviewed despite the fact that they were at odds with other people I'd interviewed. In this way an archaic experience was reproduced for me, an experience that is in part the product of my mixed cultural heritage. It is this background that also led me to concentrate exclusively on Anson's white and Mexican-American population, perhaps thereby reproducing one of the principal theses of the book.

Whatever the drawbacks, this biculturalism afforded me a particular advantage as I interviewed people from both sides of the proverbial tracks in Anson, Texas. Nearly all of them (with a few notable exceptions) seemed open to talking to me. Indeed, I was sometimes taken by surprise by the things people volunteered to tell me about their lives. Away from my consulting room, where I am accustomed to hearing intimate personal stories, I had not anticipated this kind of candor. For me, perhaps the greatest lesson of this book is that all people, not only patients, have a strong wish to talk, to be known, to be understood.

It is obvious that the issues addressed in this book have personal meaning for me, and, no doubt this meaning has infiltrated my interviews and the way in which I shaped them. However, I also believe that my personal connection to the book has afforded me unique access to the worlds that are its core. The truth is that most of the people I interviewed, regardless of their backgrounds, were open and forthright with me. Whatever the considerations that fostered such confidence in me, I am honored and grateful for it.

Acknowledgments

This project extended over several years, from my initial, tentative interviews with an Anson expatriate to the final editing for publication. Duncan Osborn first oriented me toward the little community that had been his childhood refuge. It was Duncan who set up my initial interview in Anson, and offered me the unlimited use of his Jones County ranch house, rattlesnake-infested though it was. Thus, the Osborn interviews were quite serendipitous, opening up an unanticipated universe, which at first intrigued, and ultimately consumed.

Jim Magnuson and Steve Harrigan are veteran writers whose support, critical readings, and, most of all, faith, have been indispensable to me. Steve's margin notes ("I love Jack Hornsby") and readiness to consult or console have left me indebted to him. Similarly, Jim's reliable eagerness to hear tales upon my return from excursions into deep West Texas, and suggestions for overcoming various structural and tactical problems, were continuously sustaining. José Limón has been an indispensable resource, consultant, and friend. Greg Curtis's interest in this project also deserves appreciative mention. I also wish to warmly acknowledge Betty Sue Flowers for her helpful comments on an early draft.

Nancy Scanlan, my photographer, made a wonderful contribution to the project. I am most appreciative of her work and her technical skill. She has a real knack for making her photographic subjects feel at ease.

Gemma, Roberto, and Gabriella, my wife and children, de-
serve special gratitude for enduring my various obsessions, of
which this is but one. They have been good sports, even to the
point of accompanying me to West Texas during cherished
spring breaks to witness rattlesnake roundups and to visit my
friends in Anson, many of whom they had learned to love even
before meeting them.

Guy and Jane Manaster have been steady, wonderfully dedicated supporters. Joy Bohmfalk was a true gem, bringing her
full editorial and computer skills to bear, not to mention her
considerable enthusiasm for the book. Bob and MJ Prall were
helpful with the earliest draft of this book.

I wish to thank the University of Texas' Office of Special
Research Grants for its generous support. Numerous research
assistants have helped with library work, including Nancy
Cunningham, Alison Halliday, and Kathleen Holland; I especially wish to acknowledge Jennifer Covich in this regard. I also
wish to thank the University of Texas for its grant support,
which covered a portion of the transcription expenses.

Finally, I want to thank Duke Robillard (the *Too Hot To
Handle* Robillard), T-Bone Walker, SRV, the ARC Angels,
Buddy Guy, Albert Collins, Albert and Freddie King, The Black
Crowes *(Bad luck blue eyes)*, Ian Moore *(Satisfied),* and, in a
more anthropological vein, Randy Travis (the *Storms of Life*
Travis), as well as all the others who provided a constant, abso-
lutely indispensable, medium for the mysterious processes that
operate when shaping words into stories.

" . . . to rework the pattern of social relationships is to rearrange the coordinates of the experience of the world."

—Clifford Geertz

I

THE
COLLECTIVE
WORLD

1

A Storm upon "The Big Country"

My proposal to the special grants office at the University of Texas stated, in dry academic terms, that I was interested in understanding the subjective experience of cultural transformation. I planned to explore the changing culture of rural Texas, where the reality of the post-Civil Rights Era translated into awkward engagements between peoples whose lives had once represented virtually irreconcilable corners of the social universe. Slightly more than two-and-a-half decades ago these communities had existed under the South's Jim Crow laws, which maintained a strict apartheid-like social structure. While the attitudes and emotions that were once codified in those laws may not have changed as quickly as hoped, history has significantly altered the proportions of that social geography. I had in mind a series of extended, semi-clinical interviews, distilling from them an image of the psychic hardship that frequently accompanies personal and social change, as well as the adaptive resourcefulness with which individuals and communities can at times greet new challenges. It seemed like a tidy scholarly project.

However, the truth is that at the time I was only vaguely aware of what I was looking for in the small town of Anson, situated near Abilene in the heart of what is known as "The Big

Country." At best I recognized only dimly that what I was setting out to do was more personal than that little grant proposal
could confide. Having been born of a Texan mother and a Mexican father, having lived my life within two cultural worlds that
at times could seem irreducibly alien from one another, the
extent to which I had a very personal stake in the questions I
was about to explore now seems embarrassingly obvious. However, the fact is that as I drove out of Austin headed for my initial visit to Anson, Texas, I had only the vaguest outline in mind
as to what I was hoping to accomplish or why. Such is the nature
of the unconscious.

The choice of Anson was purely a matter of convenience. A
friend who was a native of Anson had offered the use of his ranch
house, which was a few miles out of town. He had also set up
my only scheduled interview with a man named Dave Reves, a
retired Jones County sheriff. Heading northwest out of Austin
in my fading 1984 Volvo, I was driving out of my known world,
headed for the vast expanse of West Texas. Beyond the comforts
of Austin's urban familiarity, the open road descended upon me
with a rush.

I found the turnoff to the ranch the next afternoon. As indicated on my detailed instructions, a weathered, rusty cattle gate
recessed a few yards from the two-lane farm-to-market road was
the only marker indicating the entry. The cattle were impervious as I opened the gate. It occurred to me that they might
storm the gate in a frantic bid for freedom, but they just stared.
I pulled my car through, got out again, and closed the gate behind me. After another gate opening and closing, I made it to
the little two-bedroom ranch house. It was once a rural family's
home, now a city-dweller's link to his past. The sun had begun
to set, giving the western-facing windows a golden hue that
complemented the fading lime-green house. Inside, the floors
creaked at my every step. The house had an enveloping simplicity, with its inexpensive but comfortable furnishings, al-

though it seemed more suited to a group of exhausted hunters who have spent their day trying to outsmart wild turkey than to a farmer or rancher with a different tie to the land.

After unpacking, I left the house and took a walk down toward a cluster of live oaks. Although it was only late spring, the prairie grass was knee-high and already dried to a dull yellow. On my way back to the house, where some wooden slats covering the crawl space under the house had fallen, I spotted a rattlesnake curled up beneath the water faucet. Anyone reaching for the faucet would have been in for an unpleasant surprise. With darkness approaching, and not so much as a rock to be found in this smooth West Texas soil, I went into the house and hoped for the best.

The back door opened onto a screened porch that extended the entire width of the house. I could imagine, as I took up one of the rocking chairs, a family retiring there after supper, being replenished by the breezes that were steady and firm on this particular evening. It was then that I realized for the first time that I was truly alone. As I scanned the horizon in every direction there was not a single sign of human life—no houses, no flickering lights, no sounds except for the wind rustling through the brush and prairie grass. And then the last embers of sunlight suddenly vanished and a deep darkness descended. Its abruptness and intensity took me quite by surprise.

The coyotes, wind, and thoughts about the rattlesnake I had seen kept me up a good bit of that night. The next morning I made myself a pot of coffee, went back through the multiple cattle gates, and drove the seven or so miles into Anson for my first interview with Dave Reves, the retired sheriff.

In 1851, the federal government established Fort Phantom, in what is now the southern edge of Jones County, to safeguard the passage of adventurers in search of gold in California from bands of Indians, especially Comanches, who still roamed West Texas. The fort was soon abandoned, after which it became a stop on the Butterfield stage coach route. Finally, in the 1870s cattlemen started moving their herds into Jones County in search of free grazing land. The first settlers did not begin arriving until 1880. From very meager beginnings at the close of the nineteenth century, Anson, the county seat, evolved into a prosperous, thriving community. (Anson Jones, for whom the city and county are named, was the last president of the Republic of Texas.) By the 1920s Jones County had more than one hundred schools. A farmer could support his family on as little as a half-section of land (320 acres), which meant that the entire county was dotted with family homes every half-mile or so. Each of these families came to Anson or other towns in the county like Tuxedo, Leuders, Noodle, Stamford, and Hawley, to purchase goods, to get haircuts, or to eat a meal cooked by someone else. Anson had several banks, dry-goods stores, and, by the 1950s, numerous car dealerships, as well as a movie house and an ice-skating rink. On Saturday afternoons people were elbow to elbow along Commercial Street and in the square around the courthouse.

The days when Anson was the vibrant hub of a thriving Jones County were gone now, a distant memory. The transformation of this community had been gradual at first and subtle—the canaries in the proverbial coal mine appeared content enough. Then, in the 1960s, the forces of change struck sharply and with surprising suddenness. There were two factors at work, one economic, the other social.

Modern farming methods had ushered in the use of complex farm machinery that made the need for farmhands virtually obsolete. In the case of cotton farming, the economic base of Jones County, chemicals were used to kill the weeds that competed with the cotton. Other chemicals could freeze off the leaves of the cotton plant as it neared maturity, preparing it for the big reaping machines that could pluck the cotton bolls from the plants. The influx of migrant labor, for many years a prominent feature of life in West Texas farming communities, came to a halt. And most of the year-'round hands who historically were more or less permanent employees on the farms were let go.

Farming had become a one-person operation for all practical purposes. However, the machinery was expensive, fifty to eighty thousand dollars for a single tractor, not to mention the myriad sophisticated attachments that the farmer also needed for plowing, seeding, fertilizing, and stripping. It was typical for a farmer to have two or three hundred thousand dollars worth of equipment. This investment did not include the cost of seed, fertilizer, herbicides, and fuel. Many farmers also had to pay leases to the owners of the land they cultivated, or mortgages on their own lands, and none of these expenses included the costs of supporting their own families.

Advanced farming methods required that more acres had to be planted because the law of economies of scale meant that expensive machinery had to be kept in almost continuous operation to make it economically feasible to buy it. For every additional acre that was planted, the cost of the machinery was spread that much further. Every cotton farmer's dream was a bale of cotton (500 pounds) per acre, but in reality 300 pounds was considered a decent year. At fifty cents per pound (the present day price), that did not leave much of a margin, especially when one took into account the extent to which these farmers were leveraged.

However, the social changes experienced by this community, interwoven though they were with these economic changes, were even more striking. Anson, like the rest of the South, was a community once strictly segregated along racial lines. While many non-whites had lived on the surrounding ranches and farms, few non-white residents lived within the city of Anson, a circumstance that changed quickly after the passage of the Civil Rights Act in 1964. The "Whites Only" signs had come down from local drugstores, diners, and cafés, and segregated seating was no longer officially enforced in the only movie theater. However, the pre-civil rights social order lived on in the collective memory of the town and in the lives of those who recognized it in the countless derivative forms those attitudes and social processes took in the post-civil rights era.

The demographic statistics offer a telling portrait of the radical transformation experienced by Anson's residents in the short
interval between 1964 and 1990, the latest census. As a direct
consequence of the mechanization of farming in this part of
Texas,[1] between 1960 and 1970 Jones County lost nearly 17
percent of its population (from 19,299 in 1960 to 16,106 in 1970),[2]
a loss that has never been recouped (the county's current population, according to 1990 census figures, is 16,490). The city of
Anson also lost nearly 10 percent of its population during this
interval. However, while the population of Anson has remained
stable since 1970 (the 1990 census lists it as 2,644, reflecting
an increase of only 2 percent from the 1970 census figures),
Anson's ethnic composition has changed substantially. Its
African-American population has remained constant at 4 percent over the last two census counts (1980 and 1990). The
Mexican-American population, however, has increased from approximately 8 percent in 1965 to 21 percent in 1980 and 30 percent in 1990. Thus, Anson's minority population had mush-
roomed to nearly 35 percent in the short interval between 1965
and 1990.

However, these figures do not tell the full story. The 10 percent drop in Anson's population between 1960 and 1970 reflects
an emigration of Anson's white residents, mostly defunct cotton
farmers and their families seeking economic refuge in Texas's
urban centers. In addition, Anson's present white population
actually consists of a blend of long-time residents and relatively
new arrivals—individuals who have moved there to take posi-

---

1. For an excellent account of the social and political impact of changes in
agricultural methods on the relationship between Mexican-Americans and
whites in rural and urban Texas see David Montejano's *Anglos and Mexicans
in the Making of Texas, 1836-1986*. As Montejano's account makes clear, the
changes transpiring in Anson were taking place throughout Texas's rural
farming communities.
2. All census data reported as summarized in 1970, 1980, and 1990 U.S. Department of Commerce, Economics and Statistics Administration, Bureau of
the Census reports.

tions in the city or county government, married locals, come to work at one of Anson's small service or manufacturing concerns, or chosen to retire there. My estimate is that Anson had lost approximately 50 percent of its white "natives" in the twenty-seven year interval between 1960 and my first visit in 1987.

In a community of a few thousand people, where virtually everyone knows everyone else, these departures have not been mere statistics. In almost every instance they represent the loss of someone known—a family whose child played on your child's Little League team, the checker at the grocery store, a member of your church. It is members of the known, experienced community who have left, intimate friends or acquaintances, but not strangers. Whites and nonwhites have moved into the community in significant numbers to fill some of the vacancies left by those Ansonites who have sought their fortunes elsewhere. In short, Anson, Texas, as a community, has been radically reconfigured in the span of two decades, and the changes in its ethnic composition have played a central role in that reconfiguration.

Social changes of this magnitude have repercussions for everyone living in a community. Although they may have hit Anson's residents differentially—say a white farmer trying to stay afloat economically, as opposed to a Mexican-American couple trying to raise their children in town after generations of following crops across the country—everyone in Anson, rich or poor, white or non white, was struggling to come to terms with this new reality. Thus, Anson was rich and fertile ground for a psychological examination of the complexity of ethnic relations.

If different in their particulars, the immense changes experienced by the community of Anson reflect similar changes that the entire country has experienced within that same interval. The 1990 census reveals that, despite previous waves of immigration, America has never before been so diverse (Roberts 1993). Hispanics are now 9 percent of the population, an increase of 53 percent over the 1980 census. The number of African-

Americans has increased by 13 percent to constitute 12 percent of the population. Asians have doubled their numbers in that same time period and now account for 3 percent of America's population. Sam Roberts, the *New York Times* urban affairs columnist, notes in his book, *Who We Are: A Portrait of America Based on the Latest U. S. Census,* that American demographic trends are unmistakably in the direction of a shrinking white majority. These trends are even more striking regionally. In the Pacific states, for example, one in five Americans is foreign born. In 186 of America's 3,141 counties, "minorities" (Blacks, Hispanics, Asian-Americans and other groups which, individually, are still regarded as minorities) now actually constitute the majority, suggesting, according to Roberts (1993), "what the nation as a whole may look like around the middle of the twenty-first century" (p. 7).

Although whites constitute approximately 75 percent of America's residents, in many major cities such as greater Los Angeles, Miami, San Antonio, El Paso, and Honolulu, minorities actually represent more than 50 percent of the population. In many other cities including Memphis, greater Houston, Albuquerque, Fresno, California; Jackson, Mississippi; Columbus, Georgia; whites account for just over 50 percent of the population. These trends are especially salient across the South and Southwest, the area where states have shown the greatest growth in population over the past decade. (In New Mexico, for example, whites constitute only half of the state's population.) In these two regions of the country, blacks and Hispanics now represent a significant proportion of the population in most counties, and in many instances they represent the majority (Roberts 1993).

Nevertheless, despite these significant demographic shifts, in broad swaths of urban America it is still possible to hide from the social transformations that are taking place throughout the country. The suburban housewife can exist within the known territory of her neighborhood with its schools, shopping malls, and restaurants, and never engage anyone of a different race or culture except within the structured and mediated parameters of commercial exchange. The clerk at the grocery store may be black, the gardener may be Mexican, the waitress Chinese, and so forth, but rarely do these encounters enter the realm of personal social engagement. Similarly, a Cuban immigrant may live within the envelope of Miami's Little Havana (and there are corresponding enclaves for immigrants of countless nationalities in every major metropolitan area) where his Cuban cultural milieu has been reproduced virtually in its entirety, from the groceries available at the corner market, to the festivals celebrated at his church, or the newspaper he reads and the television and radio programming that air in his home. All of these cultural props may fall within the specific wavelength of that immigrant's known culture, perpetuating a sense of the world that is familiar and comforting, while simultaneously buffering and insulating him from the broader American culture within which he lives.

Personal social interactions with individuals of other ethnic and social groups tend to be unusual, the exception. Truly meaningful encounters are rare. It is not only possible, but normative in America (in the world, really) to float within subcommunities defined by ethnicity and social class, rarely encountering the Other to any substantive degree. While ethnic and social prejudices play potent roles in creating this reality, it is also true that as a species we seem to be most comfortable navigating known and familiar currents. Typically, it is only at the margins of our social groupings that opportunities to encounter difference present themselves or are sought. Hence the traditional venues of the arts and sports, for example, where such encounters with others are common and perhaps even encouraged. But these are rarefied social engagements by virtue of their taking place within cultural enclaves that are socially privileged. Within mainstream America, even when schools or employment seem integrated, social realities often adhere to the age-old practices of segregated lives. The phenomenon of the "glass ceiling" (Davidson and Cooper 1992), which sociologists have noted with regard to the vertical ascent of women and minorities within the work place, is every bit as present within the context of lateral social relations between different ethnic or racial groups. In these social relations there exists a kind of invisible but readily discernable demarcation, a "Plexiglass wall" if you will, that holds us in place (a place by turns chosen and imposed) in our ethnic and social groupings.

Notwithstanding its evident differences—its remoteness, its agricultural base, its small-town, decidedly Texan stamp—Anson's social and, to a lesser extent, economic struggles reflect America's. The particulars may vary from community to community, but America's changing ethnic character is incontestable. Anson's social transformation is emblematic of similar changes being experienced in communities throughout the country. The people who constitute America are changing and these developments must, in turn, influence what America becomes.

We are quite familiar by now with formulations regarding racism and its pernicious effects. That racism is a pervasive reality, that it translates into truncated possibilities in the lives of its victims are accepted facts. Is there something new to be said regarding this unfortunate feature of human nature? Can these waters be plumbed for fresh insights that might take us beyond the established truisms? These questions took shape in my mind as I subsequently reflected on the lives of the people I encountered in Anson, Texas.

Jones County is not the cactus-studded, arid landscape of popular Texas depictions. This is primarily cotton farming country, with a few cattle ranchers and a number of small manufacturing concerns. Following the Second World War, oil made a relatively brief splash on the economic landscape, making a few people rich quickly, but most of the oil has played itself out in this part of Texas. Wildcatters no longer search out lands to lease, and many of the oil rigs that once dotted the Big Country landscape, at least in Jones County, have been capped; it now costs more to extract the oil than it would bring in today's market.

On this late spring morning, as I headed into town for my first meeting with Dave Reves, the highway was almost devoid of traffic. The surrounding cotton fields were a rich emerald green jutting out of the orange-red clay soil characteristic of this part of Texas. Approaching Anson, the road came to a gently curving rise, at the top of which was a small white church with a bright red neon sign that announced the simple message: "Jesus Saves." The luminescence of the sign stood in contrast to the simplicity of the little church, as if to draw attention to the only thing in the universe that seemed to matter. Anson is in the heart of the Texas Bible Belt, where churches are central to every facet of the local culture.

At the crest of this hill, the road yielded to a bird's-eye view of the community below. The little town of Anson, with all of its 2,644 inhabitants, suddenly appeared. The silver dome of the courthouse gleamed against the clear sky. A statue of a young woman, sword in one hand and the scales of justice in the other, stood atop the courthouse.

The courthouse was built early in the century and is a show-piece of neo-Gothic architecture. However, it looked somewhat odd and out of place now, towering as it did over the surrounding community, and ensconced among many closed businesses. The local movie house had been shut down for years. The Anson High School seniors had painted the school's initials on the boards covering what was once the ticket window. Anson once boasted a skating rink as well, but now it served as a warehouse for the carpeting business of a former city mayor. Of five dry goods stores that were once in business, only one remained open, its merchandise mostly limited to necessities. The store's old and somewhat tattered manikins were dressed in serviceable, unglamorous apparel, and with its cracking linoleum floors, the store was a far cry from the fashionable shopping malls of nearby Abilene.

One of the main businesses still open on the town square, across the street from the courthouse, is the Slayton-Meeks feed store. Down the street, facing the courthouse, were a beauty salon, two land surveying companies, a drugstore, and a recently restored turn-of-the-century opera house. In contrast to nearby Abilene, with its glistening freeways, fast food chains, and shopping malls, Anson felt remote, even desolate. A few gas stations, a single supermarket that charged premium rates for groceries, and a couple of mom-and-pop eating establishments provided all the material comforts that Anson offered its residents.

The beauty of the courthouse and the restored opera house ("at one time the finest to be found between Fort Worth and El Paso," one resident told me) were not sufficient to offset the palpable sense of decline in the heart of Anson. One side of the street was boarded up and closed. The community had tried to make the best of it, painting onto the facades of these buildings quaint little scenes of everyday life as if to help cover the painful fact that this community was hurting. Across the square, on the other end of the street, was the city hall, a tired-looking brown brick building that was once a bank. Just off the square, but plainly visible from it, was the county jail, with its window-unit air conditioners bleeding rust onto the building's weathered stucco. A small courtyard, bounded by a tall Cyclone fence capped with barbed wire, provided the jail's inmates with a place to be outdoors. It was not uncommon to see the inmates playing volleyball (the court took up almost the entire space) while one or two deputies sat distractedly on the jail's backdoor steps. Diagonally across the square was the only surviving bank, The First National Bank of Anson. With its thickly glassed teller windows sporting microphones and speakers and those ubiquitous stainless-steel cashier drawers, the bank could have been a branch location of any suburban bank in America.

From the town square in front of Anson's courthouse, as in most small, rural communities, all of the elements of power, the key political and economic links that bind a community together, could be assimilated in one brief, visual sweep.

MY FIRST INTERVIEW

Dave Reves, a 72-year-old retired Jones County sheriff, was waiting for me on the courthouse steps, wearing a pale blue suit, scuffed boots, and a well-worn silver-gray Stetson hat. "Dave Reves," he said, as he shook my hand. Reves had a distinctly western charm about him, underscored by his thick West-Texas accent. I liked him immediately. "I've got a room set up for us up here in the courthouse," he said.

At 6'4" Dave Reves was still an imposing figure. He was large-boned, with thick hands. Few men would have the poor sense to tangle with Reves now, much less in the days when he was the sheriff. Beneath the brim of Reves's Stetson were piercing blue eyes. Dave Reves had retired from the Sheriff's Department nearly twenty years ago, but it was evident that he still made a habit of sizing up everyone he met. It was as if every stranger to town had to be assessed quickly and accurately—friend or foe, good citizen or bad, a set of physical characteristics to keep in mind and cross-check with any police bulletins that might come to his attention. Dave Reves was a native of Jones County, born and raised in nearby Leuders.

As we walked into the building, I described the aims of my project. I could not help but notice that Reves was distinctly non-committal, an attitude that only intensified once we were inside the courthouse. The formality of the room that the ex-sheriff had arranged for our interview was discordant with his personality. His initial freewheeling, inquisitive style quickly retreated into a somewhat awkward and stilted one. Within fifteen minutes I changed my strategy with him. "Mr. Reves," I said, "how about if you just drive me around a bit and show me the town?"

In the car, Dave Reves came back to life. He was now in his element. Reves was driving his wife's white Oldsmobile, having left his aging Immigration Service green Bronco at home. As we moved through town the ex-sheriff shouted at a group of teenagers in a pickup truck that they were driving the wrong way down a one-way street (the driver saluted Reves). At an-

Retired Jones County Sheriff Dave Reves at Anson's Domino Hall.
Photo: Nancy Scanlan

other point he pulled up and told a woman that she was parking in a no-parking zone. It was evident that Dave Reves was
still on patrol. Under our feet was what Reves called his "Rattlesnake Gun," a combination 20-gauge, 22 mm., "over and under"
rifle. The rifle stock was open so that it rested comfortably on
the hump that went down the center of the car's floorboard. The
bright coppered gleam of the 20-gauge shell shone up at me. Reves
said he carried this rifle with him at all times. "You never know
what you're going to run into," he noted. Mostly, as its name indicated, it was used to shoot snakes he encountered while driving around Jones County. In the trunk Reves had what he described as his deer rifle. It turned out that he also had a pistol,
which he said needed repairs, in the glove compartment. His
vehicle seemed to have weapons in every nook and cranny.

   That day I covered the entire county with the retired sheriff.
He seemed to know virtually every living creature within it. "I
even know their dogs' names," he told me only half in jest. His

reservations about the tape recorder notwithstanding, he proved to be a gold mine. In a single day he introduced me to more people than I could possibly hope to interview in one visit. More important, it was clear that his introduction carried weight. "You think he's all right Dave?" one of his cronies asked him at the domino hall, pushing his "gimme" cap from the local cotton gin back up his forehead. "Sure he's all right," Reves responded. "Let him do you some interviews."

At the end of the day, as we were heading back toward my car, I asked Reves how we would meet up the next day. He just looked at me and drawled, "I'll find you. Ain't no one else in this town drives a Volvo!"

It was not until the next day that I became aware that Anson was a town in conflict. As I drove down Commercial Street, Anson's main street, I noticed a car parked in front of the high school. It seemed to be decorated for a pep rally or something of the sort, with white shoe polish lettering on its windows. The lettering said "Let's Dance!" Dave Reves found me eating breakfast at Bea's Steak House, just a block away from the courthouse on Commercial Street. When I asked him about the "Let's Dance" sign he laughed and told me that dancing was illegal within Anson's city limits. Some of the high school kids were trying to get a senior prom organized. When I inquired further, Reves said, "That's just the way it is." He did not seem particularly interested in discussing it.

Dave Reves's remark about dancing being illegal in Anson struck me as odd, but I had my mind on cultural transformation and the evaporation of rural Texas. The controversy over a high school prom seemed curious but beside the point. Later that same afternoon I walked into the offices of the *Western Observer* newspaper, directly across the street from the courthouse, hoping to find the editor. I wanted access to their archives to research back issues. The *Western Observer* had been in continuous publication longer than most newspapers in West Texas and thus promised to be a rich source of information.

Despite the ring of the little bell attached to the door, the two men sitting behind the counter paid no attention as I entered. They were talking to a customer. I distracted myself for a few minutes, browsing over the shelves displaying pens, paper, note pads, erasers, and other office products—the *Observer* obviously doubled as the local office supply store. They also sold Bibles. When the customer left, I approached the desk and asked to speak to the *Observer's* editor. "That's me," said Don Jones, a man who looked to be in his early thirties. He had slicked-down hair and glasses that gave him a studious air. "What newspaper are you with?" Jones asked. A little surprised, I outlined the nature of my project for him. "You're not interested in this dancing issue?" he asked in disbelief. I told him that that was not the purpose of my visit to Anson, but he and Paul Davidson, the assistant editor who also sat behind the counter, proceeded to tell me about it anyway.

"This town's been crawling with media people," Davidson told me. "They're here from all over the world." Davidson looked like a semi-reformed Grateful Dead groupie, with longish hair and a creatively disheveled appearance. He was smoking a cigarette while leaning way back in his chair.

"I just talked to a guy from Australia yesterday," Jones added. Both men seemed incredulous that I was not part of the media invasion that had overtaken Anson.

It turned out that Paul Davidson was the vice president of an organization called "The Footloose Club," which was comprised primarily of a group of parents who had come together in order to change the city's anti-dancing ordinance. They had named their organization after a movie in which a group of teenagers in a rural, church-dominated community successfully rose up against the local elders. It seemed to be another example of life imitating art, for the city of Anson was primarily run by members of the Church of Christ (the mayor, police chief, justice of the peace, city council and school board members), some of whose adherents believe that dancing is sinful, and Southern Baptist churches who hold similar views. Davidson and

Jones described the machinations of the city council in its effort to keep the anti-dancing ordinance intact. The entire town was in a fury over the issue, they informed me.

It is a truism of psychoanalysis that a symptom reveals as much about underlying conflicts as it masks. However, it took me several days to translate that precept from the couch to the community of Anson. One night, shortly before I was to return to Austin, as I lay in bed listening to the coyotes and the West Texas wind, I had a realization: what appeared to be a peculiar and quaint local controversy over whether a group of adolescents should have a prom was in fact a reflection of a deeper underlying conflict about what kind of community its citizens could fashion out of a world that had changed immensely in the twenty-five years since the demise of Jim Crow and the social system of white domination it enforced. Like every community, Anson was comprised of human stories that revolved, in part, around the eternal questions posed by all communities: how to organize its members' lives into a coherent whole. There is both desire and dread in our participation in social communities. Communities give our lives comforting structure; yet we can readily find that structure binding and coercive. Communities give our lives meaning, yet we can also experience them as pre-emptive and precluding of other possibilities. Thus, they often invoke both the longed-for and the resented in the same breath. If these dynamics are true even for adaptive and well-functioning communities, they become increasingly accentuated in those where social, political, and economic forces cannot be sufficiently harnessed to create an adequate "holding environment" for all of their members. In this circumstance intergroup and individual conflicts may fester silently until they become unleashed when appropriate circumstances lend themselves to their expression.

The idea to organize a dance for Anson's teenagers was Jane Sandoval's. Jane's youngest daughter had recently become pregnant at the age of 14. Jane held a firm conviction that the pregnancy could have been prevented. "If there had been anything in Anson for kids to do other than go out and drink and park, this wouldn't have happened," Jane lamented. This pregnancy had been utterly wrenching to Jane and her family.

"Of course her real dad and I were divorced, and I wanted her to have the baby and stay at home and finish school. And then, if she decided she still wanted to marry [the boy] later, she'd be older. But her dad came down and threw a fit and said she was getting married. So she did what he told her to." The sorrow in Jane's voice made clear the extent to which this event had derailed not only her daughter's life but hers as well.

On the morning of New Year's Day, 1987, Jane and her husband were returning to Anson from a party in Abilene. "We were coming home and I said, 'You know, it's such a shame that the young people can't do this—just go to a dance, have fun, go home, nobody drunk or getting pregnant or anything like that. Just good clean fun.' And at that time my husband had a little shop out there on the hill, a garage, because he's a mechanic, and I said, 'Why can't we just clear out your shop some evening and have a dance out there for the kids?'"

The Sandovals concluded that their garage would not be big enough for a dance, so they set out to find a place that was more suitable. First Jane called her nephew, David Herring, who was close to her age because Jane was the youngest in a line of eleven children. "You can't do that in Anson," was David's reply after hearing her out. "It's against the law."

"I just laughed," Jane recalled. Then, when she realized David was serious she felt the determination rise within her. "Well, I'm *going* to," Jane declared

Jane Sandoval had lived in Anson until the age of 6, when she moved to the nearby town of Hamlin, where she lived until the age of 11, before moving again, this time to Hereford, Texas. Although Jane had been back in Anson for a few years now, she had been unaware of the city's anti-dancing ordinance until she was enlightened by her nephew. She was sufficiently the outsider that she was willing to take on the local power structure within her community.

"I got hung up on by some," was Jane's recollection of the early phone calls she made to parents she knew who had adolescent children. "Some just weren't real friendly to me. But a lot of them were real receptive." Jane invited those who seemed interested to come to Bea's Steak House for a meeting.

Mercy Torres was one of the receptive ones. When Mercy received the phone call from Jane, she accepted the invitation without a moment's hesitation. Born and raised in East Los Angeles, Mercy was also something of an outsider in Anson. She did not fit any of the standard local rules for assigning people to a place in the social hierarchy. As a Mexican-American, Mercy Torres would have been almost reflexively consigned to Anson's social margins. However, she had attended college for several years and she was a doctor's wife. On the other hand, Mercy preferred Mexican cotton dresses with bright embroidered flowers to the more fashionable clothing from Abilene's shopping malls. As a Roman Catholic in a community where anyone of *any* status at all was a Protestant of one stripe or another, Mercy Torres appeared all the more an outsider, perhaps even something of an eccentric. That some in town might disapprove of the gathering organized by Jane Sandoval did not even occur to Mercy. She had a mind of her own. When she decided to do something she did it without worrying about what her neighbors thought.

There was an unmistakable tension in the air on the cold winter night in January of 1987 when Mercy Torres and the other parents whom Jane Sandoval had invited gathered at the café, once a "Whites Only" eating establishment, to develop a strategy for their confrontation with Anson's city fathers. By the time of their first meeting, there had already been considerable informal discussion about what they were planning, discussion prompted by the negative responses by some of the people Sandoval had called. The meeting felt clandestine, and their collective vulnerability was reflected in the fact that anyone driving down Commercial Street could see them through the restaurant's plate glass windows. In a small community political acts such as this gather-

ing translate into immediate personal realities. There was no place
to hide in Anson—everyone knew everyone else.

Bea's Steak House is just a block south of the courthouse. It
was more a café than a steak house and served as the local diner,
decorated with weathered travel posters of rolling Irish coun-
trysides and dramatic Swiss alpine landscapes softened by
bright wild flowers. Four or five white formica-topped tables
were clustered in the center of the dining area, which owner
Jack Hornsby called the "community table." On any given morning gossip flowed as freely around this table as the hot coffee.
Everything from the timing of this year's cotton plantings to the
local manifestations of the darker side of human nature was
discussed daily at the community table, making Bea's the epi-
center of Anson's social universe.

People stepped out of the winter night and into the warmth
of the café for the meeting, taking seats around the community
table and then, as their numbers grew, spilling over to the surrounding tables. As each new person appeared at the door, blowing warmth into cupped hands and gently kicking boot heels on
the floor as if to shake the cold from their legs, all heads turned
to see who the newest co-conspirator was. Most in attendance
were frankly surprised at their number—some forty Ansonites
had braved the deep West Texas chill and the ire of the local
fundamentalists to attend the meeting. They included Paul
Davidson, the counterculturish assistant editor of *The Western
Observer,* and Donna Carnes, a bright, attractive woman married to a local cotton farmer. Both Davidson and Carnes would
become central figures in the conflagration that was about to
be ignited in the little community. However, one thing was
immediately apparent to any observer: virtually none of those
present at the café that night were natives to Anson.

Jane Sandoval started the meeting by giving a synopsis of
her concerns. She wanted to do something for the kids, she said.
Anson's teenagers were being swallowed in a sea of boredom that
plunged them into activities that were just not good. Something
needed to be done about it.

Others present recounted stories of prior efforts to organize proms, most of which fizzled because of a last-minute loss of nerve or because they were shut down by Anson's police, whose chief was also a member of the Church of Christ. For example, just a few years earlier, the parents of one Anson girl had tried to organize a prom at Old Pioneer Hall. The family had gone to considerable effort and expense to decorate the hall. However, shortly before the dance was to start, Anson's chief of police arrived and announced that the dance was illegal and would not be permitted.

"If y'all try to have this, we're going to have to shut it down because it's illegal to dance," one Anson resident recalled him saying.

After a last-minute scramble, the local Catholic Church, whose parish hall happened to be a few feet beyond the city limits, agreed to host the prom. Decorations were hurriedly taken down at Pioneer Hall and put up at the parish hall, but a sour taste remained for those who had been involved in organizing that well-chaperoned graduation dance. Some suspected that the orders to stop the dance had come from the top—from Mayor Gene Rogers who, like the police chief, belonged to the Church of Christ. Others at the meeting recalled prior attempts to petition the city council to change the anti-dancing ordinance, attempts that had invariably fallen prey to that most effective form of legal obstruction: they had been tabled never to be entertained again. As the meeting progressed, its emphasis seemed gradually to shift away from the mechanics of organizing a prom to the strategies for challenging the city's anti-dancing ordinance.

As these accounts of prior clashes over dancing in their community were given voice, they had a stirring effect upon those present. Like a compelling sermon that gradually picks up momentum from a groundswell of emotion, the stories and testimonials took on a certain power as people began to understand the extent to which they were being wronged by the fundamentalist city fathers. Each account added its weight to an accumulating pool of resentment at their collective predicament.

The more Mercy Torres thought of it the angrier she became.
For Mercy the matter at hand was not simply a question of
dancing. She considered herself a good Christian and a strong
supporter of her church. She felt particularly incensed by the
self-righteousness of Anson's religious fundamentalists. They
could believe whatever they wanted to, she thought, but they
had no business questioning her morals because she saw nothing wrong with her children attending a school dance.

After gathering her thoughts, Mercy Torres was ready to
speak. She was characteristically poised as she offered an incisive and compelling analysis of their situation. The city council
members were free to follow their religious beliefs in their private lives, she noted, but they had no right to legislate whether
the rest of Anson's residents could dance. Mercy stressed that
to be successful in their effort to challenge the city's anti-dancing
ordinance it was necessary to have a clear sense of direction.
"In order for you to have any clout you need to organize," she
said. "You need to have a president. You need to have a strong
board, and you need to present your issues. And then you need
to go present this at city hall."

Mercy suggested that they formally constitute themselves as
an organization with bylaws, whose aim it would be to change
the ordinance that prohibited dancing in Anson. An unusually
insightful woman, Mercy accurately sensed what lay before those
who would dare stand up for their rights. She warned that challenging the city fathers would not be an easy task; they would
have to think through their strategy with care and deliberation.

When one of the other parents asked Mercy if she would be
willing to serve as an officer, Mercy responded, perhaps disin-
genuously: "Well, I don't think you're going to want me. I'm too
much of a big mouth. I might say some things you would not
agree with." It was her way of saying that she meant business.
Were she to assume a position of leadership in this struggle, she
would see it through to the end, regardless of the consequences.

The assembled parents and teenagers agreed to elect officers
at their next meeting two weeks hence. Mercy Torres's intui-

tive assessment was a sophisticated one. She grasped the fact that the group's challenge of Anson's anti-dancing ordinance represented a complex conflict that included questions of moral values and personal rights. All who had come to Bea's café that night felt that their rights were being violated, but their understanding of that fact crystalized over the course of the discussions and testimonials. Though almost all had been cognizant of the blatant imposition of the fundamentalists' religious views on the rest of the community, this fact became undeniable and somehow more real through the telling of stories around the white formica-topped tables. However there was a deeper, unacknowledged issue at stake that few, if any, of those present could voice, namely, that almost to a person, the individuals gathered that night were newcomers to Anson. These newcomers included whites and Mexican-Americans and whites who were married to Mexican-Americans. The group represented an alter ego to the local sociopolitical establishment that had reigned over the community since its incorporation as a county in the previous century.

Whatever their understanding of the gathering's meaning, it was evident that people were moved by the experience. If they were frustrated by their circumstances prior to that meeting, many were downright angry by the time they left, filtering out of the protective sanctuary of the café into the frigid winter winds.

WHY A HIGH SCHOOL PROM?

Truly mysterious forces are at work in human communities. History provides markers for the social, political, economic, and demographic transformations that redefine collective experience. But such markers are not mere abstractions. They are, rather, vehicles that simultaneously create and reflect change. These changes, in turn, are always concretized in individual lives. Sometimes, as was the case in Anson, events that almost appear random (Why a high school prom? Why at that particu-

lar point in this community's life?) are appropriated and put in
the service of the individual and collective lives that are engaged, whether consciously or not, in great social adjustments
and reconfigurations. Conflict, tension, and discomfiture are
almost always attendant on such social processes. Change is
characteristically painful, even desired and justifiable change.
Movement brings loss.

For many of Anson's whites, change meant the loss of the
known, the familiar, the relied upon. The basic elements of their
lives—culture itself, with its holding, structuring functions—
had been altered, ushering in uncertainty and fear. Do we lose
privilege? Are our creations to be defaced or destroyed? Anson
was no less a human community for being rural and Texan. The
reaccommodation was less veiled, more pressing and raw in this
community, but no different in its essentials from the manner
in which social change is experienced anywhere else.

Anson's minority outsiders had more to gain and less to lose
by the rearrangement of the local social universe. Nevertheless,
there were costs and strains associated with such changes. Did
social progress require giving up aspects of the known world for
Anson's minority residents as well? At what cost assimilation?

The reapportionment of political and economic power is repeatedly revealed to be a conflictual process, and these conflicts
always find representation at a psychological level in individual
lives. It is perhaps a radical proposition to suggest an inversion
of the axiom that the personal is always political—the political
is always personal. In every instance the political and social are
particularized, represented within, as well as expressed as the
psychological. It is in this sense that the people of Anson, and
Anson's dance fight, lend themselves as a vehicle for our understanding of the impact of social change and the psychologies of
ethnic difference and racial prejudice—elements which, as we
will see, are inextricably linked.

2

The Dance Fight

The individuals who assembled at Bea's café that cold winter night in 1987 had been thrust into a circumstance whose full dimensions they could not perceive. This gave the meeting an air of innocence, notwithstanding the frustrations, resentments, or fears given voice. The congregants were vessels, really. Without knowing it, they were lending themselves to a purpose that spoke to the tensions within their community. For beneath the complacent surface of Anson's quaint rural existence lay other realities: Anson's minority residents were now nearly as numerous as its whites; nearly half of the faces seen along Commercial Street on any given day, whether white, brown, or black, were relative newcomers; and the days when a good cotton crop could fill the local coffers were long gone. With that prosperity had gone the trickle-down recycling of money that could sustain several banks and dry goods stores and a movie theater, a skating rink, an opera house, barbers and cafés and all of the little enterprises that hold a community together, no matter how imperfectly, giving its members that ineffable feeling of connection and place.

The individuals gathered at Bea's café were focused on one purpose: to win for their children the right to dance in their own high school so that they would not have to drive to unofficial, poorly chaperoned events miles from home. In truth, however, it was a catalyst working toward a very different purpose, one that they must all have sensed but that none could articulate. It was as if history had conspired to create this event to mark a turning point in the collective consciousness of the community.

HOW THE ORDINANCE CAME ABOUT

No one I interviewed seemed to know why dancing was outlawed in Anson in the first place. There were a number of apocryphal stories, most of which centered on the idea that in the early 1930s Anson had been a considerably wilder place. At the time, it was a prosperous, thriving community. This was especially true around harvest time, when the town was infused with thousands of migrant workers with some money to spend, and cotton was bought and sold on the courthouse steps. According to these accounts, the then-influential Presbyterian Church had lobbied for a way to control an epidemic of prostitution, gambling, and drinking in Anson—activities that were reportedly widespread at the culmination of the wheat and cotton harvests when people and money were both so plentiful in town.

Whatever its true historical origins, the anti-dancing city ordinance was passed and approved by the city fathers on the 22nd day of February, 1933. The ordinance read:

> That it shall be unlawful from and after the passage of this ordinance for any person or persons, firm or association of persons to carry on, foster or operate any public dance hall where people assemble for the purpose of dancing in any public building within the corporate limits of the city of Anson, any person or persons violating the aforesaid ordinance shall upon conviction therefore be fined in any sum not less than FIVE DOLARS (sic) nor for more than $15.00 the same for each day or a portion of a day shall be considered a separate offense.

The wording of the ordinance was ambiguous. While it appeared explicitly to forbid dance halls, the segment of the ordinance that addressed people assembling "for the purpose of dancing in any public building" gradually took on a broader connotation to include public dances of any kind, a connotation that just happened to be congenial to the beliefs of the Anson Church of Christ and the other fundamentalist congregations in town. Since the passage of the 1933 ordinance, there had been a tacit understanding throughout Anson that the ordinance prohibited dancing, period. While some townsfolk knew of individuals who had hosted small private dance parties in their homes, none questioned the fact that Anson's city ordinance prohibited dancing in public.

There was one exception to this law, an exception that only added insult to injury for those who had gathered at Bea's that winter night to discuss a strategy for changing it. Every year, just before Christmas, a large public dance was held at the Old Pioneer Hall on the southeast edge of town. This was the site of the annual Cowboys' Christmas Ball, which had a run of three nights on the weekend before Christmas. The Cowboys' Christmas Ball Association, which owned the Pioneer Hall, kept the building padlocked the rest of the year.

By local standards the Cowboys' Christmas Ball was a kind of yearly Mardi Gras. The ball had first been held in the late 1890s and was conceived as a partial antidote to the monotony of cowboy life. However, it also came into being just as the last remnants of the open prairie were being fenced in, a development that radically changed the cowboys' lot. The fenced prairie brought to a close the era of the cattle drive and substantially reduced the number of cowboys a cattleman needed to maintain his herd. The hardy Longhorn, the proud symbol of Texas because it was the only animal that could sustain the rigors of the long cattle drives, was replaced by tamer cattle that produced more beef. The emergence of the cattle "business" sharply reduced the need for the cowboy who had learned his skills from the Spanish and Mexican ranchers of South Texas.

The Cowboys' Christmas Ball was a tribute to that vanishing breed.

It was anything but a tame event. Cowboys from far and wide came to Anson in what became a kind of annual reunion. The existence of the ball in a town with an ordinance outlawing dancing was a contradiction that the community of Anson had lived with for seven years until 1940 when someone brought it to the attention of the city council. What about "that lively-gaited sworray?" as the journalist Larry Chittenden had described the ball in the 1890s. The 1933 ordinance made the famous ball illegal, too. When this oversight was brought to their attention, the city fathers quickly sought to rectify it. In the late spring of 1940 the city council passed a resolution calling for the original ordinance prohibiting dancing to be "amended, altered and repealed in so far as said ordinance applies to or affects the activities of the Texas Cowboys' Christmas Ball, Inc." Thus, the reality since 1940 was that dancing was not really outlawed in Anson, only dancing other than the annual Cowboys' Christmas Ball.

The wide acceptance within the community of the Cowboys' Christmas Ball alongside of the city ordinance that prohibited dancing was viewed as sheer hypocrisy by the group of Ansonites who had met at Bea's in 1987. It was common knowledge that a great deal of drinking went on in the Pioneer Hall parking lot during the Christmas Ball. Yet many of the Ball's most enthusiastic supporters were opposed to allowing Anson's high school to sponsor a well-chaperoned, nonalcoholic, no drugs, dancing prom for its seniors. "You've got a double standard. You have dancing in Anson. You have the Cowboys' Christmas Ball. That is a dance. It's a public dance," Jane Andruss noted heatedly during the meeting. She had been invited to the meeting by Jane Sandoval while they sat in the bleachers watching their sons in a post-Christmas basketball game.

There was a more sinister interpretation for the existence of the city ordinance and the city's intransigence. It boiled down to the simple fact that the majority of the members of the city council were members of the Church of Christ. The school board was simi-

larly constituted. Whatever motives had led to the original passing of the ordinance in 1933, it was quite obvious to everyone that
the ordinance concurred with the religious beliefs of the Anson
Church of Christ and the other fundamentalist churches in town.

THE CONSPIRATORS

The people who gathered at Bea's Steak House reflected the
changes the community of Anson had experienced over the previous two decades; few if any of them were from Anson's old
established families. Many were relative newcomers whose lives
did not fit the traditional mold within the community. For example, Jane Sandoval was married to a Mexican-American, a
fact that raised many local eyebrows. A generation ago such a
union would have been absolutely unheard of in Anson. Paul
Davidson, the assistant editor of *The Western Observer*, had a
definite counterculture aesthetic, reminiscent of the '60s.
Though married to a local, he was not an Anson native. Jane
Andruss was a divorcée who had moved to Anson to raise her
sons in a healthier community than the one she had left. And
then there was Mercy Torres, a college-educated, articulate,
Mexican-American community leader. In other words, the parents at Bea's represented a coalition of individuals who were
clearly not members of the local power elite. They were mostly
people living on the margins of Anson's social and political center. This fact alone gave the meeting an importance that few, if
any, of those in attendance could really appreciate.

At the group's second meeting, Mercy Torres was elected
president. Her election passed without ceremony. Although
unnoted, it was, nevertheless, a momentous occasion. There in
that small West Texas café a group of mostly white partisans
had elected as their president a Mexican-American woman who
a scant twenty years before would not have been served so much
as a cup of coffee.

In addition to the election of other officers, a committee was
appointed to draw up a constitution and by-laws. Donna Carens,

a non-native who was married to an Anson cotton farmer, re-called their initial strategy for organizing as follows: "Mercy felt that we needed a sound foundation, so that when people asked, 'What is it that you want?' we could point to these bylaws. One of the first things we stated was that we were building an orga-nization to promote dancing in Anson. That's what we were all about. But also, we were promoting freedom of choice to be able to dance." At the suggestion of one of the high school students in attendance, the group agreed to call itself the Footloose Club, after a 1980s movie whose plot had an uncanny resemblance to the events about to unfold in Anson.

Following this second meeting, Footloose distributed a news bulletin to the residents of Anson. The bulletin announced plans to hold a Valentine's Day dance at Welton Rainwater's barn, within the Anson city limits. In fact, the barn was just a stone's throw from the county courthouse. Footloose planned to gather donations and volunteer help to provide soft drinks, decorations, and music for the "Renegade Ball," as the dance came to be known. They also planned to have sufficient chaperones to en-sure that the seventh through twelfth graders in attendance would not get out of hand.

To counteract the accusation that Footloose's goals were at best frivolous, if not sinful, or that its aims would undermine the moral fabric of the community, Footloose launched a series of civic programs under the tutelage of Mercy Torres. For ex-ample, the group enlisted in the State of Texas's Adopt-A-High-way program. A state sign on the road into Anson announced that the Footloose Club of Anson was responsible for maintain-ing the cleanliness of that stretch of highway. The idea had been proposed by Jeff Andruss, one of the student representatives to Footloose, but it was part of the grand design outlined by Mercy Torres as part of the civic activities she had identified as appropriate targets for Footloose's efforts to better the commu-nity. Every weekend, Footloose members drove to this stretch of highway, a frequently traveled artery, and picked up trash discarded by passers-by.

Another major project involved turning the Anson hospital's basement into a tornado shelter. Tornadoes are not uncommon in this part of Texas, and many houses have shelters. Some were originally built as fallout shelters during the 1950s when the community felt a sense of stability and security within, but struggled with visions of a very different kind of threat from beyond its borders. Currently, the hospital's basement was used as a general storage area, housing dusty old medical records, discarded equipment, and furniture. Following a recent tornado, Mercy Torres brought her Footloosers to clean and repaint the basement area where they also stored donated food and water, folding chairs, and cots. These efforts all reflected a strong community commitment on the part of Mercy Torres, who increasingly saw Footloose not simply as an organization to obtain a legal prom for Anson's teenagers, but rather as a vehicle to address a broad range of issues within the community.

The Footloose bulletin announcing the "Renegade Ball" also contained a comment that foresaw the tensions that the dancing controversy would activate: "Beleive [sic] me there are people out there who are on our side, but cannot [sic] come forward because their jobs may be on the line. People who own their business, their business might suffer if they become active in 'Footloose.' These same people will help with money or any other way they might be needed. If you know someone like this let them know we understand, but they can help in any way they feel they can."

These comments contained the real anxieties and tensions Footloose members felt as they set out to challenge the local power structure. Were people's jobs or businesses really on the line because they supported a change in the city ordinance that prohibited dancing? Were Footloose members really likely to be shunned by others in the community? The concerns voiced in Footloose's news bulletin were not overwrought or hysterical. On the contrary, the unfolding of the events in Anson would bear them out.

As soon as people started learning about Footloose and its aims, tensions between the proponents of dancing and its opponents began to mount in Anson. The formation of Footloose represented a manning of the barricades. Things would not remain business-as-usual in the community.

THE LINES OF BATTLE

"It spread like wildfire," Mercy Torres observed in reference to the fact that the Anson grapevine was already buzzing with word of the group of parents with the audacity to challenge the fundamentalist city fathers. "In a small community like this, it doesn't take much to capture the imagination," she said.

Quickly, the lines became drawn between Footloose and Anson's anti-dancing forces. The members of Footloose came face-to-face with this as they were planning the Valentine's Day dance. To the surprise of some members of Footloose, many of those who offered to help or to donate to the cause requested anonymity. The experience of prior efforts, such as the aborted dance that had been discussed at Footloose's first meeting, gave fertile food for the imagination as to the kind of response Ansonites who dared challenge the local mores might receive.

Donna Carens learned early and first-hand that getting the anti-dancing ordinance changed was not going to be a simple matter. If Footloose wanted to change the law, it had some homework to do and a thorough understanding of the existing ordinance was the place to start. She was appointed to go to city hall to obtain a copy of the actual ordinance.

City Hall operated out of a defunct bank just across the street from the courthouse. A relative newcomer to Anson, Donna had never met Dottie Spraberry, the city secretary. Dottie Spraberry's desk sat behind the line of marble-topped surfaces under dark wood-spindled bars that were once the bank's teller windows. Slightly pudgy, Spraberry was a school-marmish looking woman with outdated glasses and graying hair. She had been the city secretary for as long as anyone could remember, through countless mayors and city councilmen, and throughout those years she had cultivated a degree of sophistication about the workings of the city that made her the pivotal person at city hall.

"Dottie was used to running things," was the way Donna Carens put it. "She had worked herself into a position of at least *feeling* indispensable." Dottie Spraberry who, like the mayor and a majority of the city council, was a member of the Anson Church of Christ, had a penchant for speaking on their behalf. "Never did you call up there and want an opinion from the mayor or a member of the city council did you have to wait to get it," one Ansonite noted. "Dottie Spraberry just gave it to you. . . . She was really used to calling the shots up there and if you crossed her, she was very hard to get along with."

When Carens stepped up to the teller's window and asked Spraberry for a copy of the city's dancing ordinance, her reception was cool to say the least. "She told me that someone else had already taken the page or that someone had mislaid it, which is pretty silly. I mean, even for a town like this everybody would know that you don't give out an original! Then, the next reason was that the copier was down and she said she couldn't give me a copy of anything," Carens added.

Donna Carens was not a woman easily put off. Like Mercy Torres, Donna had a spark to her; she was feisty, "stout" as they say in Texas. She was not the least bit intimidated by Dottie Spraberry's scowling disapproval. Through sheer persistence, Donna finally obtained a copy of the city ordinance.

When the members of Footloose read the actual law they were taken aback. "It was so ridiculous," Carens observed. "The ordinance didn't seem to outlaw dancing at all; it simply outlawed dance halls and public dances, which didn't cover what we were attempting to do because we would have limited dances to people by age, which would have made it a private dance for Anson's students and their guests."

Like everything in the realm of the law, this view of Anson's ordinance was a matter of interpretation. The prevailing belief in the community was that all dances, except for the Cowboys' Christmas Ball and those conducted in the privacy of one's home, were against the law. Further, whether a school dance was a public or private affair was also open to debate. In any event, such considerations were purely academic. The story that had stirred so many at the first Footloose meeting, the one about the dance reportedly disrupted by Anson's chief of police, was proof enough that whatever legal interpretations the existing anti-dancing ordinance might be subject to, the bottom line was that in Anson, public dances were not permitted.

Footloose's efforts to garner information about the city's dance ordinance only served to heighten tensions. It demonstrated the seriousness of their commitment to change the law and angered the local power structure. The open defiance of the upcoming dance only made matters worse. Mercy Torres's idea was that a substantial number of people openly enthusiastic about supervised dances for Anson's teenagers perhaps might have sufficient leverage to contain the outbreak of open warfare with Anson's anti-dancing forces. However, the reception of Donna Carens and others at city hall quickly disabused Mercy and the rest of Footloose of that hope. "We knew we were going to have to face that," Mercy reflected, "but we decided that we'd take it one day at a time, crossing each bridge as we came to it."

Footloose organized a group of volunteers to teach kids how to do country western dancing. "Lots of kids were really excited about it, and talking about who they were going to bring to the dance, what friends to invite, what relatives . . ." recollected Andrea Carens, Donna's daughter, who was in sixth grade at the time of Footloose's first dance.

Footloose printed fliers containing the rules that would govern the dance, including the ban on alcohol and drugs. Anyone who smelled of liquor would not be permitted entrance. Furthermore, once students arrived at the dance, they were to stay inside until the dance was over. No one would be permitted re-entry if he or she left the building. The fliers were distributed at the junior high school and high school in advance of the dance to ensure that everyone knew what to expect. Jane Andruss recalled the spirit of collaboration between Footloose and the students that permeated the air: "It seemed that all the kids knew the rules; they understood what we were doing and why."

The night before the Valentine's Day dance was a Thursday and it was bitter cold. Footloose had gathered a group of volunteers to clean up Weldon Rainwater's barn. Though he called it a barn, it was more like a shed the size of a city block where Rainwater worked on his farming equipment. Most cotton farmers used their barns to do repairs during the winter months, and Rainwater's barn was chock-full of shop equipment, including welding torches and large, cherry-red Sears Craftsman-style tool chests with tiers of drawers crammed full of wrenches and sockets and other tools and equipment.

Weldon Rainwater's barn was freezing—its gray sheet-metal walls and roof seemed to amplify the bitter West Texas cold rather than provide much protection from it. It was completely uninsulated. "I remember we brought in a couple of those big blow stoves," one parent recalled, referring to Rainwater's big propane heater that was fired up along with another that had been borrowed from the barn of Lonnie Carens, Donna's husband. Like two powerful dragons, they thrust a continuous flow of heat into the cavernous barn. In spite of the fact that the heat was almost immediately absorbed into the near-freezing metal walls of the barn, the blow stoves provided the volunteers with some warmth. The volunteers periodically sidled up to the heaters, standing over them with outstretched hands. However, the excitement and anticipation surrounding the big dance was enough to sustain them, fortifying them from the hostile elements.

Rumors were rampant. Some had heard that children from the Church of Christ and Baptist churches had been strictly forbidden to attend the dance. Mayor Rogers had told Footloose that he would regard this as a private dance and not interfere, provided there was no disorderly conduct and no complaints. But he made it evident that he was not pleased. Authorized or not, there was widespread speculation as to whether the dance would be permitted to proceed as a private dance, or whether, instead, Anson's police chief and member of the Church of Christ, might see fit to seize upon any pretext to shut it down, as he reportedly had a few years earlier.

Weldon Rainwater, the West Texas counterpart of Woodstock's Max Yasgur, seemed edgy about the prospect of the dance. His wife Jaynie, a teacher acutely aware of the problems facing Anson's youth, was a member of Footloose and their two adolescent children were also enthusiastic about Footloose's activities. Jaynie Rainwater talked her husband into allowing the dance, aided by strong prompting from their children. Weldon, however, was not sanguine about the project. Getting involved in such a local imbroglio was layered with all sorts of problems. Although he harbored no religious beliefs against dancing, he did own a cotton gin in Anson and there were plenty of other gins in Jones County where farmers could take their cotton if they were displeased with Weldon. Rainwater had to live with the people in this town. Reluctantly, then, he allowed Footloose the use of his barn, which was no minor coup, given that in a town the size of Anson there were very few places that fit the bill.

The barn's cement floor had years of accumulated dust and oil when the volunteers went to work. First they moved Rainwater's equipment, which they covered with tarps, to the side walls. Next they swept and mopped the floors clean. There was going to be smooth sailing for the couples drifting across the dance floor. A local rancher lent Footloose enough bales of hay to line the entire barn and provide seating for those too timid or too tired to dance. Finally, they decorated the barn with bright red fold-out hearts, cupids, and pink, white, and red crepe paper. By the end of a long evening of preparations, Weldon Rainwater's barn was transformed into a festive setting that eagerly awaited the crowd of Anson's teenagers the next night.

Throughout Thursday evening, as volunteers worked feverishly to get the barn ready, groups of teenagers kept driving by, curious to see how the preparations were going. The Footloose members got mixed prognostications from the kids. "Some of them would come by and say, 'Well, nobody's coming, none of the kids want to come.' No sooner had that batch of kids left, than another group would show up and say 'Oh, everybody in town's coming! Even kids from Hamlin are coming to this thing!'"

Exhausted from their work, the Footloosers finally retired to their homes, not knowing for sure if they would be sitting in an empty barn surrounded by Valentine's decorations when Friday night arrived, or swamped with a throng of teenagers ready to party hard.

THE RENEGADE BALL

On Friday there was no letup from the freezing temperatures, and a steady wind made it feel that much colder. Footloose knew that their activities had drawn a great deal of attention in the community. Everyone in town was talking about them. Between the anti-dancing forces and the frigid temperatures, Footloose had no way of gauging how many people would actually show up for the Valentine's Day dance.

They were not disappointed. Suddenly, it seemed that kids were sweeping in from everywhere. "We had at least 400 kids," Jane Sandoval recalled. "More than I ever dreamed!" Donna Carens took a turn collecting tickets and could hardly keep up with the throng. Rainwater's barn was packed to the rafters.

At almost every Footloose meeting Mercy Torres had underscored that it was imperative for the dance go off without a hitch. Everyone understood that any incident would be used to discredit them. The dance was to be a strictly chaperoned event, free of drugs and alcohol. The hay provided an excuse for a ban on smoking inside the barn. Outside, Footloose members patrolled the street around the barn to ensure, as Mercy put it, "that there was no hanky-panky." "The children were under our supervision," she noted, "so we set the guidelines about their coming and going. We treated them as if they were our own children and expected the kids at the dance to behave as we expected our own children to behave."

The patrols around the perimeter of the barn were not exactly cherished tours of duty that evening. It was so cold that the chaperones could only tolerate being outdoors for twenty or thirty minutes at a time before seeking refuge inside the barn again, sidling up to one of those big propane heaters to thaw out before taking up some other assignment. While on one of those frigid outdoor tours, Donna Carens first spotted the police cruiser, traveling at a snail's pace toward Rainwater's barn. Reflexively, her heart leapt. However, Donna felt confident that Footloose's activities were right and she was prepared to challenge whatever authority might think otherwise. The patrol car reappeared periodically throughout the evening, the police officers trying to make discreet inquiries of the teenagers on their way to their cars. At one point the police hinted to Donna that a neighbor had complained about the noise, but she was skeptical of the report. No one who lived close to the barn gave evidence of being the least inconvenienced.

The "noise" was coming from a local band called Bitter Creek, led by Paul Davidson. The core of the Bitter Creek band had been playing together for a number of years, during which they had established a fairly reliable circuit of engagements in locales beyond the reach of the local fundamentalists who viewed dancing as sinful. They played regularly in towns such as Hamlin, Coleman, Breckenridge, and Aspermont, where they actually made better money than they would have in Abilene, which had too many competing bands.

"The guys in the band were worried about getting arrested, and I kept explaining to them that even though this ordinance was in place, that to my knowledge no one had ever been arrested for playing in Anson. But they sure as hell didn't want to be the first! They were real nervous about that," Davidson remembered about that night.

The band members were dressed in brightly colored T-shirts, which sported their logo, a cow skull mounted on an Indian shield with eagle feathers tied to the end of it with rawhide. The logo's southwestern motif was appealing in the West Texas towns that were the band's mainstay. At intervals, the band members hawked their T-shirts from the stage.

Bitter Creek played mostly country western music, Top 40 tunes, and a medley of '50s songs that included such numbers as Elvis's old hit "Blue Suede Shoes."

Initially, the kids seemed shy. After all, most of them had no idea how to dance. The Footloose-sponsored country western dance classes had not exactly been overfull. Bitter Creek played a few numbers while people mostly just stood around and watched—a party band's greatest nightmare. But gradually a few took courage, especially after some of the adults stepped onto the dance floor, and before long, the floor was full. "They just had a ball!" Jane Sandoval remembered gleefully.

The Valentine's Day dance was Davidson's dream come true. "The band was so hyper, partly because the guys had been worried about getting arrested, that they were energized and just cookin'. That night even the gags on stage were working. Everyone was really communicating. We were really working hard as a band."

For Andrea Carnes, who had never heard a live band before, one of the lasting memories of the dance would be seeing Paul on the little make-shift stage, singing his heart out. "While Paul was singing he was smiling real big. I could tell he was really happy," Andrea would later reminisce.

The one sour note that evening, musically speaking, was the band's playing of Eric Clapton's "Cocaine," which caused debate even among Footloose's staunchest supporters. "There was a lot of disagreement over whether or not they should have done that song since we were trying to sponsor a chemical-free atmosphere," one of them later recollected, adding with a tone of forgiveness, "but it was a popular song at the time! So . . . "

A sprinkling of suggestive songs notwithstanding, the consensus among Footloose's members following the Valentine's Day dance was that it had been an unqualified success. Anson's teenagers seemed to have sensed what was at stake. Their behavior, as a consequence, had been impeccable. Not a single youngster was caught sneaking liquor, or smoking, or necking in the back seat of a car.

However, for Davidson there was more to the Footloose Club than just having a teenagers dance:

> I think there were people there that night for whom that was really it. They just believed if they could accomplish this—it was like damnit! They were going to have a dance in Anson! But for me it was just the beginning. From the small nucleus that came from those meetings at Bea's to "Here's an actual dance," you know, and seeing all these people and being part of the band and looking out at those kids out there having such a good time. For me it was more like "All right, something is really happening here. Something is really going on." So for me it was more of a beginning, like crossing a starting line in the race.

Paul Davidson also recalled a special feeling in the air following the dance: "I remember cleaning up that night and how it was almost strange, because usually, the hardest thing is to get people to stick around afterwards and help clean up. But not only did people stay, it was almost like they were happy doing so! It was like they really didn't *want* to leave! There was this sense of accomplishment for what had happened."

Footloose and Anson's teenagers had demonstrated that they could be trusted to have a dance that was "clean" and free of activities that everyone in this community, not only the fundamentalists, was concerned about. The dance was a bold challenge by Footloose. Even at that early stage in the events that were unfolding, it was becoming clear to many that for the anti-dancing forces, especially the members of the Church of Christ, Footloose's activities were viewed with considerable displeasure.

Paul Davidson had been especially struck by this fact:

> I remember at that first dance people were parking elsewhere and using one car to bring people over so that their

cars would not be seen out front. Now, these people wanted
to be there, they wanted to be part of the dance, but they
were so scared that their boss just might come by to check
out the situation, or that their kid's school teacher or principal might come by and see their car . . . and back then I
thought that was hypocritical of them, but now I see their
point, because I wasn't afraid of anybody, which was probably my mistake, but these people had jobs, homes, they'd
lived here all their lives, and so they were taking a big
chance, much bigger than I thought I was taking. . . . They
were really on the line.

In retrospect he admired them for that.

From the very first meeting Mercy Torres had made it clear
that her intention was for Footloose to take its concerns to
the city council in an effort to get the city's anti-dancing ordinance changed. While some, seeking to avoid an outright confrontation with the city fathers, believed that a low-keyed
approach might be best, Mercy was adamant about her strategy. If the city ordinance was not changed, they would be perpetually reliant on the unpredictable good graces of the ruling powers.

Support for Mercy's argument came when Jaynie Rainwater
announced at the next Footloose meeting that her husband,
Weldon, had told her in no uncertain terms that he would not
allow the use of his barn for future dances. His property had
been well cared for, but that was not the basis for his concerns.
Some within Footloose believed that he had been pressured by
the anti-dancing forces. One of them would later recall:

We felt that this was the plan, that the city council had
turned their heads for *this* dance, knowing that we couldn't
do anything else. If Weldon wouldn't let us use the barn,
then more than likely someone had told him that he had
better not. See, some of the business people were more or
less told that they wouldn't have business done with them

if they associated with Footloose, and Weldon had a cotton gin here, so people could just take their cotton somewhere else. Now I don't know that for a fact, but that was the rumor. And the people from the flower shop, who had been supporting Footloose's activities prior to the dance, they withdrew from Footloose after the dance and I think it was because they were being shunned, you know, people weren't using their services as much.

Rainwater's defection meant that Footloose had no setting within the city limits available to them for "private" dances except for Old Pioneer Hall, which had also been denied them. Whether the allegations of fundamentalist pressure on Rainwater were true or simply the threads of paranoia beginning to surface in the mounting tension, it was clear that Footloose people were beginning to feel some heat. Such pressures heightened the tensions within Footloose, with some members feeling less convinced of the merits of staying the course. The potential personal and economic costs were becoming apparent.
Some within Footloose thought they had already accomplished something with the Valentine's Day Dance. Maybe Rainwater would let them have another dance next year? Why push their luck? Mercy Torres, however, argued compellingly for the necessity to continue the struggle and she won the day.

THE LEGAL TEST

By the end of February Footloose elected to take the legality of the dancing ordinance into the lion's den and put themselves on the agenda for the next city council meeting scheduled for March. As the time approached, tensions within the community became increasingly palpable. What had been a series of guerrilla skirmishes was about to become a frontal assault on the local power structure.
Anson City Hall faces north toward the county courthouse across the street. Years ago, it was a thriving bank, and the main

vault now stores supplies for city hall, as well as a coffee maker. The vault's heavy steel door is permanently open, exposing the wheels and gears of its locking mechanism that once protected the wealth that local residents entrusted to it. To get to the council chambers, one must walk past the vault and through another door, leading into what was once the bank's board room. The room was furnished with a single, brown, metal table, standard bureaucratic issue, with a number of imposing highbacked swivel chairs arranged around it. The room was bare, except for three mass-produced paintings: one depicted an oil well, another was a stylized portrait, the third a seascape.

On the evening of March 15, 1987, the city chambers were packed. As she stepped out of her car, Donna Carens was quite surprised to see that people were already spilling out onto the sidewalk, well in advance of the 7 P.M. starting time. Because of the overflow crowd, a set of doors opening directly onto Commercial Street were being used for entry rather than the usual route through the city hall offices.

Donna was dressed in her "power outfit," a dark suit with a white blouse. "I probably looked more like a bank vice president than anything else. I wasn't going to show up in your typical polyester stretch pants!" she recalled. She was not accustomed to speaking in public or being the center of attention. However, there was also a clear inner strength in evidence: "I was determined to be taken more seriously than we had been," she noted, because of the prevalent insinuation that members of Footloose were at best a collection of bored housewives, if not "low life" trouble makers.

Donna pressed her way through the crowd into the chambers to find city council members passing additional metal folding chairs into the crowd. The room was already teeming—the city council meeting was clearly going to be standing room only. Someone had saved Donna a seat two or three rows back from the table where the council members would be sitting. She spotted Mercy a few rows over and Paul Davidson as well. She felt ready.

The strategy that Footloose had fashioned for the meeting
was quite simple. They would present their views in an objective, unemotional manner. Mercy Torres would be the primary
spokesperson for the group, with the other three adding commentary as needed. Mercy would make it clear that Footloose
was not interested in setting up dance halls or anything of that
sort. Indeed, Footloose was prepared to meet with the city council to figure out a compromise that would make sense for everybody.

"We were willing to limit ourselves, too," remembered Paul
Davidson, adding "because in all honesty, we didn't want just
anybody coming in and throwing a big dance downtown. We
wanted some kind of control. We understood that's the way a
city has to be run."

The second part of Footloose's strategy was immediately in
evidence by the throng of Ansonites who had shown up. "Our
idea was for those people who *could, and would* to show up,"
Paul Davidson said, "and that was our strength. It was a delib-
erate strategy, you know, strength in numbers. That fell to
Mercy and Donna; they're the ones who got out in front of the
organization and said 'If all you're there for is to sit and look
pretty, that's great!' They're the ones who motivated people to
come."

Jane Sandoval, too, was surprised by the number of people
who had come to take a stand on Footloose's behalf. Something
else, however, surprised and unsettled her and that was the
presence of the Abilene media. The bright strobe lights of the
television crews panning across the gathered multitude and into
the faces of the city council who were beginning to take their
seats suddenly made it clear that this meeting was not going to
be business as usual.

Mayor Gene Rogers, sitting at the head of the table, called
the meeting to order. Protocol at the city council meetings was
not what it is in Dallas or Houston. Under ordinary circumstances these meetings were a laid-back affair. But being in the
spotlight, quite literally, made everyone tense. Like everyone

else on the city council, Gene Rogers was rapidly approaching retirement age. He was known throughout the community as a good politician with a quick smile. He also had the reputation of being a shrewd businessman—he owned a construction company—who liked to be in control of things. These character traits made the present situation all the more distasteful for him. The other chairs around the table were occupied by the five city council members and Dottie Spraberry, the city secretary.

Footloose had prepared well for this meeting. Mercy Torres presented their position clearly and firmly: they wanted the city ordinance banning dancing changed because it represented a violation of the civil rights of those residents whose religious beliefs did not prohibit such activity. Further, she made it clear that Footloose, while willing to work with the city council to find an acceptable compromise, was prepared to take the issue as far as necessary to remove this unreasonable restriction. Most of all, she noted, Footloose wanted Anson's high school graduates to have a legal prom just like other teenagers in America had. Mercy made it clear that Footloose was not interested only in dancing. She spoke of the many plans they had, some of them that neatly depicted the group's ambitious ideas for reaching the community's children outlined on poster board. In the end Mercy's tone was conciliatory, inviting the city fathers to join with Footloose in a cause that she knew must be of concern to them just as it was to the members of her organization, namely, the well-being of Anson's youth who were increasingly facing the temptations and problems that adolescents elsewhere in America were facing.

Davidson recalled: "There were a lot of stiff smiles. No one got hostile or anything, but to me, even the people I was with, it was like children who have reached the age where 'I'm finally going to have to rebel.' Well, that's how the side I was on felt. The other side was pretty straight-faced." Everyone seemed to remember it the same way. "Gene just kind of glared," one Footloose officer recalled. "And Dottie Spraberry, I mean if looks could kill, we'd have all been dead!"

Gene Rogers had his pat response to the entire affair, which was to suggest that Footloose's efforts represented a threat to the community. If they allowed the kids to have dances, how could they prevent any Tom, Dick, or Harry from waltzing into Anson to set up a nightclub, a bar, or a dance hall?

Jane Sandoval tried to reason with him. "No one's going to want to do that when they can just go into Abilene a few miles away and dance and get drunk and do all they want." She also tried to appeal to Roger's nostalgia. Anson had once been a bustling town with an opera house and a movie theater. Gene Rogers had owned a roller skating rink during this heyday. Jane reminded Rogers of those days. "You know, you did a lot for the youth when you were younger, with the skating rink, and that's all we want to do."

"Since I was a child I'd known him and I just *loved* him. When we were little we'd go to this skating rink and I thought that he and his wife were some of the nicest people I ever knew," Jane said.

Such pleas were clearly falling on deaf ears. The fundamentalist-run city council seemed as completely impervious to reason as it was to impassioned pleas. It was as if their minds had been made up before the meeting had even begun, which, of course, was precisely the case.

However, the denouement came shortly after Jane's remarks. Bob Evans was preacher at the Northside Baptist Church, an especially fundamentalist group of Southern Baptists. He was tall, with striking looks, broad shoulders, and a distinct preacher's demeanor. He held himself erect, readily flashing a quick smile. One of the few members of the "opposition" in attendance at the city council meeting, Evans happened to be sitting next to Paul Davidson.

"You're with the opposition aren't you?" Davidson had asked, voicing the obvious.

"Yes," Evans replied.

"Would you like to talk? Gene, would it be OK if we let Reverend Evans talk?" Davidson asked the mayor.

This was a point of pride for Davidson. He was aware of the fact that since no one from the opposition had requested a place on the council's agenda, technically they could not speak at the meeting. It was a fortuitous gesture for Footloose. Reverend Evans stood up to speak and his words made the evening news: "In thirty-one years of counseling," declared the preacher, "I've talked to young people who were unwed mothers and unwed fathers, and I've asked them, 'Where was the point of your downfall?' Nine out of ten told me, 'It was on the dance floor.'"

Davidson stole a glance at Mercy and Donna. He could not believe what he was hearing. Neither could they. All three had been awed by this man of the cloth who exuded such an air of dignity. But what he was saying now was utterly preposterous. No one was more surprised than Jane Sandoval, however, since she and her husband attended Evans's Northside Baptist Church. "The only way I know how to say it," Jane would later recall, "is to say that he made such a *fool* of himself. He came across as, you know, holier than thou, and it made him look ridiculous." In Jane's view, her preacher's pronouncement was a rhetorical loss of footing that reflected the tensions in the meeting, tensions that were substantially amplified by television cameras and reporters.

Brother Evans's comment was more than Donna Carens could bear. She had not come prepared with any kind of formal statement; Mercy was to be Footloose's spokesperson, but after Evans was through speaking she found herself standing to respond. "You're making it sound as though we have a utopian society that's going to be corrupted if we have dances," she said. "The truth is that we *already* have all of the problems you're mentioning. Outlawing dancing has not prevented them!" Donna was poised and articulate. Her ire was fueled, in part, by thoughts of her good friend, Jane Sandoval, whose daughter had become pregnant when she was 14. Donna knew the pain and anguish that the Sandovals had endured over that situation. Donna Carens's response was received by a murmur of approval from a packed chamber trying to keep the decorum the mayor had requested.

Evans was not the only one to make outrageous statements that evening. Another memorable quote came from P. B. Middlebrook, a city council member, a former Anson mayor, and a third-generation Ansonite. Middlebrook had left the Anson Church of Christ, where he had been an elder, after a disagreement with fellow church leaders. He was now the preacher at a Church of Christ in nearby Truby. In his inimitable West Texas style, and in a tone of ironic humor, Middlebrook also responded: "The unlawfulness of prostitution is an effort to legislate morality. There are many people in this town who feel that card playing is a sin. In my opinion, dancing is somewhere between card playing and prostitution!"

(By Middlebrook's later report, things had been moving smoothly at the meeting that evening until Davidson got up to make what Middlebrook termed his "You're trying to legislate morality" speech. To Middlebrook, the premise of a personal morality—that each individual was entitled to do whatever he or she felt like doing—was totally alien. Middlebrook was proud that he had never taken a single drink of alcohol or smoked a single cigarette in his life. Dancing, in his view, carried all of the dangers of such temptation. It made no sense to him to foster such circumstances; life was full of enough temptations as it was. Middlebrook had spent years as a Church of Christ missionary in New Mexico and on an Indian Reservation in Utah, an experience that had transformed his views on a number of important theological questions. He remained committed to the view that there was right and there was wrong in this world, and the two were clearly delineated. Davidson's relativistic stance was quite alien to Middlebrook.)

It was clear that Footloose and the city council were at loggerheads. Some sort of compromise had to be hammered out. One council member suggested that the issue be tabled until further review. Footloose, however, was leery of this strategy for they had anticipated this night's fateful confrontation. There had

Paul Davidson, Footloose vice president and assistant editor for Anson's *The Western Observer*. Photo: Nancy Scanlan.

been much discussion about prior efforts to work with the city council; once items were tabled they never saw the light of day again. Mercy Torres and her group demanded a specific time-table.

Mayor Rogers told Footloose that he and the council members would review their proposal and give it some deliberation. Jane Andruss responded for Footloose: "Do you mean a month? Do you mean two months? We want to know when, because we're going to give you a deadline and then we're going to come back!" She said later, "because that's what they'd always done. . . . We weren't going to let them table it. They were going to tell us 'yes' or 'no.' They weren't just going to put us off." The council acquiesced to this request, promising a response at the next scheduled meeting one month later.

Clearly, a major storm had broken. Footloose's course of action had brought about this confrontation. Immediately following the meeting, Footloose regrouped at Bea's café. There were high fives and whoops of victory. When Donna Carens arrived she received an ovation for her response to Brother Evans's remark about dancing leading to pregnancy. People could not believe he had said that. Although Donna responded to Evans, she actually felt kindly toward the man. "He is a very nice man," she would later recall. "He has a *wonderful voice* when he preaches. And I think that if he'd stated things differently he would not have come across as such a comic cliché. I didn't know him well, but I'd always felt he was a very personable, distinguished man, and he'll probably never live that quote down. He's probably sorry he stated it that way, because I think I know what he meant. . . . "

THE WAITING GAME

No one had really known what to expect from the city council meeting. Many had anticipated nothing more than a door slammed in the face. Instead, preposterous pronouncements notwithstanding, the consensus was that the city council would seriously entertain their petition and even work out a compromise that might be acceptable to all.

"I thought they were really going to consider it," Jane Sandoval recalled. "I felt they were really considering what we said and at the next meeting they would vote and we'd be able to have some input." It was clear that everyone felt the council meeting had gone exceptionally well.

With quotes like those of Middlebrook and Brother Evans to work on, the ground was fertile for media coverage. That night, the Abilene TV station carried Bob Evans's comments on the evening news. In addition, a reporter from *The Abilene Reporter News* wrote a somewhat patronizing story about the dancing controversy in Anson. But it was only when a writer for *The Fort Worth Star Telegram* picked up the Abilene reporter's piece from the AP wire that momentum really started to build. The *Star Telegram* reporter, Barry Shlachter, whose beat was small towns in Texas, came to Anson to do a story. Paul Davidson remembered his visit vividly:

> When he hit town it was almost like, I mean it was like the guy who rides into town on a horse and the windows start slamming shut. When he went to talk to various people, basically they said "No comment! get out of my office." So he got a little resistance. He was originally from Boston, so you can imagine someone with a Bostonian accent coming over here saying, 'I'd like to interview you about this stuff'. But that's what kicked it off. Then *The Dallas Morning News* had to compete, and they came, and then the Footloose officers were suddenly getting calls from all over.

Paul Davidson was a newspaper man, but he also loved an opportunity to *be* the news. *Texas Monthly* magazine, in an article on the dancing controversy in Anson the prior December, had featured a picture of Paul posing with his steel blue Fender Stratocaster guitar behind bars in Anson's County Jail. After the March city council meeting, *The Dallas Morning News* reporter brought along his own photographer and took a picture of Davidson and his guitar on the courthouse steps. "Just at the time that I was there taking this picture," Davidson would later recall, "people who usually weren't out at this time of day were driving by and when I got back people had called and asked, 'Can't you find Paul something to do?' And by this time the newspaper had a new owner who was a member of the Church of Christ. They knew what I was going to do. So that's when our opposition started heating up."

Newspapers from everywhere carried the story about a group of people who were fighting the local establishment to gain the right to dance. A reporter from England came, another from Australia. In addition to all the major Texas newspapers, many newspapers throughout the country, including *The Washington*

Post, *The San Francisco Chronicle*, *The Arizona Republic*, and *The St. Petersburg Times*, ran extended stories on the dancing controversy in Anson. National Public Radio's news program, "All Things Considered," also interviewed Footloose members.

A DEEPENING WEDGE

In the atmosphere of a media spectacle, things grew increasingly serious. Especially sensitive was the notion, frequently invoked in newspaper accounts, that Anson was a town run by the Church of Christ. For example, Dottie Spraberry, the city secretary, bristled at the suggestion that the Church of Christ, of which she was a member, ran the city. Spraberry was angry at what she termed "inaccurate portrayals" in the media coverage. In particular she disputed one newspaper report that said that three of the five city council members belonged to the Church of Christ. "That is not true," she told *The Dallas Morning News*, "two are members of the Church of Christ, two are Baptists, and now there's a Methodist, and he's a very fine fellow, and, of course, the Mayor is Church of Christ, but he's not on the five-member council." (The response was clearly disingenuous. The Methodist had only recently been elected to the council.) Just a few months earlier, when the whole matter had still seemed rather innocent, Leon Sharp, the Anson Church of Christ preacher, had boasted to reporters of the church's political power and influence.

The dancing controversy was creating deep divisions among the residents of Anson. Brother Bob Evans was quoted as saying that outsiders were "driving a wedge between some fine country folks who have always settled their differences between themselves." Indeed, things were getting personal and quite ugly. In a letter to the *The Western Observer*, one Anson resident pleaded with his fellow citizens: "I have heard all of the name-calling, insults and boycotting of business going on over this ordinance . . . please, Anson, let's go back to being the happy, friendly town I know we can be, and allow each person to choose his or her own forms of recreation." Another resident wrote to the same newspaper: "Cut it out! It's getting extremely embarrassing to go anywhere anymore and tell people I'm from Anson, 'cause everyone knows about the dancing situation. They just laugh right in your face."

Spraberry was no less pointed: "We're sick and tired of this issue," she told a *Fort Worth Star Telegram* reporter. "It has split the town, ended friendships. Nobody but Anson should be interested in this. . . . We don't worry about whether they dance in Fort Worth so why should they worry whether we dance in Anson?"

And it was true. Friendships, family ties, and work relationships were all being taxed and strained. Every social nexus became a forum for discussing the controversy. From the conservative fundamentalist pulpits, preachers gave sermons questioning the moral fiber of anyone who supported Footloose and its aims, no matter how indirectly. Members of Footloose were described as rebels. One preacher even implied that they were doing Satan's work. The attacks also became increasingly personal. Paul Davidson noted that Footloose members were described as "the trash of the town," and he was furious about it.

The St. Petersburg Times quoted the following conversation with two Anson residents on their opinions of Footloose: "It's not your better class of people," one woman said, to which her friend reportedly added, "It's not your main citizens." "It's your low-renters," the first woman concluded.

If Jane Sandoval had any questions about how serious things were getting, they were cruelly dispelled one evening when she arrived home. Jane owned two dogs, one an 8-year-old Schnauzer, the other a 4-month-old Eskimo Spitz. Typically, when she pulled into the driveway, the dogs received her enthusiastically from the fenced-in back yard. But that evening the dogs were uncharacteristically quiet, and she opened the door to the back yard to find both dogs dead.

"They were poisoned," Jane said later bitterly. "We did do an autopsy on Pepper, my Schnauzer, and she was definitely poisoned." Jane paused momentarily to pull herself together. She had been very attached to her pets, especially Pepper, her steady companion for eight years. "I have no proof, we could never prove anything," she said, still angry about it, "but to think that people can be . . . " Her voice trailed off. Jane Sandoval had witnessed an ugly manifestation of the dark side of human nature, which she presumed had come from within the camp of the anti-dancing forces.

At the conclusion of the council meeting in March 1987, Mayor Rogers announced that he and the council would postpone a decision on changing the ordinance until it could be established whether the ordinance was unconstitutional. They would seek the opinion of the Texas Attorney General's office in Austin. It was anticipated that by the next scheduled meeting on April 23rd, some resolution would be likely. It is clear that the council felt embattled.

On Tuesday, April 14th, *The Fort Worth Star Telegram* carried a story which read in part:

> The first public word of a possible change in the 1933 ordinance came in an anonymous statement read along with other announcements during Sunday services at the Anson Church of Christ. Dottie Spraberry (the city secretary) said the statement was written by the mayor, himself a deacon in the church. The statement said the move was made necessary by a finding by Texas Attorney General Jim Mattox's office that the no-dance ordinance is unconstitutional, church members said.

The story continued, citing a city council member as saying that a new ordinance was being prepared with some restrictions to be decided later.

Footloose members reacted cautiously to the announcement. "I am reserving judgment," Jane Sandoval remarked. "If they don't change it we might have to take other steps," she said. "We're not going to lay down and play dead like the rest of the town has for the last fifty-four years. I am hoping the council

will come up with something agreeable to everyone . . . all of
them are embarrassed and tired of seeing Anson made fun of,"
she concluded.

Precisely what happened next is not clear. The statement at
the Church of Christ that the ordinance would need to be
changed was made on Sunday, April 12. Dottie Spraberry claims
she posted an announcement at city hall, some time late afternoon or evening on Monday, notifying the public that the council had decided to schedule an emergency meeting for Tuesday
morning at 8 A.M. Evidently, it was an announcement that no
one else saw. In spite of the widespread interest in the dancing
controversy throughout the community as attested to by the
huge attendance at the council's March meeting, only the mayor,
city secretary, and some council members (P. B. Middlebrook
was out of town) were present. The only nonofficial person in
attendance that morning was Don Jones, editor of *The Western
Observer*. During this "emergency session" a new city ordinance,
which had clearly been drafted prior to the meeting, was passed
by majority vote of those present.

THE NEW ORDINANCE

The result of that secretive, early morning meeting was Ordinance Number 663, titled "Dance and Dance Halls." It was a six-
page, single-spaced document with twenty-two separate "closely
reasoned" clauses governing the conduct of public dances in
Anson. The new ordinance did permit dancing; however, the
bewildering array of stipulations made it all but impossible to actually hold one. Among these was the requirement that a permit
be obtained from City Hall. In addition, sponsors of a dance would
have to be found "of good moral character" by the city secretary
before a permit could be issued, of which *The Sunday Telegraph*
of London later said: "Many think that even a saint would fail to
pass through the eye of that particular needle."

But the most restrictive clause in the new ordinance appeared
in Section 4 under "Issuance of Permit or License." That clause

stipulated that the premises where a dance could be held, in addition to having "suitable and sufficient toilet and conveniences and facilities" must also be "so located with reference to other buildings and private residences as not to constitute a nuisance to other citizens and residents of the community; nor shall the premises be located closer than three hundred feet (300') to a church or hospital." In the small town of Anson, with its fourteen churches sprinkled up and down Commercial Street, that pretty much excluded every potential dance location. It most definitely excluded the high school, which was across the street from the Church of Christ and abutted the First Baptist Church. It was obvious that the city fathers had implemented this legal strategy in an attempt to regain control of an out-of-control situation.

As news of the new ordinance spread, Footloose members were enraged. They felt betrayed. "Stabbed in the back," Paul Davidson told me. Calling an emergency meeting of their own, they retreated to Bea's café to formulate a course of action. Mercy Torres was not prepared to accept defeat. On the contrary. Sensitive to questions of honor and pride, she felt belittled and disregarded by the city fathers, a feeling that only reinforced her determination. She was not about to back down. The city fathers would, in the end, have a clearer understanding of the person with whom they were dealing, whatever the outcome of this legal dispute.

At Bea's café that night in mid-April, fourteen members of Footloose huddled to plan their strategy. It was evident that they had little leverage against the city council from within Anson. In recent elections held earlier that spring, candidates associated with Footloose had received a thorough trouncing. It was outside resources, such as the media that had covered the dancing controversy, that might provide their only influence on the city fathers .

One other resource had been mentioned at prior Footloose meetings, namely, a legal suit against the city of Anson, possibly backed by the American Civil Liberties Union.

The American Civil Liberties Union. Its very name evoked
the soul of the underlying struggle in Anson. The implications
of such a step were potentially enormous. Few in this conservative rural town (even among members of the Footloose Club)
viewed the ACLU as a guardian of human liberty. The majority of Ansonites saw it as a defender of leftist and liberal causes,
anathema to all they held dear. Thus, to bring the ACLU into
this quarrel risked confirming all the overt and covert accusations as to the "true" purposes and aims (serving prurient interests, undermining wholesomeness) that had already been
ascribed to Footloose. This group of parents had worked hard
to defuse such innuendo through its conscientious community
works and through its strict regulation of the dance it had sponsored. The good will Footloose had garnered through those
efforts would be placed at risk were they to enlist the aid of the
American Civil Liberties Union.

In short, playing the ACLU card had many potential ramifi-
cations that Footloose wanted to avoid, but their backs were
against the wall, and their options had narrowed considerably.
Either they reinvigorated their cause (and themselves), and
carried on the fight, or they would have to fold up their tents
and go home. As Mercy Torres surveyed Footloose's predicament, it became obvious that there was no other alternative, no
recourse left but to bring in the biggest gun they could find. That
gun was the American Civil Liberties Union.

Not without some reluctance and anxiety, Mercy Torres
called the ACLU offices in Austin. She first spoke with Gara
LaMarche, then Executive Director of the Texas Civil Liberties
Union, an affiliate of the American Civil Liberties Union. Almost immediately Mercy sensed that she had done the right
thing. LaMarche was clear, firm, and supportive. He had read
the *Texas Monthly* article and had followed some of the newspaper reports on the conflict in Anson. Thus, he was familiar
with the situation Mercy Torres described over the phone. He
urged her to obtain as much documentation of Footloose's case

as possible. More important, however, LaMarche told her that in his view Anson did not have a legal leg to stand on.

"This isn't a joke," LaMarche told a *Washington Post* reporter in mid-May, not long after his initial contact with Mercy Torres. "The Supreme Court has already decided that topless dancing is a form of civil expression protected by the First Amendment, so I can hardly imagine that the courts will deny people [in Anson] the right to organize dances."

That same month, LaMarche told *The National Law Journal* that he did not believe the issues involved in the Anson case represented "a complex legal question." He termed the Anson ordinance "anachronistic" and said it was ripe for challenge because dancing had already been held to be constitutionally protected as an expressive action. LaMarche zeroed in on what he viewed as the primary issue in the dancing controversy: "a religious majority imposing its view on the minorities."

THE ACLU STEPS IN

Bringing the ACLU into the controversy had the immediate effect of further straining already existing tensions. For many in Anson it represented the ultimate outside intrusion. Reflecting those mental processes that blend political views with moral positions, the ACLU was not far removed from sin itself.

On May 17, 1987, in his sermon "The Absence of Awe," Jerry Paulding, pastor at the First Baptist Church, the second largest congregation in Anson after the Church of Christ, warned his congregants that the American Civil Liberties Union was "one of the most humanistic, seculistic [sic] organizations in the entire world and their major concern, and [that of] the people that are involved in them, is to overthrow the idea of one God, Christianity ruling in our world today." Reaching an angry crescendo, the preacher instructed that *anything* that the ACLU became involved with "I must stand against because of the Godless organization, the satanically motivated organization that they are!"

The message was powerful and clear. Those residents of Anson who were involved with Footloose, and therefore consorting with the ACLU, were doing the work of Satan, regardless of their avowed intent. They were furthering the efforts of those who would try to overthrow the idea of one God. They were undermining Christianity itself. It is evident that the preacher was trying to intimidate Footloose into relinquishing the one bit of leverage available to them, namely, the possibility of a lawsuit against the city of Anson for an ordinance that violated the First Amendment to the Constitution.

Jerry Paulding audio-taped his sermons so that members of the congregation unable to attend church could listen to them. Footloose obtained a tape and mailed it to the ACLU offices in Austin. In response, the ACLU sent the preacher some pamphlets describing its own history and its aims. In his cover letter, Gara LaMarche tried to be evenhanded. "I understand that you recently made some comments criticizing the American Civil Liberties Union for our plans to sue the City of Anson over its restrictions on dancing. I would like to think that your views of the ACLU are based on misinformation, not prejudice, so I am enclosing some literature which will explain our goals and our activities. . . . "

At the evening sermon of May 31st, Jerry Paulding's message centered on Peter's "faith failure." "What causes faith failure? . . . David warned us centuries before . . . 'Blessed is the man that walks not in the council of the ungodly nor stands in the way of sinners nor sits in the seat of the scornful.'" Once again, his message was clear and strong: " . . . anytime we begin to company with the wrong people . . . it's going to cost us and . . . we're not going to be blessed." These reflections served as introduction to his reading of portions of LaMarche's letter as well as portions of the pamphlets he had received. Mockingly, he read from a pamphlet that described the ACLU's past accomplishments, including the fact that their first case involved the defense of John Thomas Scopes for daring to teach evolution in

Tennessee, a state that officially favored the biblical view of creation and sought to impose that view in the schools. (The year was 1925. Fifty-six years later in Arkansas, the battle was renewed with the ACLU again fighting to keep the state from imposing creationism in the schools.)

"This is from *their* pamphlet!" the preacher declared with incensed incredulity, his voice reaching a penetrating pitch. It was as if the pamphlet constituted a kind of inadvertent confession by the ACLU of their debased morality. He went on to read, in a tone laced with derision and disapproval, about the ACLU's defense of civil rights activists, anti-war demonstrators during the Vietnam War, and their special interest in such topics as reproductive freedom, national security, women's rights, prisons, and lesbian and gay rights. Finally, the preacher quoted the findings of a 1960s congressional committee to investigate communism, which he said documented the fact that the ACLU was closely affiliated with the communist movement in the United States, with "fully 90 percent" of its efforts on behalf of communists who have come into conflict with the law. He also cited a report from the California State Committee on Un-American Activities which he said had classified the ACLU as a "communist front." Even the *World Book Encyclopedia* made the communist undergirding of the ACLU clear, since it described one of its founders, Elizabeth Gurley Flynn, as "the first woman to head the Communist party in the United States."

"I refuse to be intimidated by the letter that I received from the Texas Civil Liberties Union," Jerry Paulding asserted, looking over the assembled congregation. His demeanor now reflected a mixture of persecuted hero and fiery defender of the flock from the teeth of the voracious infidels. It was clear, however, that the intimidation was not coming from the ACLU but from Paulding. This was the message he wanted his congregation to hear and hear clearly. He concluded with the following admonition: "One of the reasons that Peter had a faith failure was because he distanced himself from Christ and began to company with the wrong people. There are places that Christians cannot go . . . there are organizations that Christians cannot belong to . . . when we compromise our walk with Christ we're in for a faith failure. And that has everything to do with who we company with and how close we walk with Christ."

The message was unmistakable. Individuals who were active in, or even sympathetic to the aims of the Footloose Club were playing with fire. They were toying with "a faith failure" which could only lead to a fall from a life with Christ. One could not be involved with a "Godless organization," or a "satanically motivated" organization and hope to have a positive reception by God when the day of reckoning came. Similar messages were being heard from every fundamentalist church in Anson, including the Church of Christ, where Mayor Rogers reputedly apologized to the congregation for failing to retain Anson's anti-dancing ordinance.

Mercy Torres had not underestimated this pressure, however and had constituted the board of Footloose with people who were "good speakers and whose minds would not be manipulated or changed because of their religion or work or whatever." She had anticipated that their leaders would come under heavy pressure from various quarters within the community. She sat down with Salvador, her husband, and asked him: "Are you prepared to have the people boycott you if we go through with this?" Salvador's reply was immediate and unambiguous: "Listen, Mercy, when they come to the emergency room and they're sick, they're going to want to see the doctor on call . . . don't worry about it."

Throughout the spring of 1987, and into early summer, the city council remained intransigent. Little direct communication occurred between them and Footloose. By June, the ACLU and Footloose were ready to turn up the heat. Paul Knisely, a lawyer from Austin who had agreed to take the case for the Texas Civil Liberties Union, fired the first salvo in the form of a letter to Leon Thurman, the Anson city attorney. The letter read, in part:

Our law firm has been contacted by Ms. Mercy Torres of
Anson with regard to the possibility of representing her
and other residents of Anson who comprise the "Footloose
Club of Anson, Texas" in a legal challenge to the City Ordinance No. 663 which regulates and severely restricts
public dancing in Anson.

We have carefully reviewed Ordinance No. 663 and we
believe that there are strong grounds for challenging the
constitutionality of the ordinance as a whole or certain
portions of it. Ms. Torres has requested, however, on behalf of her organization, that we refrain from instituting
any formal legal proceedings for the time being so that a
reasonable effort can be made to convince the City Council of Anson to address their concerns and, we hope, amend
the ordinance and avoid the necessity of a lawsuit. Neither
Ms. Torres nor the other members of the Footloose club
wish to create any problems, embarrassment, or unneces-
sary expense for the City of Anson. However, they also feel
strongly that the existing ordinance unreasonably and un-
fairly restricts their right to engage in conduct which is
clearly protected by the First Amendment to the United
States Constitution.

A week later, Paul Knisely received a response from Leon
Thurman. Thurman's letter suggested that neither Mercy
Torres nor other members of Footloose had availed themselves
of the opportunities to "give them any input . . . regarding the
Ordinance that they would like to have changed." The fact that
the city had demonstrated a clear disinclination toward dialogue
by virtue of their "emergency" meeting was obviously not taken
into account in the city's response to the ACLU.

Leon Thurman's letter further suggested that the City of
Anson held firm to its stance regarding the new city ordinance.
"[We] wish to advise you," the letter said, "that the Mayor and
City Council of Anson has passed this Ordinance in accordance
with the laws of the State of Texas." Thurman also indicated

that the Anson ordinance was in keeping with those of other communities in West Texas. But the main point of Thurman's letter read:

> The City of Anson does not wish to get involved in a law-suit of any type, and we are sure that the Footloose Club does not wish to create any problems or embarrassment. Please feel free to contact Mayor Gene Rogers and City Council at any time. They are willing to work with these people but would first need some input from them what (sic) they would like to change in the Ordinance.

In spite of the tone of the main body of Thurman's letter, this concluding paragraph revealed the truth of the City's situation. They knew they were in trouble. The city, with a shrinking tax base and an extremely weak economy, could ill afford to have a major lawsuit on its hands. Bravado notwithstanding, it was clear that Anson was willing to negotiate with Footloose. With national media attention and the involvement of the ACLU, Footloose had raised the stakes to the limit. A meeting was scheduled in which the two opposing camps would try to hammer out a compromise acceptable to all that would avoid the looming threat of legal proceedings.

ANOTHER COUNCIL MEETING IS SCHEDULED

The final meeting with the city council was preceded by a confusing turn of events. It was set off by what Paul Davidson termed "the famous 'We don't want Davidson there'" phone call from the mayor to Mercy Torres when he tried to set up a meeting that would exclude Davidson. Mercy had refused to go along with what she felt was an effort to get her and Donna Carens alone against the all-male council, and insisted on Davidson's attendance. The meeting had originally been set for midday on Wednesday, July 15, a bad day for Davidson because Wednes-

day was the day that the newspaper was laid out. In anticipation, Davidson had stayed up until 3 A.M. so that on Wednesday
his work was complete.

By all accounts, Jerry Wallace, owner of *The Western Observer,* is a fairly easy-going man. But that Wednesday morning when Davidson announced that he needed to attend the city
council meeting, Wallace "exploded." Davidson pointed out that
he had made all the preparations the night before, but Wallace
wouldn't hear of it. "Under no circumstances can you go,"
Davidson recalls him saying.

Davidson suspected foul play. It was clear that Jerry Wallace
had been under some pressure from his fellow Church of Christ
parishioners who did not want the newspaper supporting
Footloose's activities. He had already received a barrage of calls
when Davidson had been photographed by *The Dallas Morning News* on the courthouse steps the previous April. Davidson
now suspected that perhaps the mayor had orchestrated the city
council meeting so that it fell on a day when Davidson's respon-
sibilities at the newspaper would interfere with his attendance.

Davidson called Mercy Torres to let her know that he would
not be able to attend the city council meeting. Torres's response
reflected a sophisticated grasp of the underlying dynamics of
the situation: "Well, what they're trying to do is get me and
Donna there, in other words, two women. They think that these
five men can overpower these two women and get everything
settled without you there." She then called the mayor and refused to attend if Davidson could not be present as well. With
some reluctance, he rescheduled the meeting for the next day,
Thursday, at 5 P.M.

As had become her trademark, Mercy Torres did not leave a
stone unturned in preparation for this meeting. For Footloose
members who would accompany her, she prepared packets containing copies of every important document related to Anson's
dance fight that they might need. In addition, she contacted a
number of persons she felt might have some expertise on the
question of dancing and whose opinions the city council might

listen to, asking them to write letters endorsing dancing as a positive activity.

The county's chief probation officer, for example, wrote that, in his opinion, if "supervised dancing was allowed within the city of Anson, it would deter other activities, both negative and unsupervised, that the youth of this town are already or could easily become involved in, both locally as well as in traveling to Ablilene for entertainment . . . I feel [dancing] would contribute to the prevention of these young men and women from entering into the criminal justice process." The probation officer concluded his letter noting that, as a parent, "the future of our town as well as the social activities of our young is (sic) of importance to me."

A licensed physical therapist at the local hospital also wrote the mayor and city council, extolling the virtues of dance as a form of physical exercise, noting that dancing "takes control, coordination, balance, trunk stability, strength and endurance—and we could all use more of these skills."

Finally, a counselor at the Pastoral Care and Counseling Center in Abilene wrote an extensive letter in which she argued, among other things, that "movement is God's gift to us" and that, were the city council members to look back in history they would find that dance was used to worship God:

> . . . and is still used today in the church. This liturgical dance enables the worshiper to release his 'earthly ways' and have a direct "spiritual" communication with the Lord, something that cannot be described in words. This spiritual high is also used by the dance therapist when trying to free the psychotic patient from his own personal world.

The counselor concluded by attributing to dance the potential for instilling in children confidence, security, trust, and a great enthusiasm for life.

These letters were mailed just prior to the final city council meeting with the Footloose representatives.

In the thick heat of the West Texas summer, on July 16, 1987, the final round of the dancing controversy was played out. The council chambers had a hollow feeling that Thursday afternoon. Since it was after work hours, none of the regular employees were there. As people arrived for the meeting, they filed past the huge bank vault. The aroma of fresh coffee wafted out through the open vault door. Only the three Footloose representatives and most of the city council members sat in the council chambers.

There was considerable tension in the air, with little trust remaining between the two sides facing each other. Too much had transpired in these few months to pretend otherwise. Mercy Torres was accompanied by Donna Carens and Paul Davidson, the faithful allies who had stood with her throughout their collective ordeal. All had been the object of considerable pressures, all had held firm in their resolve. Mercy knew that neither would be easily intimidated by the powerful and influential men of the city council.

The trio sat across from Anson's mayor and several council members. The setting was a portrait of contrasts: all but one of the council members (the newly-elected Tom Isbell) could trace their lineage in Jones County back several generations. None of the Footloose representatives had been there even a decade. The city's authority was embodied in a group of older white males, sitting across from the likes of Paul Davidson, the counterculturish country western band member with an iconoclastic bent, and Donna Carens, a bright young woman with a sense of her role that differed from the traditional farmer's wife. And then, of course, there was Mercy Torres, a dark-skinned Mexican-American with a penchant for Mexican cotton dresses. In fact, the circumstance could be seen as a parody of postmodern antagonisms, but the stakes extended beyond the question of dance. The participants were from different worlds, though they spoke the same language and lived in the same community. Their meeting marked a turning point in that community, an irreversible shift in its self-understanding.

Mercy Torres was the first Footloose member to speak. She proposed that City Ordinance No. 663 be scrapped. In response,

Gene Rogers indicated that the ordinance was now a law on the books and the legal steps to remove it would be too involved. The ordinance could readily be amended, but it would be too difficult to void. Besides, the city needed some kind of ordinance to regulate dancing, he argued, just like every other neighboring community in Jones County had.

Mercy Torres grew especially angry when the mayor indicated that his primary reservations centered on the cost of insuring public dances. She was fed up with the council's obstructionism. She reminded them that no one had said anything about insurance when she had raised funds to install some children's toys at the little park off Commercial Street several years ago. "When I had those little toys put in the park, you never stopped me. There's no insurance. A kid could fall off of one of those toys much faster than he could from the dance floor!" Mercy told the mayor.

At that moment, the recently elected Tom Isbell broke ranks with the mayor and other council members. "That's right," he told them, "that's discriminatory." Isbell pointed out that the city condoned a yearly fall festival when vendors sold merchandise on the sidewalks and streets.

Footloose attempted to systematically cover the new ordinance. It was established that the ordinance actually did not cover private dancing. "What about the dances we're having for these kids?" Donna Carens remarked. "You're talking about dance halls. You're talking about profit-making things that you're trying to regulate and legislate, but what about private dances?" This was the line of reasoning Footloose was trying to pin down.

"We really weren't getting a straight answer," Carens recalled. Finally, Tom Isbell spoke up again. "We cannot regulate private dancing. That's a private thing. The only thing that would regulate it would be disturbing the peace or any other law that is broken. But it wouldn't be constitutional to try to regulate a private dance at a private party."

Isbell's sharp, clean delineation of the issues left his fellow city council members momentarily speechless. "I got the impres-

sion that they didn't have an answer to that," one of the Footloose members later recalled. "Everyone puts on a face, you
know, and keeps up a front. But the mayor was very displeased
that Isbell said that."

Isbell had been an unknown quantity to the members of Footloose. "He's a dear, dear man, but we weren't sure of him at the
time," one of them remembered. They were anticipating that he
would side with the mayor. When he broke ranks with Gene
Rogers, he did it politely, as this Footloose member continues
to describe Isbell's stand:

> He just very graciously agreed with us, but he stood up for
> the facts, the facts and the law, which is what he was con-
> cerned about and what all of us should have been con-
> cerned about. And I think that opened Tom's eyes enough
> that he began to examine both sides with an open mind.
> That was really the turning point. Tom Isbell is not a pushy
> man. He's a very gracious man. But he gets things done.
> And I think he really persuaded the rest of the city coun-
> cil that they were potentially in for a lot of trouble if they
> continued like they were going.

Isbell's position took the Footloose members by surprise as
well. He had run against a pro-dancing candidate, and during
the campaign had subtly positioned himself to garner anti-
dancing votes without actually advocating an anti-dancing position: "There's more to the position [of City Councilman] than
whether or not you want people to dance," Isbell had noted. Now,
with his support of Footloose, the tide turned and most of
Footloose's objections to the existing city ordinance were removed. By the end of the meeting, the city council and the Footloose Club had arrived at a mutually acceptable ordinance. It
was an ordinance that now clearly and definitively permitted
dancing within in the City of Anson.

For Davidson, unfortunately, the Footloose Club's momentous accomplishment was bittersweet. The day after the coun-

cil meeting, while at work, Davidson noticed that Jerry Wallace seemed aloof. "Usually, I had to run him out of my office because he liked to talk so much," Davidson recalled. At about two o'clock that afternoon, when Davidson went to pay some *Western Observer* bills, he noticed that the newspaper's checkbook was gone from his desk, which was where it was usually kept. The next day, Jerry Wallace called Davidson into his office and fired him on the grounds that he was not selling enough advertising. Both men, however, knew better.

DANCING IS LEGALIZED

At its next meeting in August, the city council ratified the amendments to the dancing ordinance that had been hammered out with Torres, Davidson, and Carens. Eight months after their first meeting on that chilly January evening at Bea's café the members of the Footloose Club had succeeded in overturning the City Ordinance that had made the moral choice of the fundamentalist churches the standard for all the town.

Members of Footloose were elated. They immediately set out to plan a victory dance to celebrate. In May of 1987, Marc Oswald, the manager of a well-known country western band, Mason-Dixon, had written to the mayor after reading about the dancing controversy in *The San Diego Union.* He offered the services of Mason-Dixon to "lend a hand to our fellow Texans in Anson . . . We are willing to waive our performance fee . . . in the interest of putting a little pep into the step of your youth," Marc Oswald's letter said. Finally, he sought to assure the mayor that "alcohol, drugs and promiscuity are not at all a part of Mason-Dixon's show or lifestyles."

"From what I gather, Gene just threw that letter in the trash, but for some reason Mason-Dixon had also sent a copy of the letter to the high school and Jaynie Rainwater's daughter was the class president or something like that so she got us a copy. That's when we decided to write Mason-Dixon ourselves and see if they would have a dance for us," Jane Sandoval recalled.

A date was set for early October for the first legal public dance to be held in Anson since 1933, not counting the annual Cowboys' Christmas Balls, and, ironically, their association consented to Footloose's use of their location, Pionner Hall, for this event.

A local tragedy provided Footloose with another opportunity to serve the community. In the summer of 1987 Laurie Hornsby, the daughter of Jack and Bea Hornsby, who owned Bea's café, died under confusing circumstances. It was rumored that Hornsby and his daughter had feuded over her involvement in an interracial relationship. The Hornsbys were convinced that Laurie's death had been an accident, but the police investigator had concluded that it was a suicide, which meant that the Hornsbys' medical insurance would not cover the three days of hospital treatment prior to Laurie's death. The medical bills had come to $36,000, an enormous sum for the Hornsbys. It was a tragedy that deeply affected the entire community. Laurie was a popular girl at school, and almost everyone in town loved her parents. Jack was a consummate raconteur and an ever-ready host, and the café was the center of Anson's social world.

Footloose's victory dance generated all the excitement one would expect from an event that had been so contested in this small community. Tickets were five dollars, with proceeds going to benefit the Hornsbys and the youth of Anson. The 700 available tickets were sold out early in the evening, but the demand was so great that people manning the ticket counters started selling more tickets. No one wanted to be left out. It was Footloose's moment of glory.

It was also a personal moment of glory for Paul Davidson. His band, Bitter Creek, had played at the Valentine's Day dance and a Footloose-sponsored unofficial prom that was held in the Roman Catholic church's parish hall, which happened to be a few feet beyond the Anson city limits. Bitter Creek opened for the Mason-Dixon band the night of the victory dance. With his pre-1965 Fender guitar strapped over his shoulder ("that's when they still made them in the U. S."), Davidson and his band stepped onto the little stage at Pioneer Hall to the screams and cheers of the packed house. He and the other band members were a bit awed by the sound system provided by Mason-Dixon, which was far superior to the comparatively skimpy amplifiers they were accustomed to. This really felt like the big time. With his wry, mischievous little-boy smile, Davidson looked out over the sea of faces. He knew nearly everyone. Bitter Creek started their set playing for the first time Davidson's own composition, "Ain't No Dancin' in Anson." The crowd went wild.

If people were stirred up, it was nothing compared to the emotions that ran through the crowd when Mason-Dixon came on to begin their set. "They were real professionals," Davidson noted, "and they really got the crowd going." One of the band's well-known songs was "353 West End Avenue" in which the street numbers were repeated in a refrain. A little boy named Rudy Perez was hoisted up on stage to sing the numbers into the microphone. One person in attendance remembered: "They'd hold the microphone down for him and he was as cute as he could be. He was just putting on a show! He'd prance and he'd do these little turns, and you could tell he was really into it." The crowd was into it, too, screaming, hollering, and clapping.

"The audience was great. This was the *victory* dance," Paul Davidson recalled. Everyone who had had anything to do with Footloose was at the Pioneer Hall that night. However, it wasn't only the Footloosers. What impressed Donna Carens about the dance more than anything was that it had drawn from a broad cross-section of the community. People who had not attended any of Footloose's previous functions were there. And, because of the character of the band, the dance attracted at least as many adults as it did teenagers.

For Donna there was something distinctly conciliatory about that night, and she remembered that "the politics seemed to stop. It was no longer 'I'd like to go but I don't want to be seen' kind of attitude. There was just a large cross-section of people." Everyone in Anson seemed to have come out to celebrate the end of the civil war that had nearly torn their community to pieces. It was a dance of peacemaking.

Then came the grand finale. As the emotion peaked, the Mason-Dixon band called all the key members of Footloose onto the small stage at the Pioneer Hall. The band and their Footloose guests now filled the stage in its entirety. Davidson's recollection:

> I'll put you in my frame of mind. I had been released from my job. I had made enemies in a town that I really cared about. I hadn't had any luck as far as jobs were concerned. But it was like, "Was it all worth it? Yes it was worth it!" And that, that moment was my reward right there. That was all I wanted . . . , that feeling right there that I had of being on stage with everybody who had gone to bat, you know, they were all on one stage right there. It was almost like sheer exhaustion. It was like I'd run this big race and *finally* crossed the finish line. Just like the first dance back in Rainwater's barn had been the starting line, this was the last dance. My whole purpose had been fulfilled.

With the stage crowded with victorious Footloose members, with Pioneer Hall bursting at the seams with an ecstatic crowd, Mason-Dixon started their last song; "Proud to be an American." A roar went up from the crowd. It was one of Mason-Dixon's most popular songs and practically everyone was singing, whether or not they understood its political statement. Davidson recalled the faces of other Footloose members who were on the stage:

> Maybe Mercy kind of felt the same way I did. She had this glow of enlightenment over her face and she wasn't looking at the audience, she was looking up. I remember that. Like at the ceiling. And I remember Jane Sandoval. She was in closer proximity to me than anybody, and I remember her crying. And I remember her turning to me and, it's like you've got to remember the part that Jane played in this. She had started all this. She was the one who had organized the first meeting at Bea's. So I can only imag-

Augie and Angelica Mata at Anson's Pioneer Hall. Photo: Nancy Scanlan

ine what it felt like for her to be there in the middle of all this and she was crying. But, you know, it was like that bittersweet, painful smile when someone's crying on their face, where she's trying to hold it in but she can't, and she's smiling, grinning ear to ear. And what I remember about Donna is that she had just a hint of skepticism on her face. Those are the faces I remember.

Many of Anson's residents felt they had come of age somehow. "We made the *Today Show* this morning, so l guess we're big time," noted one local to a *Dallas Morning News* reporter. "Anson is finally catching up with the times," said another, "and it's a wonderful thing for the kids."

One Anson teenager stripped the meaning of Footloose's victory down to the bare bones. She told *The Dallas Morning News* that night, "This means we can finally have fun. Normally, what we can do in Anson is nothing. Now, we can have a prom, just like everyone else."

3

Dance Fights, Cockfights, and Other Forms of Enactment

What to make of this curious drama enacted on the desolate plains of West Texas? Clifford Geertz, the cultural anthropologist, tells us that small acts speak to large issues. In the context of America's immense social struggles, Anson's skirmishes seem remote and quaint. In fact, however, they are an extension of the conflicts taking place today in nearly every American community. Anson's rather absurd debate over the morality of a high school prom was symptomatic. It betrayed a deeper debate, one regarding the kind of community its citizens could fashion out of a world that had changed radically since the early 1960s when, as in the rest of America, virtually the only citizens "of standing" were white and the economy was prospering.

In psychoanalysis, the concept of enactment refers to a piece of action within the treatment situation in which the participation of both analyst and analysand is ripe with meaning (Chused 1991, McLaughlin 1991). Though Freud never used the term, its meaning is not far removed from his contributions in the arena of transference and countertransference. Transference, of course, refers to the analysand's projection of unconscious conflicts, desires, anxieties, and so forth onto the analyst. It is a process whereby the patient brings to the analytic situation the variegated emotional "constituencies" of his life history. Transference represents an imposition of those unconscious realities onto the analysis. Conversely, the psychoanalytic conceptualization of countertransference refers, in its original sense, to the analyst's unconscious response to the analysand and/or the analysand's transferences.

From this perspective, the analytic situation is a convening of two psyches, each with a different role, or function in the unfolding analytic process. The concept of countertransference has been expanded in recent decades to include the broad range of conscious and unconscious reactions that the analyst has to the analysand and the analysand's life story (Kernberg 1976). The effect of this expanded view has been to bring closer attention to the interactive elements of the analytic situation. Rather than Freud's simile of the analyst as a well-polished mirror reflecting back to the analysand the meaning of the analysand's life, psychoanalysis has moved toward a co-constitutive, or narrative model (Schafer 1983) in which meaning is constructed by analyst and analysand together within that most peculiar dialogue that is psychoanalysis.

The notion of enactment, however, while a direct descendant of transference and countertransference, highlights the element of action within the psychoanalytic situation. It refers more specifically to some piece of behavior in which both analyst and analysand have unconsciously participated—a piece of behavior that carries substantial meaning, which is only understood by the two participants within the context of the unfolding analysis. Thus, psychoanalytic enactments are actions (albeit sometimes actions cloaked with words [Chused 1991]) laden with potentially revelatory significance. However, these actions must be analyzed if one is to grasp their meaning. Otherwise, enactments remain entangled or hidden within the more superficial layers of social convention, or they become "lost" as analyst and analysand attempt to set them aside and continue "the real work" of the analysis. In psychoanalysis, the social convention may be the analyst's silence (McLaughlin 1991), which is itself a kind of ritualized practice. However, an enactment may be "carried" in any number of ways within the analysis as analyst and analysand respond to implicit, that is, unconscious realities in which they are both participating.

Especially useful for my present purposes is Chused's observation that enactments within the analytic situation often signal that a change has occurred in the material that organizes the analysis. Chused suggests that this shift, because it may catch the analyst by surprise, could provoke an enactment of a process that the analyst is unable to "objectify and observe" (p. 636), a failure that leads to the analyst's participation in the enactment. I am suggesting, of course, that Anson's dancing conflict was a kind of collective enactment—an event that erupted at a point of social change within the community, giving expression to what its participants could not clearly articulate or fully comprehend.

The psychoanalytic notion of enactment has a collective corollary in the concept of symbolic action. In his classic anthropological work, Clifford Geertz (1973) set out to understand the social meaning embedded within the Balinese cockfight. "As much of America surfaces in a ball park," wrote Geertz, "much of Bali surfaces in a cock ring" (p. 417).

In a brilliant examination of the social ritual that is the Balinese cockfight, Geertz uncovers the "deep play" lurking within this competitive event when a variety of factors become activated. When the cockfight is a "deep" one, that is, one infused with social and cultural significance, it becomes dense with resonances that refer back to the players' social position, conflicts, tensions, historical enmities, and so forth. "In deep ones," Geertz tells us, " . . . much more is at stake than material gain: namely, esteem, honor, dignity, respect—in a word . . . status" (p. 433). In other words, those in attendance are participating in a piece of symbolic social action the meaning of which they are at best only partially aware.

Geertz continues:

What makes Balinese cockfighting "deep" (is) the migration of the Balinese status hierarchy into the body of the

cockfight. Psychologically an Aesopian representation of
the ideal/demonic, rather narcissistic, male self, sociologi-
cally it is an equally Aesopian representation of the complex fields of tension set up by the controlled, muted, cer-
emonial, but for all that deeply felt, interaction of these
selves in the context of everyday life. The cocks may be sur-
rogates for their owners' personalities, animal mirrors of
psychic form, but the cockfight is . . . a simulation of the
social matrix, the involved system of crosscutting, overlap-
ping, highly corporate groups . . . in which its devotees live.
[p. 436]

Geertz concludes his thesis concerning the underlying crosscurrents represented in the cockfight by noting that it "is fundamentally a dramatization of status concerns" (p. 437). In this
way, he sets out to decode the hidden social realities at play in
the Balinese cockfight, realities in which struggles between
different factions within the community are played out, through
which alliances are affirmed and animosities expressed, however subtly, within the confines of another reality, namely, that
they are participating in a culturally sanctioned competitive
game. "You activate village and kin group rivalries, hostilities,
but in 'play' form, coming dangerously, and entrancingly close
to the expression of aggression . . . but not quite, because, after
all, it is 'only a cockfight'" (p. 440).

Geertz describes a variety of practices that indicate these
underlying elements. For example, there are very involved networks of alliances that are "played out" or expressed via the betting practices at the cockfight. Geertz further notes that when
people are involved in what he terms "an institutionalized hos-
tility relationship . . . in which they do not speak or otherwise
have anything to do with each other," (for example, because of
wife-capture, inheritance arguments, or political differences) they
will often "bet very heavily, sometimes almost maniacally, against
one another in what is a frank, direct attack on the very mascu-
linity, the ultimate ground of his status, of the opponent" (p. 438).

With the benefit of Geertz's reasoning, the cockfight has shifted from a peculiar, regional form of entertainment, to a piece of highly symbolic, social action containing multiple acknowledged, partially acknowledged, and unacknowledged social meanings. The structure of the cockfight is thus revealed to be much more than the simple betting game that at first glance it appears to be. Symbolic action thus is a social or collective corollary to the dyadic enactments of the psychoanalytic situation. Both speak to a particular kind of action which carries unconscious meaning for the participants.

Though different in some important respects, Anson's dancing conflict was an American version of the Balinese cockfight. Beneath the apparently absurd dispute over the moral status of dancing at a high school prom lurked issues of much greater import, which utilized the dance as a vehicle for expression. Anson's dance fight was not the ritualized, "competitive sport" that the cockfight is in Bali. In its own way, however, it was a kind of ritualized encounter, using political and legal conduits to play out the very kinds of "rival kinship group" tensions, conflicts, and hostilities found in Bali's cockfights. As Geertz describes the cockfight, so was Anson's dance fight a "migration" of its "social hierarchy" into the political imbroglio of the dance question through which differing allegiances, and ethnic, religious, social, and economic commitments could be played out.

What were these forces that vied, beneath the surface, for position? A central issue revolved around the question of ethnic relations. So much had changed in Anson beneath the business-as-usual appearance at city hall. More than one-third of the community's residents were now non-white. Wherever one turned in Anson the manifestations of this social change were evident. Mexican-Americans were now clerks at the dry-goods store, highway patrol officers, policemen, and tellers at the bank. Even Anson's doctor was Mexican-American.

The impetus for the influx of minorities into Anson was two-fold: the mechanization of farming that had untethered them from work in the fields, and the passage of the Civil Rights Act, which paved the way for their move into town. Anson's minority population, most of whom were Mexican-Americans, either came into Anson after generations of working on Jones County farms and ranches, or because this was where they had chosen to get off the migratory trail that seasonally carried families from South Texas into the farming regions of America following the crops in a great human wave.

For all of these changes, the community of Anson had not really come to grips with their implications. As long as these "immigrants" complied with an unspoken expectation that they remain on the social and political margins of the community then a social and emotional status quo could be preserved where Anson's "old line" whites maintained the illusion that life could go on more or less as it always had. The dancing controversy represented, then, a clear-cut shift in the "status hierarchy" in which the minority community, embodied by Mercy Torres, demanded a degree of social and political parity heretofore unknown. She may have believed in her right to sponsor a well-chaperoned prom for her son's graduation, but everything about her—her activism, her ethnic pride, her hopes for what the Footloose Club should be (an active organization inspiring its members to participate constructively and broadly in the social welfare of their community)—spoke to a more ambitious vision.

Anson's population had changed dramatically, yet the political structure of the community had remained intact: the white power structure that had run Anson for generations still held every position of consequence. Mercy Torres, as spokesperson and leader of the Footloose Club, conveyed succinctly the message that Anson's minority residents could no longer be considered mere "hands"—uneducated and powerless in a hierarchy where white *patrones* could grant or withhold largesse. Nowhere in Footloose's declarations or bulletins could be found a single statement about ethnicity or Anson's changed demography. Nowhere in the sermons of Anson's fundamentalist preachers or in the pronouncements from city hall was there a single reference to race. But there was Mercy Torres sitting across from

Gene Rogers, a deacon at the influential Church of Christ, and clearly an embodiment of the privileged sector of Anson's social world that had held power for generations. The two now sat across from one another as social equals, and it is this, more than whether or not Anson could have dances, that was at issue within the community.

DANCE PROVIDES THE MEDIUM

The dance question was fortuitous for the forces of change in Anson because it provided a medium that was quite broad in its ability to enlist adherents. Thus, what developed was a Rainbow Coalition of sorts. It is only fitting, then, that Jane Sandoval was inspired to gather a group of parents to discuss sponsoring a prom dance for their teenagers. Sandoval, a white woman married to a Mexican-American who was a local mechanic, represented, in her own way, the social crosscurrents and, for some, the anxieties ripping through Anson, Texas.

Footloose represented the aspirations of Anson's minority community, but it was predominantly comprised of whites who were newcomers like Donna Carens, Jane Andruss, and Paul Davidson. These whites existed outside of the networks and alliances, which in Anson were also tightly linked to membership in its elite churches—especially the Church of Christ and the First Baptist Church. The fact that these newcomer whites shared the same social margins as Anson's minority residents created a common standing from which Footloose-as-social-alliance could be formed. The crystallization of such an alliance required a common ground, however, and Anson's dance fight was made to order. At the same time, like Geertz's Balinese cockfights, the utility and convenience of dancing as a focal point for their participation was immense, since it masked the real underlying tensions and conflicts at stake in this piece of social action, in favor of the more conventionalized, even quaint reading of the situation: a group of parents organizing themselves to secure a senior prom for their sons and daughters.

Conversely, the real anxieties of Anson's ruling elite concerning ethnic change and economic woe remained subterranean, hidden under the posturing over the question of whether dancing was sinful. The media coverage colluded with this disguise by trivializing a political encounter in which citizens actually had a great deal at stake. One article in *The Dallas Morning News* began, "The debate has nothing to do with municipal corruption, property taxes, or freeways cutting through property. It has everything to do with the future of the Two-Step and the Cotton-Eyed-Joe." Although this article did briefly state that the controversy had also stirred arguments about religion, morality, and civil rights, virtually every news account of the dancing controversy in Anson was similarly patronizing.

No media accounts, for example, spoke to the fact that Mercy Torres was representative of a radical social transformation that had swept through Anson, or although the fact that Mexicans and blacks were considered low status, marginal members of the community, social categories were becoming increasingly difficult to define in those terms. If the majority of Anson's minority residents remained part of the poor underclass, there was a clear emerging middle-class among them, most notably among the Mexican-Americans. The Torres family represented the spearhead of just such a development on Anson's social landscape, but it was a development unacknowledged in either local or national renderings of these events.

THE ROLE OF THE CHURCH

Most of Anson's fourteen churches can be found on Commercial Street, visible from one side of the courthouse or the other, but the most important church in Anson was the Church of Christ located two blocks south of the courthouse. The church was a large, one-story building constructed of cream-colored brick, sporting a fading sign that invited passersby to attend the Sunday morning, Sunday evening, and Wednesday evening services. This was clearly a prosperous church. Over the years the congregation has added to the original structure a newer, more commodious building that housed the church offices, Sunday School rooms, and other rooms for church-related activities. A carport-like structure connected the old church with the new addition, but the architectural contrast between the two structures made this union seem visually awkward, even implausible.

Many in Anson could remember the days when teachers hired by local schools, who coached the football team, and the recipients of city contracts were dictated by which church was in power. In West Texas, this typically meant a struggle between the Church of Christ and the Baptists. However, in recent years the Anson Church of Christ had taken the definitive lead in these skirmishes. With membership at 300-400 people, the congregation could count on a solid voting block when its interests were at stake, making them by far the most powerful and influential.

Anson's roster of civil servants followed the same pattern. Virtually all the members of the city council, the mayor, the chief of police, the city secretary, the justice of the peace, as well as numerous county commissioners and members of the school board, were either members of the Church of Christ or one of the Baptist churches. Clearly, there was an intimate linkage between religious affiliation, and economic and social power. Within this religio-political power structure, however, the Church of Christ was first among equals, and its members held most of the town's key positions. More moderate churches, like the Methodists, were on the margins of the local power structure, while liberal churches had gone out of business altogether. One such church, the Presbyterians, ceased to exist, according to one local informant, "when they decided to ordain women and homosexuals."

The families who attended the Anson Church of Christ were clearly among the most prominent and influential in town. Many were descendants of the early settlers of Jones County. Their great-grandparents had encountered this desolate, harsh land alone and against the greatest of odds. (The prevailing wisdom in the early 1880s, when farmers first settled the county, was that this land was unsuitable for farming.)

Inside of the Church, the aesthetics are quite striking. An austere simplicity characterizes its decor—its members believe that decoration distracts worshipers from their communion with God. A large, solitary cross hangs at the front of the church, providing its sole focal point. The use of musical instruments is also considered a distraction and is forbidden. Only the human voice, untainted by inventions such as the piano or organ, is believed worthy of God. In fact, not permitting distractions was a cornerstone of Church of Christ worship and the basis for countless debates and at least one major division just before the turn of the century, within what was then called the Disciples of Christ. That division had created two groups, the Disciples of Christ and the more conservative Church of Christ.

As is true in many communities, religious categories were blurred with economic, ethnic, and political categories. This reality, reflected in the membership of the Anson Church of Christ, was just as clearly reflected in Mercy Torres's church—she was a devout Roman Catholic. In Anson, being Catholic was virtually synonymous with being of Mexican descent. Indeed, I encountered a number of people who referred to Anson's sole Roman Catholic church as "the Mexican church." The Catholic church's location, on the outskirts of town, with its parish hall actually a few feet outside city limits, revealed its social location within the community. Within the poetics of Anson's struggles, it is only fitting (not to mention the obvious irony in light of the circumstances under which Luther launched the Reformation in the fifteenth century) that it was the Catholic church that hosted several of the Footloose Club's "underground" dances at its parish hall. This circumstance simply reflected the socio-ethnic-religious standing of the pro-dance movement in Anson.

The Anson Church of Christ represented the core of the local power structure, but it was a power structure under siege. The social and economic problems of rural America were harsh enough, but for the members of the Church of Christ there was another layer of concern. They not only saw the financial base of their community rapidly eroding, but they believed that the moral base was eroding as well. Anson was situated deep in the heart of the Bible Belt. The city ordinance that had banned dancing and the fact that Jones County was still dry were sources of pride to many Ansonites, not only members of the Church of Christ. However, more than most, the members of this congregation viewed themselves as holdouts against the incursions of the twentieth century, proud to count themselves in this select group of individuals with the courage to stick to their beliefs.

For generations most of the people of Anson had been raised on a steady dose of a particular kind of religious world view. They believed that they were among the last stalwarts standing their ground against a changing social world they did not understand and they deeply distrusted and feared. Up until the 1960s, communities such as Anson were extremely isolated. Few had television sets, and the distances to any major metropolitan area kept them almost completely insulated from the great social transformations sweeping across America. What they heard of these, though, they definitely did not like. Issues such as the Civil Rights Movement, the Anti-War Movement, and the Women's Movement cut very much against the grain of the majority of Anson's residents, who had a very different sense of how the universe should be organized. In the vernacular available to them for articulating the nature of human frailties, they viewed this collection of social changes in large measure as anti-Christian, immoral, and sinful.

From a waning-days-of-the-twentieth-century perspective, such views might seem so reactionary as to be a form of evil themselves, and perhaps some of them were. But human realities do not lend themselves to simple formulas for dividing the world into good and evil as we would sometimes wish. Most of the members of the Church of Christ were good people. The

truth is they were frightened that they were fast losing ground
to a modern world that made absolutely no sense to them. Contemporary American culture offered little that most of the people
of Anson could grab hold of. The categories which structured
their world were entirely different. They were genuinely concerned with questions of values and morality, issues that became entwined with the dance fight.

Anson may have been a community with a nineteenthcentury world view in many respects, but increasingly it had
to face twentieth-century problems. The community was suffering from myriad woes. Not only was the economy steadily
declining, a slump with no end in sight, but they were challenged
by a variety of social problems. Many of Anson's teenagers, white
and non-white, were succumbing to the same ills as their urban
peers: drugs, alcohol, and adolescent pregnancies. Petty crimes
and acts of vandalism were on the upswing. The declining tax
base meant fewer resources to keep city services afloat, not to
mention the difficulties of addressing increasingly complex
social problems. The percentage of Anson's population gainfully
employed had decreased substantially. Between the elderly and
Anson's primarily Mexican-American minority population,
more and more people were depending on some form of aid. As
political leaders, business leaders, and farmers, members of the
Church of Christ were especially cognizant of the changes their
community had already experienced, and, perhaps more than
most, they understood the bleak picture that lay before them.
Like others in the community, they feared for their future not
only in economic and social terms, but in spiritual terms as well.

Thus, the Church of Christ was the self-designated point man
in Anson's confrontation with a twentieth-century *modus
vivendi*. Its members, like those of other fundamentalist
churches, viewed their West Texas communities as the last
repository for true moral values not only in their own region,
but perhaps in all of America. They could see the daily encroach-
ment of the twentieth century into their lives and there was little
that could be done to fend it off. Anson had no barbershop but

now it could boast of two thriving video stores where the full array of contemporary culture as captured in cinema was at the fingertips of anyone in town. Now, even the poorest families had TV sets from which spewed the sitcoms, soap operas, and talk shows that carried the values and temptations most feared by the conservative mind. Anson was no longer insulated against those powerful forces, yet the rural culture of West Texas did not provide a ready means of absorbing these new models for living that were so discordant with local realities.

Thus, another feature of Anson's dance fight centered around the tension between traditional and "modern" world views. What was Anson to be—a traditional, isolated, rural town, entrenched in mores and values no longer typical of American society, or a modern community, in step with a contemporary American outlook? One resident, in a letter to *The Western Observer* stated the case this way: "It's high time you people of Anson lighten up, swallow your pride, and MODERNIZE, with the '80s, but most of all give life a chance." Another Anson resident seemed more philosophical: "It may seem trivial to outsiders," he commented to *The St. Petersburg Times*, "but to me what this is all about is whether Anson is going to come of age or stay in the past."

In this context, modernity was implicitly viewed as a kind of recipe for salvation, as if Anson's difficulties—social, moral, and economic—might find resolution if only the community could "modernize" itself. It was a fantasy that spoke to the contemporary ideal of a suburban America with its access to shopping malls and infinite choices on cable television. Of course, such a position tended to accept, without critical examination, the notion that shopping malls, fast-food restaurants, and the myriad distractions available in contemporary urban America truly represented meaningful progress.

ADOLESCENTS EVERYWHERE

Finally, there is the particular meaning of dancing itself in the collective unconscious (at least in the social, if not the Jungian

sense) of the people of Anson. The specifically adolescent focus
of Footloose's efforts further links the dance fight with the problem of managing the world of taboo and forbidden impulses.
Adolescence is a developmental juncture in which such impulses
flood the adolescent's universe (Blos 1968). Like adolescents
everywhere, Anson's adolescents were struggling with hormonal
storms. Like their peers in urban America, Anson's adolescents
were quite familiar with alcohol, drugs, and sex. At the same
time, their parents faced the universal struggle to raise their
children to be constructive participants in society. To imbue
children with a sense of values and to help them address the
human realities that threaten productivity and happiness is an
immensely difficult challenge.

Even the problems that Anson's parents viewed as somewhat
unique to them, the boredom of rural life, the lack of distraction (ironically, the very qualities that had drawn some of these
newcomer parents to Anson in the first place) were related to
this same conundrum: how to shape a child into a solid participant in our social world. Many members of Footloose wanted to
help dilute the deadness of their adolescents' smalltown life by
finding more constructive outlets for them: "We've got as good
a bunch of kids in Anson as anywhere, but the truth is, there
just isn't anything for them to do," one parent said. Adolescent
pregnancies were not uncommon. One young woman voiced concern about the pressures that teenage girls in particular experienced, noting that currently five girls from the freshman class
at Anson High School were pregnant. If her statistics were accurate, this would represent a significant percentage of the
freshman girls in a school its size. Following a rural norm, many
teenagers married soon after high school, thereby truncating
the possibility of further education. Footloose Club parents were
not so naive as to expect that school-sponsored dances could be
a cure for all of these problems. However, they did view such
dances as a step in the right direction, a good way to provide
Anson's adolescents with a means of entertainment and social
activity. They hoped that the dances would be an outlet for the

pent-up feelings that led their adolescents to drive up and down
Commercial Street on Friday and Saturday nights, feelings that
all too often led them to self-undermining activities.

As Jane Sandoval had once put it: "I saw kids sitting there
in the high school parking lot drinking and throwing their beer
cans you know, night after night after night! And the police saw
it too, but they didn't seem to want to do anything about that.
And this is what made me angry when I started getting involved
with Footloose, because I had watched that, and I *knew* about
the drugs—at that time drugs were *terrible* in Anson. But
nobody seemed to care. I mean the police would turn their heads
as if everything were peachy-keen. And, I mean these Church
of Christ and hard-shell Baptist people drove right down that
main street *every* night and saw these kids sitting there drinking, and that was fine, but then when these parents decided they
wanted something better, and tried to get together and organize a good, clean, chaperoned dance, I mean we were scum of
the earth! That's how they made me feel."

When the national and international media descended on
Anson, a repeated motif in interviews with teenagers and their
parents was that Anson's youth were simply bored. "We need
something to do," one adolescent complained, "a bowling alley
or a movie theater or a skating rink, or *something!*"

The St. Petersburg Times would subsequently quote a local
teenager's all-too-common solution to this plight. "There's nothing to do. After I graduate I'm going to get married and get out
of this town." Another girl described the dire consequences of
this boredom more poignantly. She had dropped out of school
one semester before graduation and now worked behind the
counter at a local diner. At 18, already married with an 8-month-
old baby, she said, "I honestly believe that people get tied down
too fast because there's nothing else to do in this town but go
out and get pregnant and get married. . . . I love my baby girl
and my husband. But I wish I could start all over."

Anson offered its teenagers two football fields, three tennis
courts, a couple of baseball fields, and a community pool in the

summer. More cynical citizens would add to this paltry list the
parking lot behind the Church of Christ, a favorite hangout for
local teenagers. This choice seemed to represent a kind of
shadow self to the moral views of the church that unwittingly
hosted their late-night activities.

The people of Anson did not agree on a solution to this dilemma. The conservative fundamentalist congregations viewed
Footloose as quickening the moral demise of Anson's youth and
the rest of the community. It is clear that for the conservative
churches dancing was equated with a libidinized, taboo activity. They devoted their efforts to repress such impulses and
ensure that they remained repressed.

In his book *Dancing with the Devil: Society and Cultural
Poetics in Mexican-American South Texas,* José Limón (1994)
underscores the links between dancing, the world of forbidden
impulses, and ethnicity. Specifically, Limón cites Arnoldo de
Leon's observations:

> Whenever whites discussed the Mexican's moral nature,
> references to sexuality punctuated their remarks. The fan-
> dango, for instance, was identified with lewd passions and
> lasciviousness. The erotic nature of this traditional Mexi-
> can dance often led to prudish comments from onlookers.
> . . . The ones who gathered to enjoy the obscene dance were
> described as the lowest species of humanity—the poor un-
> educated mixed-bloods. [p. 37]

Limón also cites Franz Fanon's comments regarding the
importance of understanding the meaning of dance in "any study
of the colonial world" because dances are really what Limón
terms a formed social text, the analysis of which yields "a political unconscious, the huge effort of a community 'to exorcise
itself, to liberate itself, to explain itself' in a context of colonial
violence" (p. 57).

Finally, Randy Martin's observations on the meaning of choreo-
graphed dance might be as apposite to the question of dance in
Anson, when he states that dance can act "as an organized re-
surgence of desire, in which art and collective will are mar-

shalled to a transcendent end—transcendent, that is, beyond the 'normal,' dominated character of society" (quoted in Limón 1994, p. 55).

Dancing in Anson, already had a very specific, socially constructed meaning. It stirred such anxiety in some quarters because it was seen, to a greater or lesser extent and with greater or lesser conscious awareness, as a manifestation of the darker aspects of human nature. Anson's preachers from the fundamentalist, conservative churches were quite direct in making this association as they pointed to its sinfulness. Earl McCaleb, an elder at the Church of Christ, told a reporter: "The Bible teaches that the dances lead to drinking and other things that are immoral." McCaleb wasn't just quoting Scripture; he truly believed this to be the case.

Similarly, Leon Sharp, the Church of Christ preacher, distributed a pamphlet titled "Is Dancing Christian?" as the dancing controversy heated up in town. "I believe dancing is an activity that promotes what the Bible calls the sensual nature of man," Sharp said. (When Mercy Torres first heard Sharp's description of dancing as "lascivious" she had to look the word up in a dictionary, and discovered that it meant "tending to excite lustful desires." She told one reporter, "I was incredulous. I was a professional dancer and these things never occurred to me."

When I interviewed him, Brother Sharp said: "Basically, there are those who read the New Testament at points where morality is the subject and they conclude that the dance, as we usually know it in the social sense, is a sinful thing in itself and would promote other immoral possibilities." He dismissed the proponents of dancing as newcomers who wanted to change Anson's values, and believed that "it goes back again to the attitude toward what's stated in the Bible whether it's human law or divine law."

When a reporter from London's *Telegraph* tried to interview Bob Evans, the preacher of the Northside Baptist Church, he got a dose of what many of Anson's families were hearing from the pulpits of the conservative churches. In Evans's view, close body contact and rhythmic swaying to music aroused emotions and impulses that encouraged heavy petting and more sinful promiscuous activity. "It can lead to just about anything that human emotion can lead to," he said. "Some of the finest kids I've ever seen are in these high school classes. But human emotions are not changed since God created Adam and Eve and put them in the Garden of Eden. . . . I don't care what kind of supervisors you have at a dance, you can't regulate people's emotions. . . . The Bible says 'the lust of the flesh and the pride of the eye is not of God,'" Evans continued. He had a very different solution to the problems faced by Anson's youth: "How many of you have considered starting Bible classes for your kids?" he asked the Footloose parents at one of their meetings.

In other words, dancing was an extension of the forbidden, the sexual, the taboo. For this reason, those who agitated for it became morally tainted in the minds of their detractors. It was a small step from there to making Footloose and its supporters the receptacle for all sorts of projections. They were viewed as evil, as ushering in perversion and indulgence, and thereby corrupting the children of the community and robbing them of their innocence. A fundamentalist preacher portrayed the "real" interests of Footloose members: "They want to dance with each other's wives, and that's not all they want to do." From the pulpits of Anson's fundamentalist churches, members of the Footloose Club were clearly identified with the work of the Devil—a prurient group that would wreak havoc on the moral fiber of the community.

Thus, via the sexualization of the dance, the pro-dancing partisans were linked to the loss of control of sexuality. The markedly adolescent context in which such impulses were, by definition, already as ubiquitous as they were tenuously organized and "dangerous," further linked the dance fight, at least unconsciously, with other taboos, such as adultery and interracial relationships. Those who ventured to question the premises behind the city ordinance against dancing quickly became morally suspect.

As I will discuss in Part II of this book, Anson's Mexican-Americans and African-Americans were particularly vulnerable to such projections, given that ethnic prejudice typically revolves around just this kind of psychological mechanism (Kubie 1965). To the extent that Footloose and its supporters could be increasingly experienced as the embodiment of the dark side of human nature, to that extent, through a bit of superego subterfuge, the opponents of dancing could experience themselves as purer, cleaner, and closer to righteousness.

Behind the dogmatic fundamentalist pronouncements were genuine, if distorted concerns for the well-being of Anson's adolescents. The fundamentalist religious view contains an implicit theory of personality within which the ego is seen as extremely weak and vulnerable. Individuals must therefore be shielded from sin and life's many temptations, while they remain ever alert against such possibilities. The view of the ego as deficient, when added to a view of the world as teeming with dangerous sexual and aggressive impulses, is a construction that can sometimes reach paranoid proportions. Such a circumstance creates substantial anxieties when even derivative impulses, such as a well-chaperoned high school prom, are activated. In that context, all sorts of restrictions and injunctions are not only felt to be desirable but absolutely necessary.

For the fundamentalist congregations, dancing could only serve to kindle base emotions and impulses, thereby making Anson's teenagers more vulnerable to self-destructive, sinful activity. In the minds of many people within the community, the dancing controversy boiled down to a theological debate between two opposing views as to the nature of human beings and the pervasiveness of sin. However, this difference of opinion produced concrete, tangible consequences: public dances had been illegal in Anson.

Vamık Volkan (1988) notes the tendency within nations and communities toward more regressive forms of ideation and behavior when stresses act to strain established realities. In such circumstances, more primitive defensive processes, such as primitive splitting and projection, take over. With splitting mechanisms (typically found in borderline personality disorders and other so-called lower character disorders), the tendency is to bifurcate the world into good or bad, idealized or devalued, elements as a means of managing "internal" tensions. The tendency is then to project upon the Other all of the unacceptable, anxiety-provoking features and characteristics that may exist within the self. In Anson, such processes manifested themselves in the linking of Footloose with the dark side of human nature, with the world of impulse and taboo. Footloose became a receptacle for all the anxieties and fears of a community in transition. It was as if people were saying, "Contain Footloose and perhaps we can succeed in controlling the social transformation and the economic unravelling of our community and the cultural intrusions of modernity into our lives."

Defensive processes such as projection and splitting radically undermine understanding and accommodation, for they prevent other facets of reality that might mitigate against highly distorted perceptions from coming into play (Kernberg 1976). In this manner, Footloose members came to be viewed as a form of evil, rather than well-intentioned fellow citizens who simply differed in their views as to how to address the problems both factions agreed their adolescents faced. As Footloose was cast into the role of Satan's handmaiden, its opponents could then view themselves as morally cleansed and superior. In their minds they were fighting to preserve their adolescents' innocence, an innocence some believed Footloose threatened.

Such distortion and conflict come at the expense of a more effective engagement with real concerns. In Anson, distorted anxieties disrupted the effective engagement with a real problem, namely, the fact that a legacy of prejudice and marginalization, combined with the erosion of the region's economy, had left gaping wounds that prevented a constructive community engagement with a changing social world. When the members of Footloose presented their concerns to the city council, what could have been a healing, conciliatory opportunity became instead a further wounding that invited deeper resentment and mistrust. A greater obstacle to cohesion was created, embroiling the community in a divisive, fragmenting confrontation that tore it to the very core. Whether acknowledged or not, almost every collective enactment in communities across America presents its residents with this kind of choice.

THE NEED FOR CONFRONTATION

As it slowly gathered momentum, beginning with Jane Sandoval's phone calls and culminating with the showdown with the city council, the dancing controversy took on a certain utility for the participants on both sides. It became an organizing metaphor that could unite the diverse interests and allegiances at play within the community into a confrontation, a face-off of factions with different histories, different intentions, and different needs. However, this was a confrontation mediated and, perhaps most importantly, *modulated* by the veil of illusion provided by the collective belief that what they were engaged in was a local conflict over the semi-preposterous question of whether or not dancing should be legal in a contemporary American community—an analogue to the tempering effect upon Geertz's cockfighters of the fact that, despite the intense feelings they were "only engaged in a cockfight."

Anson's dancing conflict differs in one important way from Geertz's cockfight, however. As we will see in what follows, the outcome of Anson's symbolic action was important and full of implication for the future well-being of the community. It is here that the dance fight as social process more closely resembles the issues at stake in the psychoanalytic enactment than it does the cockfight as symbolic action in Geertz's depiction. He maintains that ultimately little is at stake in the latter: "The cockfight . . . makes nothing happen. Men go on allegorically humiliating one another and being allegorically humiliated by one another, day after day, glorying quietly in the experience if they have triumphed, crushed only slightly more openly by it if they have not. *But no one's status really changes*" (1973, p. 443).

In the psychoanalytic enactment, on the other hand, a great deal is at stake in how the enactment is ultimately understood and resolved. Recurrently, in virtually every community in America, incidents are appropriated by different constituencies, incidents which come to represent a form of collective enactment. These incidents are infused with meaning. The beating of Rodney King by the Los Angeles police, for example, came to embody all of the accumulated resentment of the African-American community. The initial failure of the judicial system to bring justice meant that this enactment could not lend itself to a healing resolution of long-standing animosities. Instead, it devolved into continued and exacerbated internecine warfare. Such circumstances are increasingly divisive, fragmenting, and destructive to the national identity, wreaking havoc with our ability to maintain a coherent sense of community in the face of the immense social transformation this country has experienced.

II

THE
INTERNAL
WORLD

4

The Persistence
of Prejudice

It is likely that, in terms of the relations among its people, no single legislative event of this century has had a greater impact upon American society than the Civil Rights Act passed by Congress in 1964. Race has become one of our national obsessions; it saturates one's consciousness. Fortune 500 companies offer training programs, seminars, and retreats to explore the dimension of ethnic difference within the corporate structure. Every government agency at the local, state, and federal level is engaged with the question of affirmative action and equal rights in every facet of life from housing to employment to commerce. Every major university offers courses in multicultural studies. Indeed, virtually no facet of our contemporary lives is unaffected by the consideration of our cultural and ethnic differences, even though, arguably, those of us who live in the United States have more in common than we seem inclined to think.

In Anson, as is true everywhere, there were historical antecedents that defined the particulars of this region's prejudices—the social organization of Jim Crow laws, the legacy of the South, and the historical, economic, and social relations between whites and blacks and whites and Mexican-Americans. The extensive cotton farms of East Texas were the original basis for the introduction of slaves. This region of the state is virtually indistinguishable from other parts of the Old South in terrain and economy, as well as culture and social structure. Slavery was an important impetus behind Texas's war of independence from Mexico, since Mexican law prohibited slavery and the landowners of East Texas demanded it (Fehrenbach 1968).

A different set of historical circumstances governed the relations between whites and Mexican-Americans. The fact that Texas had once been part of Spain and then Mexico left a strong legacy of resentment among Mexican-Americans. In addition, there was the potent symbology of the Alamo for partisans of both sides. Thus, relations between whites and African-Americans were the legacy of the master-slave relationship, while relations between whites and Mexican-Americans were governed more by the tensions attendant to the victor–vanquished relationship. However, each of these separate lineages produced a common or shared psychological staple. For more than a century Mexican-Americans and African-Americans had been social, political, and economic outsiders in Texas —the Other to the region's whites.

This history represents brute, inescapable facts. It holds fertile ground for profound, perhaps even indelible resentments and animosities. Similar or related histories play a role in setting the stage for that collection of thoughts and feelings we term ethnic or racial prejudice in every corner of the world, where prejudice is always to be found embedded within a particular, unique historical circumstance. However, our habit of dichotomized thinking clouds our understanding of the social and, especially the psychological processes underlying the phenomenon of ethnic prejudice. For example, we tend to view prejudice almost exclusively in terms of those who carry it and those who are its victims. That is, we view prejudice as one element of a two-part (victimizer–victim) relation. The origins of such a formula are obvious: history brims with the most unsettling acts of barbarism in which one group, fueled by its prejudices (and the economic, cultural, and political elements which form their backdrop), has wrought unspeakable cruelties on the objects of that prejudice. However, while any specific condition or instance is readily understandable in the victimizer–victim relation, such a view simultaneously masks another reality we would prefer not to engage, namely, that as a psychological process, prejudicial thinking is ubiquitous.

Every person engages in prejudicial thinking. This fact is reflected in the many historical instances when the oppressed, given the opportunity, readily become oppressors who committed atrocities equal to those they once endured. The relations between the Hutus and the Tutsis in Rwanda serve as one among countless illustrations. The ultimate sin of ethnic prejudice lies in its capacity to completely dehumanize the Other. The recent case of an innocent black man in New York who was hunted down by whites and bludgeoned to death for straying into their neighborhood is one example of such dehumanization. The near-murder of an innocent white truck driver by rioting African-Americans in South Central Los Angeles is another. Both of these events are reflective of the psychological processes at work in prejudicial thinking. While the origins of such dehumanization may vary in ways that suggest that one reaction is more justified than another (in these examples, accumulated resentment over chronic mistreatment and inner city hopelessness in East Los Angeles versus anxieties about interracial relationships in New York), the psychological mechanisms that facilitate such dehumanizing outcomes are the same.

In proposing that there are deep-seated psychological processes at the root of all ethnic prejudices, universal processes from which no one is spared, I am not suggesting there are no true grievances, or that there are not peoples who have suffered severe and chronic injustice. Obviously, history is replete with these. I *am* suggesting, however, that only historical circumstance dictates who becomes the victim and who becomes the perpetrator. All of us carry that propensity, and every society must find ways of subverting the emergence of such propensities into open practices of dehumanization.

THE RESPONSE TO THE UNKNOWN

Having stated that our reaction to difference is deeply rooted in our psychological development and that it plays itself out via psychological processes and mechanisms that are ubiquitous and commonplace, I will now suggest, drawing primarily from psychoanalytic contributions, a model for the origins of this unfortunate aspect of the human condition. The infant's anxious response to the unknown Other is the first encounter with these processes. The anxious reaction to strangers is as universal as the need to attach oneself to caregivers (Bowlby 1958, Spitz 1965). The human infant experiences love and hate as fundamental organizers of subjective experience at the dawn of its emerging consciousness, the juncture that Margaret Mahler and colleagues (1975) have termed "the psychological birth of the human infant" between approximately 6 and 36 months of age. Although the anxiety reaction to strangers may vary in intensity from mild wariness to acute fear, most infants develop such responses when they are approximately 8 months old.

From this vantage, fear of the Other is an innate given with its roots in earliest experience. When a good family friend comes to visit and tries to pick up or simply caress our 8-month-old, the baby may recoil as if our guest were the most threatening of monsters. Those who do not have the clear sanction and blessing we extend to family and friends may fare worse in such encounters. The experience of stranger anxiety constitutes the emergence of the experience of the Other as enemy (Fornari 1966, Volkan 1988).

It is precisely at this time in our lives when we first experience the Other as enemy that we also experience our deepest intimacy with another human being. An infant's attachments become singular (Ainsworth et al. 1978). If the 2-month-old may accept substitutes readily, the 6- to 8-month-old is absolutely particular about who has access to its heart. At this point in development, infants are cementing a special, individualized attachment to whoever is playing a substantive role in their caretaking (Ainsworth 1978, Mahler et al. 1975). Bowlby (1958) argued that such responses represent a fundamental, instinctual mechanism with evolutionary and adaptive functions, namely, to keep the infant in close proximity to maternal figures who can ensure survival. The character of the emotional enclosure of these earliest attachments marks us for life and we are destined to seek it, derivatively, in subsequent attachments. However, no human relationship will ever again match the warm satiation of those first bonds where with no boundaries, intimacy reaches its zenith—that point in development in which, psychologically, mother and child are momentarily one and the same being—what psychoanalytic theorists have termed *normal symbiosis*.

Thus, within the first year of life we concurrently experience the two most fundamental organizers of our social experience: the deepest love for the "we," and the deepest dread of the "not-we." Winnicott (1953) describes this point in development as one in which the infant is immersed in the realm of illusion. The reality of the maternal object's separateness from the self is only gradually acknowledged.[1] Indeed, Spitz (1968) theorized that it was precisely the threat to that illusion of oneness-with-mother, embodied in the presence of the non-mother stranger, that was the source of the infant's reaction of fear and anxiety to the unknown Other. Gradually, however, the separate existence of the maternal object as another aspect of reality beyond the self is conceded.

From this beginning, development unfolds as an increasingly inclusive process. Broader aspects of the world in which we live gradually come to be included within the phenomenology of who we are. The infant moves, then, from an experience in which illusion permeates the relation to the Other (and the external world in general) to an experience in which the reality of the

---

1. I use the term *object* in the psychoanalytic sense, that is, as an intrapsychic representation of "other." Hence, maternal object refers to the intrapsychic representation(s) of those who tend, comfort, and nurture us.

Other is increasingly acknowledged, notwithstanding the fact
that the experience of the Other is never entirely free from elements of illusion. Within the realm of awareness, the external
world becomes increasingly implicated in our subjectivity.
Maternal objects are gatekeepers for this process; they increasingly name experience, defining not only who but what counts
as "we" (and who and what do not). Increasingly, as Volkan
(1988) notes, the categories that define identity, both individually and collectively (the "I" and the "we"), come to include
broader cultural elements that take on specific meaning.

As a child develops, what is included within the band of significations that are collected within the self extends beyond the
bounds of immediate family relationships to include other social
categories such as language, neighborhood, religion, country,
and, of course, ethnicity, among others. These come to play an
increasingly important part in that definitional experience of
ourselves we term identity. To take one of Volkan's illustrations,
chicken soup becomes not only how mother shows her caring,
love, and nurturance, but also a cultural signifier—chicken soup
may become emblematic of what it means to be Jewish as well.
Quintana's (1994) work on the evolution of a sense of cultural
identity supports this observation. Quintana suggests that
children's understanding of the meaning of ethnicity develops
over time. The 2-year-old has virtually no concept of ethnic identity, while by adolescence ethnic identity has reached levels of
signification that are readily available and that play an important role in identity development and organization.

There is a parallel developmental trajectory with reference to
the Other. Thus, when it comes to enemies and other forms of "not-
we" experience, we move from having what Volkan (1988) terms
individualized enemies, those whom it is impossible for all children within one's group to share (the "stranger" who instills such
anxiety, for example, is actually mother's best friend), to shared
enemies, those outside the boundary of a more collective "we"
(those who do not speak our language, for example, or who are
not of our neighborhood, religion, country, ethnicity, and so on).

Each human group defines its enemies and allies out of the matrix of its social conditions. Everything within a given culture is a potential candidate for use in this manner, a potential "target of opportunity" (Volkan 1988). The artifacts that become signifiers of enemies and allies range from the subtle to the prosaic, but once so delineated these signifiers may become highly charged—even something to die for. On the island of Cyprus, or in South Central Los Angeles, the signifiers may be color and/or dress codes. In Northern Ireland and Bosnia it is religious affiliation. Skin color is a ready marker of difference that in some cultures is appropriated and infused with multiple meanings and connotations. The United States is illustrative of this, but not uniquely so. Here, it may also manifest itself in a Northerner's unexamined, reflexive response to a Southerner's accent, which may connote assumptions regarding education, sophistication, politics, or attitudes toward race. To these and other signifiers are affixed, directly or indirectly, narratives of a people's experience, the deceit or treachery endured, the collective subjugations and abuses experienced, or the heroic deeds accomplished.

Whatever their particulars, signifiers are learned responses that bind us to the group with whom we primarily identify. Whether they point to national, ethnic, religious, or some other cultural subgrouping such as a gang, the signifiers represent a revolving sequence of self-identifying commitments that organize the social world of every human being. All elements that give a culture its distinctiveness, even (or, perhaps, especially) its art, its food, and its music, become candidates for the definitional processes through which we establish our group identities and allegiances. Since identity (with both its individual and collective elements) is so vital to our survival and sense of well-being, threats to its stability engender deep anxieties. In adults, such anxieties are derivative (now elaborated and structured by knowledge of received historical and cultural enmities) of the raw, undiluted anxieties so aptly described in reference to infants by Spitz (1968).

Prejudices of all kinds tap this archaic root of original anxiety and apprehension toward the Other, an apprehension that
gradually, over the course of development, is given further and
more subtle delineation and definition as we become increasingly aware of the world in which we live and the meanings those
most important to us attribute to its constituents. The problem
of human prejudice is but a variation of the problem of our engagement with the Other and the feelings stirred within us by
such engagement. As Gordon Allport (1954) noted in his classic
study, *The Nature of Prejudice,* prejudice is a universal disease.
It is part of the fabric of the human condition.

NOT ALL ANTAGONISMS
ARE PSYCHOLOGICAL

Every ethnic grouping experiences these struggles and internal conflicts. To propose such universality in our ambivalent
engagement with otherness is not to suggest that all antagonisms and resentments are merely "psychological" in the sense
that connotes something less objective or real. The Nazi Holocaust and the institution of slavery constitute objective facts and
consequences that will forever resonate in the psychologies
of their respective victims. Similarly, the ethnic genocide in
Africa between the Tutsis and the Hutus, or in Bosnia between
the Serbs and Muslims are extensions of long-standing, historical enmities—old wounds once again torn open (and each tearing, of course, makes these wounds deeper and more difficult
to heal).

Indeed, history repeatedly creates the circumstances that
activate or strengthen certain individual and collective psychological responses. Collective histories provide the fuel for the
extended, perennial animosities we witness between human
groups and their attendant prejudices. However, these facts of
history find representation within individual psyches. There,
at the level of subjectivity, they are appropriated in highly idiosyncratic ways. Within the same generation the same collective

history can produce a Martin Luther King Jr. and a Malcolm X, for example—two men emblematic of different approaches to the problem of race and difference in America.[2] It is my contention that these two men reflect two contrary tendencies within all human beings and their culture groups. They became signifiers within the entire culture for these two psychological elements: union and engagement versus separation and autonomy. In other words, Martin Luther King Jr. and Malcolm X were vessels for the expression of two very different impulses within the African-American community with respect to the question of race and prejudice. These impulses find a parallel expression within all human groups, including America's white community with its partisans of racial integration and those who advocate separation of the races.

As human proclivities, however, these social/political strategies find a resonant expression in the universal childhood task of separating from, yet remaining meaningfully connected to those who play a defining role in our existence. The work of Mahler and her colleagues (1975) on the developmental unfolding of the separation-individuation process, and its normal and natural ambivalence with regard to the experience of connection versus autonomy, reflects, in psychological terms, the very dynamics we see in broader social-cultural contexts.

These and other elements of the psychology of prejudice will be explored in the remainder of this book through an analysis of the lives of individuals who, knowingly or not, participated in a community's effort to engage the complex problems of social change and ethnic difference. The dance fight itself was a tumultuous collective symptom within a community whose eth-

---

2. In this respect it is the pre-1963 Malcolm X who embodied this separatist spirit–that is, before Malcolm X's differences with Elijah Muhammad led to his ouster from the Nation of Islam. In the ensuing two years, before his assassination in 1965 at the Audubon Ballroom in New York City, Malcolm X espoused a more universalist vision (a vision closer to that of Martin Luther King Jr.) a position that further flamed the enmity between Malcolm X and the Nation of Islam.

nic character had changed radically, and whose economic under-
pinnings had shifted and eroded. However, it is in the lives of
the people of Anson that we see the more immediate meaning
of these struggles. If sociological and psychological treatments
of these issues have typically remained at the level of the collective and the general rather than the ideographic and intrapsychic, it is my hope to bridge these two levels of discourse
through more interior portraits of some of Anson's residents.

5

The Torres Family:
From Pre-existing
Categories to Ambiguity

On an exceptionally hot summer day, a year after the Footloose Club, under the leadership of Mercy Torres, had mounted its assault on the local political establishment, I pulled in across the street from her home and parked under a mesquite tree. The mesquite provided welcome shade in the middle of the afternoon, although, in this heat, any benefit derived was minimal except perhaps in one's imagination. The only true relief was in a well air-conditioned space.

The Torres family lives in a red brick house on Anson's west side, in the same part of town as Anson's successful farmers and business proprietors. Their home had considerable street appeal; its Spanish architectural style was reflected in a set of arches facing the street and yielding to a small courtyard at the entrance to the house. Mercy's maroon Lincoln was in the semicircular driveway. I was eager to meet this woman whose prominent role in the Footloose Club seemed exceptional given that in Anson, Texas, Mexican-Americans were still often reflexively considered low-status, marginal members of the community. Although there was an emerging Mexican-American middle-class, the majority of Mexican-Americans continued to subsist at or below the poverty line. The Torres family represented a spearhead of the Mexican-American community that was moving up within Anson's social landscape.

Mercy, a woman who appeared to be in her late forties or early fifties, greeted me warmly at the door. She had a rich smile that extended almost to the frame of her black, horn-rimmed glasses. Footloose's former leader was wearing a Mexican cotton dress, her trademark, which hung loosely from her body like the old muumuu dresses of the '60s. One of her grandsons was holding onto her leg as he stared up at me with marked curiosity.

"This is my daughter's littlest one," Mercy said as she playfully ran her fingers through his brown hair, and then, "What's your ancestry? Ricardo Ainslie is an unusual combination. Is your mother Mexican?"

I was not surprised by the direct questioning from a woman who had known me for less than a minute. Mercy had an established reputation for her forthright, no-nonsense approach to things. I answered with a short synopsis of my background: my father was Mexican, my mother from Fort Worth, I was born in Mexico City, where I lived until coming to the United States for college.[1]

Having placed me on an unspoken set of ethnic coordinates, Mercy started sprinkling her discussion with Spanish phrases, as she offered me a Coke. In the living room, a long bank of modular furniture was arranged around a large television set inside a credenza. On top of the credenza were many family photographs, and above it a painting of a bullfighter by Mercy's brother-in-law. There were numerous crucifixes in the living room, underscoring the family's devout Roman Catholicism.

Mercy had grown up in East Los Angeles, married Salvador Torres, and earned an Associate Arts degree in social planning shortly afterward. The couple then moved to Mexico, where Salvador studied medicine at the Universidad Autónoma de Guadalajara. After he passed his medical boards, they moved

---

1. As a young man, my paternal great-grandfather migrated to Mexico from Scotland in the 1850s. He married into a Mexican family and his descendants were raised as Mexicans. My mother, whose maiden name is Croxdale, is of English ancestry.

to Houston, where Salvador was practicing when he was re-
cruited to work in Anson. At first, the local gentry had struggled
with the cognitive dissonance created by what for them was
an unlikely circumstance, a Mexican-American family with a
father who was a physician and a mother who was college educated. While there may not have been a better educated couple
in the entire community, the situation had no parallel in their
experience. Gradually, however, locals assimilated this awkward fact. Mercy became an accepted community leader, and
had even been invited to join the Anson Garden Club, historically an all-white organization for the wives of the local elite.

Mercy Torres was the sort of ideal citizen depicted by Bellah
and colleagues (1985) in their book *Habits of the Heart.* Her
personal psychology combined her ethnicity, religious identification, and dedication to broader community and civic participation into a seamless weave. For example, during one of our
interviews she brought out some materials related to Footloose.
Proudly, she showed me the original poster she had made for
an early Footloose Club meeting. Following the steps learned
in her social planning classes in college, Mercy had designed a
"Variables Chart" that formed the core of Footloose's goals. The
chart revealed an ambitious organization whose aims extended
beyond dancing to an effort to improve the community via the
active participation of Anson's youth.

FOOTLOOSE: AMBITIOUS VISION

"One of the things that I wanted Footloose to do was not just to
make money so they could get a place to dance—but to help the
parents and children get involved in the city, in the state, in
everything. On the Variables Chart, we wrote that the kids
would help with civic activities. So, the kids would go out and
clean up the highway (as part of the Adopt-A-Highway program), and then we helped with the County Care Center that
helps indigent families. Another was the shelter in the hospital
in the event of a tornado," Mercy explained.

Mercy Torres, Footloose president and social activist. Photo: Nancy Scanlan.

In fact, all of these ideas came into fruition under her leadership during the 10-month interval between the formation of the Footloose Club and its Victory Dance in October 1987. It was an impressive list. One particular vignette demonstrated Mercy's nerve and intrepidness in these efforts.

Jerry Paulding, preacher at the First Baptist Church, liked to tape his sermons so that church members could hear them if they had to miss services. In May 1987, when Paulding had given the inflammatory sermons against Footloose and the American Civil Liberties Union, Mercy had called the church and requested copies of the sermons. A few weeks later, the church secretary notified Mercy that they were ready. Mercy pulled into the church's driveway and ran inside, assuming she would be on her way in a few minutes. However, when she announced that she was there to pick up the promised tapes, the secretary said that Brother Paulding wished to speak with her. Did she have a minute? Ever the congenial one, Mercy said she

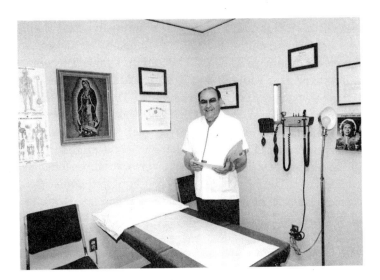

Salvador Torres, Mercy's husband and a physician in Anson. Photo: Nancy Scanlan.

would be glad to speak with the preacher and was led into his office.

As she reflected on it later, Mercy felt she had been duped into meeting with Paulding under the ruse of getting the tapes. She recalls the encounter:

> I walked into his office and he said "Come on in!" Very friendly. And then he sat back very arrogantly and talked down to me. He unleashed a torrent of accusations against Footloose's involvement with the ACLU and the fact that Footloose's actions were tearing the town apart. And so I heard everything that he wanted to say, but I was steaming, and I was burning up because he had tricked me into it. I said, "I don't think it's very fair what you're doing to me. You had already planned what you were going to say. I don't have the answers for you. I just know that the ACLU is the best counselor I could go to at this time because I

feel our civil rights are being infringed upon." And then he said, "I'm afraid of the ACLU." I asked if he had read the city ordinance and he said he hadn't. I said, "Do yourself a favor. Get yourself a copy and read it and then you tell me if you're still afraid of the ACLU. Because the ordinance is too dictatorial." He didn't know how to answer and finally said, "Well if there's any way I can help you, Mercy, you let me know." I said, "Sure there is!" [She laughed here in the telling.] "Do you think you can get two chairs for that basement at the hospital? Footloose is helping with the tornado shelter there." He'd already read about that in the newspaper and he said, "Sure."

The irony was not lost on Mercy that the preacher of one of the churches most staunchly opposed to dancing and the Footloose organization, the same individual who had preached about the sinful, satanic evils that Footloose was promulgating, was helping her out the door with two folding chairs to support their civic efforts. With sheer chutzpah, she had turned an attempt to humiliate her into a moral victory.

Mercy Torres had a vision for Anson, one that transcended ethnicity, religion, or social class. Her dream was to harness the emotions around dancing and channel them into more meaningful, community activities. In fact, Mercy's leadership in Footloose was only one of a string of projects and involvements. She had led a move to create a public park on vacant city property and had obtained children's outdoor games for it, and had headed the community's effort on behalf of the newly restored opera house—an immense project that required writing grants, establishing the historical uniqueness of the building, and enlisting the support of a wealthy family in Dallas with roots in Anson. Presently, Mercy worked with a variety of county programs designed to help the poor and needy.

Although the Torres family succeeded in establishing a firm foothold on Anson's social ladder, they had encountered numerous painful, ethnically related tensions in the process. One of their sons, a troubled young man, had committed suicide after being rebuffed by his white girlfriend. He had been struggling for years (indeed, Mercy implied that his problems may have led to the family's decision to move to a smaller community). One of the immediate precipitants to his suicide (although not the main cause) may have been the complications encountered in this biracial relationship. Under the circumstances, it seemed inevitable that his death would have racial overtones. Another factor linking their son's death to local racism was the family's experience when they made arrangements to bury him. They discovered that twenty years after the repeal of Texas's Jim Crow laws, Anson's cemetery was still strictly, if no longer officially, segregated by race. Incensed, they refused to comply with the practice. Their son was buried in the better-maintained white portion of the cemetery.

One of their daughters had married "into a good [white] family" but was now divorced. Mercy recalled with some irritation a white friend who, following her daughter's divorce, had said, "Oh, I feel so terrible about it, but I think it's wonderful that she now has that name because it's such a classy name." Mercy noted the obvious implication that "Torres," a Hispanic name, was not nearly as classy to her friend's ears. "That's the mentality," Mercy noted with a laugh, "[but] not everybody is that way."

Salvador Torres was a genial, balding man with a warm handshake. Like Mercy, he was born and raised in East Los Angeles. As a boy, Salvador helped support his family by selling ceramic figures door-to-door in the public housing projects. In our discussions regarding ethnicity, Salvador made it clear that he did not subscribe to some contemporary views. For example, he derided those Mexican-Americans who used the more militant and separatist term "Chicano" to describe themselves, which he saw as a desperate effort to regain some link to a mythic past. Salvador stated that he was proud of the fact that he was an American. He considered himself an American first, he said, Mexican-American second. But it was also clear that he was

proud of his ethnic heritage, as evidenced by the large, framed
picture of Our Lady of Guadalupe, an image that is virtually
synonymous with Mexican-American ethnic identity, hanging
on the wall of his consulting room. Dr. Torres recalled an experience at the clinic shortly after arriving in Anson, when a
patient walked up to his receptionist's window and asked,
"Do y'all have a *Meskin* doctor working here?" "Well," Salvador's receptionist responded, "he's not Mexican; he's Mexican-
American. His name is Dr. Torres." The patient refused to see
Salvador, insisting on seeing Salvador's colleague, a physician
from India, instead.

In spite of these experiences, Salvador and Mercy felt that
for the most part the community had received them warmly and
cordially when they arrived in the late 1970s. Rural Anson was
desperate for a physician, and most in the community were
delighted to have the services of Dr. Torres, Mexican-American
or not. He now served on the Anson Independent School Dis-
trict School Board and was the physician for the high school
football team, an especially esteemed position in Anson, where
during the season, Friday night football is the focal point of the
community's interest to a degree that few urban dwellers can
appreciate.

The Torres's youngest son, Peter, walked in during one interview and took a seat next to Mercy. He had just graduated from
high school and was going to Texas Tech University in Lubbock,
where he planned to be a pre-med major and follow in his father's
footsteps. Peter was a good-looking, bright, articulate young
man. He had been the senior class president and the president
of the student council at Anson High School, a first for Anson's
Mexican-Americans.

Peter reflected on his experiences in Anson, shedding light
on some of the costs of assimilation not often acknowledged
in sociology courses. Culturally, Peter had inhabited a kind
of no-man's land, retaining an ambiguous social status. "You
know," he told me in tones laced with irony, "here in Anson
the Torreses aren't considered Mexican." I asked him what he

meant, and he said, "It's like 'You're different. You're Spanish.'
They try to do that, and I say, 'No, I'm not. I'm Mexican-American.
I'm of Mexican descent.' But they say, 'But you're different.' It's
almost like I'm an exception, like 'Y'all are like white people.'"

NOT EASY TO OVERCOME

Peter Torres's experience with his friends reflects our understanding of an important element that organizes ethnic and
other forms of prejudice. Social interactions are deeply structured by cognitive processes. A prejudice is, in Allport's (1954)
words, a tendency toward "thinking ill of others without sufficient warrant." It further refers to a prejudgment that turns a
deaf ear to counterinformation. In this respect, as I have noted
earlier, a prejudice is a form of stereotyped thinking, a cognitive schema that structures as it defines social experience. For
this reason, there is a fixity to prejudices; they are not easily
amended or transformed, even when counterinformation is
available (Pinderhughes 1979).

The rigidity of prejudice, its categorizing or schematizing
aspects, is a facet of prejudice that Allport found noteworthy in
his classic examination of the subject. In a manner that closely
parallels Piaget's conception of cognitive schemes, Allport notes
that the processes underlying stereotypes of all kinds, not only
ethnic ones, involve the clustering of larger masses of information that guide our engagement with reality. "We spend most
of our waking life calling upon preformed categories for this
purpose," (p. 20). He further states that these categories tend
to join new information to existing clusters (rather than shifting the category to fit newer information). In Allport's view, individuals find ambiguity taxing. It is easier to fit things into pre-
existent categories than to develop new ones. "There is a curious
inertia to our thinking," he states (p. 20). Further, the categories
that organize our thinking have a close and immediate tie with
what we see, how we judge, and what we do. This is especially
true for categories infused with emotional meaning, such as with

ethnic prejudice. Finally, Allport asserts that these categories may be more or less rational (p. 21). Stereotypes vary to the degree that they do violence to reality, or in the extent to which they translate into destructive thoughts and feelings. Indeed, one of Allport's radical formulations in this regard is his assertion that prejudgment is as normal as it is ubiquitous. In other words, the cognitive processes at work in ethnic prejudice are a subset of mental processes all of us use. Indeed, they are indispensable to our normal engagement with reality. Peter Torres's white peers found it necessary to make Peter white, or at least not Mexican, in order to accommodate his presence, in psychological terms, within their social group. He did not fit their preconceived notion (prejudgment) of "what Mexicans are like."

Also at play here is a variation on the psychological processes typically termed splitting of mental representations, a process by which similar mental representations of self and other are clustered together. This is a near-universal conceptualization of the earliest experience of self and others in reference to good/bad affective states, idealization/devaluation, and so forth. In psychoanalytic theorizing, it is a hallmark of normal development during the first two years of life that the human infant moves from a state of undifferentiated experience with respect to self and others, to increasingly differentiated experience in which others are gradually seen as having their own needs, feelings, capacities, and so forth.

Similarly, during this time the experience of self is increasingly differentiated. Such intrapsychic differentiation of self and object (other) representations, which is partly a function of cognitive maturation, is foundational to a more realistic capacity to experience the self constructively, as well as to engage others in increasingly mature, healthy ways (see Fraiberg 1969, Mahler et al. 1975). Splitting of mental representations, as a cognitive maneuver, is intimately linked to Allport's notions regarding categorizing or stereotyping processes, for these organize or cluster the developing child's world into "good" and "bad" experiences on the basis of their affective commonality. Similarly, these processes are related to what Pinderhughes (1979) terms the "drive to dichotomize," in which avoidant-differentiative-aggressive behavior stands in opposition to the tendency toward seeking-joining-introjection, the wish to make someone else a part of the self (p. 35).

Prior to the establishment of such differentiation, the integration of a sense of identity remains tenuous (Giovacchini 1986, Pine 1990). That tenuousness actually accentuates the reliance on defensive splitting of self and object representations as a mechanism for maintaining an intact sense of self (Kernberg 1976). An example may help illustrate the processes being described: a 3½-year-old child was struggling with a variety of concerns, which he managed, in part, by focusing on the fact that his mother was Jewish and his father a Gentile. In the context of a particularly stressful time in his life, he blurted out at one point: "My father is different from us. Mommy and I are Jewish, he's not." While this vignette might readily be viewed as more oedipally based, that is, reflecting the little boy's wish to exclude his father and have his mother to himself, it was my impression, in context, that the youngster was needing to consolidate a fragmenting sense of self. He was attempting to accomplish this by reinforcing the experienced links to his mother, an effort that led in part to a need to exclude (paternal) identifications he was not yet in a position to integrate. This little boy's sense of identity, at this point in his development, was as yet unstable. However, by artificially disconnecting himself from his links to his father, he sought to stabilize a sense of himself via his mother.

The issues at stake for him, in reference to those paternal identifications, were complex and multi-determined. For example, the struggle between remaining primarily identified with mother and gradually admitting paternal identifications as central to defining his identity is universal for little boys. Unlike girls, whose primary object of identification remains the mother, boys must shift their primary object of identification to their fathers if they are to successfully consolidate a sense of male gender identity (Greenson 1968). As Greenson makes clear, such a shift is anxiety-producing and temporarily destabilizing for boys, in part because it entails abandoning (or, more precisely, the *fear* of having to abandon) early, fundamentally organizing attachments to mother. In the present illustration, the child condensed these concerns, among others, into the issue of ethnic identity. This is an example of how ethnic stereotyping lends itself to defensive use. It becomes a convenient receptacle for a broad array of concerns and anxieties that must be managed. Volkan's discussion (1988) regarding the function of differentiation from the Other as an essential step in identity consolidation is especially apt here since he links the intrapsychic elements described by theorists like Mahler to broader cultural identifications not typically examined by psychoanalytic theorists.

This same dynamic is at play in Peter Torres's predicament with his peers. Apparently, his white friends needed to see him as white, too, in order to maintain their collective social (ethnic) identity. That group identity was threatened by the "intrusion" of a "foreign object" (a Mexican-American). Peter was accepted by them in large measure. However, that acceptance was predicated on a particular psychological maneuver: He was redefined as white by his peer group as a precondition for his integration into it. Peter's attempts at clarification were met with "but *you're* different."

Thus, his status as a studious, middle-class Mexican-American adolescent in his West Texas community entailed a challenge to the assumptions and preconceptions regarding what Mexican-Americans "are like," which in this rural community was for the most part confined to less than complimentary adjectives. In fact, it is evident that the entire Torres family posed this same classificatory dilemma for Anson's white community. This, of course, is to be expected in the context of evolving definitions within which questions of ethnicity and social class are embedded. Insofar as a stereotype is partially a habit of thought, a way of organizing certain social information (correctly or not), then people who violate that set of expectations must be seen as "different." Psychologically, that is a more economic (if at times destructive) way of handling those discrepancies than the alternative requirement, namely, to reexamine the cognitive schemas that organize that body of social information. Such are the psychic economies of ethnic and other forms of prejudice.

THE ONTOGENY OF RACIAL PREJUDICE

In what has become one of the classic psychoanalytic treatments of the subject (one that nevertheless reflects the limitation of early psychoanalytic voices with their singular focus on psycho-sexual development), Lawrence Kubie (1965) examined the unconscious meanings often associated with differences in skin color in his article "The Ontogeny of Racial Prejudice." In particular, Kubie argues that one of the universal roots of prejudice lies in early human development, in the child's "oscillation between a secret, guilty pride in his body and hidden feelings of profound aversion toward his body" (p. 265). Kubie notes the fact that early in life children have no "derogatory" feelings about themselves:

> They delight in nakedness and (the body's) free display. They delight in all of the apertures of the body and in all body products. They like the feeling, the sense of move- ment, the warmth, the smells, and tastes of their own bod- ies and of its products, and they have the same joy in the bodies of others. They know no hierarchy of dirtiness, lead- ing from that which is so clean that it can be taken into the mouth to that which is so filthy that it cannot be touched, looked at or named or thought about even to one- self and not even in solitude and silence. [p. 268]

Notions of "clean" and "dirty" become fundamental organiz- ing constructs for the young child. "Clean" is whatever can be taken into the body, while "dirty" is whatever comes out of the body. It is this radical psychological shift in feelings and attitudes toward one's body and its products that partly "civilizes" the human child, transforming the child from a biologically dominated existence to one that is increasingly socially defined.

Such a transformation, however, has its costs. One of the hallmarks of the psychoanalytic narrative of development is the notion that those earliest investments in what we come to view as the "dirty" or "bad" parts of ourselves remain with us unconsciously, to become the subject of a variety of defensive processes. The classic example is accomplished during the anal phase of psychosexual development, in which a child's pleasurable feelings associated with feces and other body products are transformed into their opposite via the defense of reaction formation (Freud 1908).

From this point onward, body products are consciously repudiated and associated with anxiety, shame, and revulsion, feelings that must be managed in a variety of ways. Humans develop complex feelings regarding these conflicts that unconsciously define one aspect of our experience of the world. Kubie specifically argues that differences in skin pigmentation may become a screen upon which a variety of meanings from our earliest developmental resolutions regarding cleanliness and dirtiness are projected. Kubie quotes the hymn that says, "Wash me clean of my sins and I shall be *whiter* than snow," as an example of how, in this culture at least, skin color can take on other, unconscious meanings. Light and dark, for example, are common symbols for good and bad. The light of day, is juxtaposed against the darkness of night, and the latter associated with many fears and anxieties characteristic of early childhood but also, one imagines, with the predawn of mankind when darkness made one vulnerable to predators and enemies.

Clearly, these are attitudes where color is infused with psychological meaning and connotation. In this context, Kubie argues, the psychological elements of prejudice are brought into play "out of the defense against the initial concept of an untouchable 'I' with untouchable, unmentionable, unthinkable body parts comes the concept of an untouchable 'You.' From the taboo

of our own bodies . . . comes the caste system of people who are
as untouchable as are the forbidden untouchables of the body"
(p. 272).

Kubie's argument speaks to one possible dynamic at work in
the motivation behind skin-color-based prejudicial attitudes and
feelings (namely, projective and identificatory processes as means
of managing conflictual feelings about one's body). Further,
people "of color" may, and often do, identify with such projections, making "the problem of color" one that resides, psychologically, within both whites and non-whites. In this manner,
certain conflicts become contained and managed, and certain
feelings about one's "cleanliness" (in all its connotations) can be
enhanced or depleted, by the social meaning of skin color. It is
a social construction that implicates whites and non-whites
alike, if in different ways and for different reasons.

Within a cultural milieu in which all sorts of moral and cultural values are paired with skin color, it is likely that individuals of darker skin pigmentation might identify with those projections, to consciously and/or unconsciously viewing themselves
as "stained" and aspiring for ways to feel more "white." For
example, in the Broadway play, *Jelly's Last Jam*, based on the
life of Ferdinand "Jelly Roll" Morton, the African-American who
was seminal to the evolution of jazz, a central thesis is that
Morton's light skin color played an important role in his psychology. His family, of Creole descent and relatively affluent,
considered itself superior to darker-skinned blacks. Morton felt
exceedingly ambivalent about this issue, on one hand spending
every minute he could in the forbidden music scene that "lower
class" (and, typically, darker-skinned) blacks frequented, while
simultaneously feeling superior to them because he was lighter
skinned. Similarly, Malcolm X in his autobiography (1964),
makes a great deal of his light-colored eyes, his attempts, early
in his life, to straighten his hair, as well as the meaning of his
interest in white women, all of which, he argues, were symptomatic of his identification with the devalued meaning of dark
skin in the eyes of black and white societies. Such meanings do

not by any means originate exclusively in the realm of psycho-
sexual development. Indeed, as illustrated in Jelly Roll Morton's
life, social processes, including economic well-being, the legacy
of slavery, the potent impact of active, present, unavoidable
experiences with prejudice, all contribute in ways that are conscious and unconscious, to the psychological representations of
self and others (within and outside of one's group). The psycho-
sexual contributions to which Kubie points are partly a bodily
receptacle for these broader social meanings—an immediate, at
times wordless substantiation of how one experiences that which
is acceptable and that which is not.

Kubie's work is among the limited number of earlier psychoanalytic contributions to the topic of racial prejudice. While
helpful in illuminating features of the psychodynamics of racial
prejudice, especially those related to psychosexual development,
his work also represents the kind of psychoanalytic formulation
frequently criticized for its narrow and exclusive preoccupation
with *internal* contributions to prejudice, while all but ignoring
the broader social-cultural elements at play in creating such
realities. In my view, psychoanalysis offers an unparalleled
vehicle for an in-depth understanding of the internal experience
of prejudice as well as the origins and vicissitudes of such attitudes. I am referring, of course, to the opportunities afforded
by that uniquely intimate life-examination that an analytic
process represents. Unfortunately, much psychoanalytic theorizing, like Kubie's, tends to be less interested in the internal
representation of these social forces than in the more traditional
dyadic, familial experiences that organize individual psychology even though, as Freud's (1923) formulation of the superego
makes clear, such experiences always and of necessity contain
traces (whether highlighted or subtly implied) of an individual's
broader cultural world.

Mercy Torres seemed particularly conscious of skin color.
Once, while the family was living in Mexico and Salvador was
attending medical school in Guadalajara, Mercy had been mis-
taken for a servant because she was dark like many of the maids

who worked in the Torres's neighborhood. While she found humor in the incident, it had also affected her. All her life her dark skin color had been something she had had to contend with: "My mother was very fair," Mercy noted one afternoon while sitting in her living room, "but we [her brothers and sisters] were all *morenitos* [dark skinned]. When we went to look for a house with my mother [in Los Angeles], it was, 'Well you can live here but your children can't.'"

This story, too, was told with an thread of humor, although it is evident that for Mercy it spoke to uglier truths. In his book, *Days of Obligation,* Richard Rodriguez (1992) observes that in Mexico, to be fair skinned (a *güero*) defines a high status within the hierarchy of social possibilities, while to be dark skinned (an *indio*) is synonymous with being dirty, messy, undesirable, unsocialized. One of the country's leading beer commercials for decades extolled its product as "La rubia de categoría" (The blonde with class). Octavio Paz (1950) also observed the implications for the Mexican psyche of La Malinche, the Indian woman who betrayed her race by consorting with Cortez and becoming his indispensable translator and cultural interpreter. Mexico is the product of countless unions captured by that emblematic story, since relatively few contemporary Mexicans are of pure Indian blood. For this reason, however, skin tone becomes a kind of color coding for one's social class and status within the culture. It goes without saying, of course, that Mexico is in no way unique in this regard. It seems inevitable that within each society or social subgrouping signifiers are found to indicate power, influence, success, attainment, and so forth. In societies where skin color becomes easily paired with discrepancies in these socially valued elements (regardless of the origin of these discrepancies), then skin color becomes available as a quick reference for one's social standing within that society, thereby readily making an individual the target for the immensely dehumanizing processes of ethnic prejudice. However, skin color is clearly not the only possible marker available for such processes. In some cultures it may be religious affiliations, in others it may be the means by which one's group sustains itself (cattle herding versus farming in Africa), or (and perhaps most typically) it may be a combination of these or other elements.

Three of the Torres's living children had all married whites. The meaning of such unions is obviously not reducible to the question of ethnicity and skin color. However, in a social context where skin color is linked to success in a culture's eyes, in which social status, income, and education for minority groups are highly correlated with variations in skin color, one could speculate that marriage to whites carried social and psychological meaning, even though it may not have been *the* pivotal or central consideration in those decisions. Limón (1994) notes, with respect to Mexican-Americans, that, typically, "those at the bottom are noticeably *darker* than those at the top" (p. 101). Empirical studies of Mexican-Americans, such as those of Relethford and colleagues (1983), Arce and colleagues (1987), and Telles and Murguia (1990) support the thesis that lighter skin color is significantly correlated with indices of higher social status.

Within the Torres's social milieu, whites were more prevalent than Mexican-Americans and African-Americans. Nevertheless, there was ambivalence about this issue within the Torres household. In the midst of a discussion regarding the difficulties faced by this family with regard to questions of ethnic identity and assimilation, Salvador had broken the tension with a telling remark: "Hopefully, I'm still going to have a Mexican grandbaby." He smiled good-naturedly as he looked straight at Peter, his sole unmarried child. "I have a dozen grandbabies and they're all half-breeds!" he added. Everyone laughed, but it was a joke that carried a definite edge.

ASSIMILATED AND ETHNIC

The Torres family was at a social crossroads, fully immersed in a kind of ethnic no-man's land. Culturally speaking, they were neither Mexican-American nor white in any exclusive sense.

Their grandchildren, being of mixed parentage, were even less so. They inhabited a simultaneously assimilated and "ethnic" cultural world. Mercy could be invited to join the Anson Garden Club but still head the Women's Guild at the "Mexican" Catholic church.

Their son Peter was a particularly good example of this predicament. One afternoon he reflected on his difficulties in growing up in this ambiguous world where he did not fit social stereotypes. In the cafeteria at school, Mexican-Americans sat on one side and whites on the other. The truth was that Peter had more friends among the white kids at school "because when I first moved to town, they're the ones who came up to me. The Mexican kids didn't appreciate me not hanging around with them. Like, 'Are you too good for us?'" Peter added, "They always called me a *bolillo* [a derogatory term for white person]."

Probably, more was involved in Peter's social choices than who happened to approach him on the first day of school. Mercy wondered if it was envy that spurred such criticism of her son, while Salvador interpreted his son's tendency to hang out with the white kids as a matter of social class, suggesting that Peter simply had more in common with the white kids. For Peter, his family's social status and his academic success had carried costs: he was estranged from most of his Mexican-American peers while simultaneously not entirely accepted by some who could not imagine a Mexican-American as anything but a low-status field hand. Derided as being a *bolillo* by his Mexican-American schoolmates, Peter was at the same time not quite white enough for the others. He recounted a recent incident in which a neighbor was hosting a foreign exchange student whom Peter had wanted to take out. The girl's host denied Peter's request.

"He just looked at me and said, flat out, 'No, I'm not going to let her go out.' And it shocked me, and I just said, 'Why? Give me a reason.'" Finally, under pressure, the man acknowledged that he did not "think there should be intermingling here of relationships." Peter saw this for what it was, namely, the man's way of saying that he did not want the girl going out with a

Mexican-American boy. Peter was still angry about it: "And I was thinking all the way home, 'Pretty Christian, Huh?!'" The man had a leadership role at a local Baptist church.

Within this family, ethnicity was a conscious, ever-present form to be engaged—part of an ongoing conversation that naturally folded into its reflections about the events in their lives: whom their children were dating, what it would be like at college, outings with friends, and so forth. The Torres family had taken the plunge. They are emblematic of a family in transition. But there were costs as well as gains. On one hand, they were stranded, hanging loose in the wind of a West Texas culture that did not know what to do with them. On the other, they were accomplished, successful; their children were educated. At what cost? The statement that "the Torreses aren't considered Mexican," reflected the cost. What, then, were they? White? Mexican-American? Or were they, simply, American?

RACE AS SOCIAL CLASS

One complication in any attempt to pin down such designations is that in the eyes of many in contemporary American society, white and middle-class are sometimes interchangeable or equivalent categories. Thus, to move up becomes unconsciously equivalent to becoming white if you are an ethnic minority. This fosters a tremendous ambivalence with regard to such social ascendance. An interesting window into this fact is a book by Jhally and Lewis (1992), *Enlightened Racism: The Cosby Show, Audiences, and the Myth of the American Dream,* in which the authors interviewed black and white respondents as to their reactions to the popular television sitcom depicting an upper-middle-class black family. Many of the book's black respondents expressed very favorable feelings because it portrayed a strong, positive, accomplished, black family. However, at the same time, the authors skate on the margins of suggesting that, by virtue of their middle-class status, the Huxtables (the show's protagonists) are, well, almost white.

Behind the preference for *The Cosby Show* (among African-Americans) lies a subtle interaction between race and class in the context of an American culture—displayed on television and elsewhere—in which to be working class is a sign of failing in the meritocracy. In the upwardly mobile world of popular television, it is only when black people are presented as middle class that they become normal and are assimilated into the succession of images of social success. [p. 119]

And a little later: "The question of whether the Huxtables are typical or atypical, black or white, real or unreal, is resolved in terms of the broader concerns of the black audience, the desire to overcome TV racial stereotyping" (pp. 122-123).

The authors are more explicit about this link in their commentary on white responses to the popular television show. One of them observed: "You can't [notice color], really! I mean, it wouldn't be any different if they were white" (p. 99).

"Perhaps," the authors conclude, "white people do not actually see the Huxtables as a black family at all. Perhaps they see them as white or as some shade of gray in between." (p. 98) They suggest that perhaps the Huxtables represent "the compromise between black and white culture that is unconsciously seen as a prerequisite of black success" (p. 99).

The blurring of social status and middle-class values with ethnic categories seems to produce confusion for both minority and white populations. For minority people to be successful, they all too readily become "white" in the eyes of *both* whites and their minority group peers. This is clearly the fate suffered by Peter Torres who was told by his white friends that he did not really seem Mexican-American, while being called a *bolillo* by his Mexican-American peers. Under such circumstances, it takes a great deal of psychological fortitude to persist in one's aspirations.

This circumstance also readily produces destructive consequences sometimes not acknowledged within minority communities where the external sources of prejudice and oppression are given greater play (for obvious reasons), while internal, within-group issues that also contribute, albeit secondarily, are minimized. In the eyes of others within one's ethnic group, such ascendance is often viewed as a kind of betrayal, evoking such derisive epithets as "Oreo," "Uncle Tom," "Tio Taco," "bolillo," or "Coconut." An illustration of the problematic nature of such conflicts is reflected in an academically successful 12-year-old Mexican-American boy from a Texas public housing project who was repeatedly beaten up by his peers and chided for being a "school boy." The boy's grades took a precipitous fall. One newspaper account (*The Austin American Statesman*, June 11, 1994), described a young, single, African-American mother who felt compelled to leave for work every day wearing a T-shirt and shorts. The woman went from her home in a housing project to a bathroom in the public library, where she changed into her work clothes. On her way home after work the woman reversed this sequence. By her report, this elaborate process was necessitated by concern that her ambition would make her the object of her neighbors' scorn.

As a member of an ethnic/social class outside the usual designations, Peter Torres is reminiscent of Leonce Gaiter's (*New York Times Magazine*, June 26, 1994) experiences as an African-American student at Harvard. A white classmate once said to him, "Oh, you're not really a black person." "In her world," Gaiter noted, "black people did not attend elite colleges. They could not stand as her intellectual equals or superiors. Any African-American who shared her knowledge of Austen and Balzac—while having to explain to her who Douglass and Du Bois were—had to be *willed* [Gaiter's emphasis] away for her to salvage her sense of superiority as a white person." It may have been, however, that rather than an expression of superiority (or perhaps in addition to it), Gaiter's classmate was giving voice to an unconscious statement of solidarity. It was a statement that said, in effect, "You must be white, too, since we seem to share certain cultural signifiers." His response, of course, spoke to the experience of violation when the precondition to such solidarity is the effacing of an aspect of one's identity.

Gaiter's experience parallels that of Peter Torres in another respect. At the junior high school he attended in the mostly white Washington suburb of Silver Spring, Maryland, a black girl stopped him in the hallway and asked belligerently, "How come you talk so proper?" "The girl was asking," Gaiter observed, "why I spoke without the so-called black accent pervasive in the lower socioeconomic strata of black society, where exposure to mainstream society is limited." In short, Gaiter's middle-class attributes elicited from some of his black peers an accusation similar to the one leveled at Peter Torres—that he was not really black. Similar to Peter Torres's being called a *bolillo,* Gaiter was, by implication, labeled an "Oreo" for seeming to be too white (middle-class).

I am certainly not suggesting that the primary factor keeping poor and/or ethnic minority individuals in poverty is the pernicious effect of intragroup envy. But such envy exists within minority communities as it does in every social grouping, and it plays a destructive role. Mercy Torres was suggesting this when she wondered if the verbal assaults on her son were a function of envy. While there is no shortage of objective factors that contribute to the entrapment of poor and ethnic minorities in the American underclass, within-group psychological elements are rarely acknowledged. Yet minority individuals who face scorn and ostracism from their own group because of their middle-class strivings pay a great price for appropriating the cultural signifiers of those who historically have been considered the Other. Such transitions in social class status are inevitably linked to access to greater economic resources and privileges, and, therefore, lend themselves readily to the universal psychodynamics associated with having something that another does not—the issues of envy, greed, reparation, and gratitude. These psychodynamics cut across every social definition and every social grouping.

Citing census figures, Leonce Gaiter notes that between 1970 and 1990 the number of black families with incomes under $15,000 rose from 34.6 percent of the black population to 37 percent, while the number of black families with incomes of $35,000 to $50,000 rose from 13.9 percent to 15 percent of the population. The number of African-Americans living in such dire economic circumstances is overwhelming. However, Gaiter draws attention to figures indicating the significant increase in the number of blacks with incomes of more than $50,000 (from 9.9 percent in 1970 to 14.5 percent in 1990). Nearly one-third of American blacks are middle-class or upper-middle class (Gaiter's argument, in his *New York Times Magazine* article, "The Revolt of the Black Bourgeoisie" (June 26, 1994) is that the reality of this black middle class is for the most part ignored by the media in favor of portrayals of the black underclass, which has come to represent the whole of the African-American community). However, because of the social history within which these considerations are embedded, a minority person's economic success places him or her in conflict. All too often, to become middle class is synonymous, consciously and unconsciously, with becoming white in the eyes of the minority and the white communities. Such reflexive pairing of ethnicity with social class is an encumbrance to minority individuals seeking to find a place within the American Dream.

6

Jack and Bea Hornsby: "If I wanted to keep the white business, I wasn't going to mix them."

Jack and Bea Hornsby's café is strategically located on Commercial Street, a block south of the county courthouse and a block north of the Anson Church of Christ. Jack does all the cooking, and many in Anson consider his culinary talents inspired. Bea's Steak House has no menu, but Hornsby prides himself as a café man who is a master of home-cooked, family-style cuisine.

The large windows facing Commercial Street are filled with various plants in plastic pots placed in an odd assortment of straw baskets and hats. The plants appear to be a trifle neglected, with dead and yellowing leaves alongside new shoots. On any given morning, or at lunch time, local gossip swirls from one end of the café to the other, as do matters of importance, such as when to plant this year's cotton or when the next cold front, or "blue norther" might blow in. Jack and Bea typically close after lunch; there is no dinner business in Anson. Bea's became a kind of unofficial headquarters for me during my visits to Anson. Taking up a strategically situated table, I could peruse my notes, think about my upcoming interviews, and visit with people I had already met.

Although raised Church of Christ, Jack had always been something of a maverick. At 74 his reputation as a man who

Jack and Bea Hornsby at Bea's Café. Photo: Nancy Scanlan.

followed his own inclinations was firmly established throughout
Anson. All his life he had been something of an amiable rebel.
Yet he was tolerated, even loved, by some whom he had offended
the most. While fourteen churches in town vied for people's souls,
only two eating establishments (not counting the Hatahoe and
Dairy Queen, both of which served mainly hamburgers) vied to
meet their gustatory needs, and Jack Hornsby's was arguably the
better of the two. Hornsby was not only personable and well-liked,
he also had deep roots in Anson where his mother had also been
a restaurateur. Most important, however, he provided the community with an essential function—a place to meet and visit with
your neighbors. No doubt, all of these reasons helped Jack maintain his status regardless of how he behaved, including the fact
that he had played host to the Footloose Club's meetings.

"Ninety percent of my business is local," he said, leaning back
in his chair. He reached into his shirt pocket and pulled out a
round container. Popping the lid open, Hornsby stuck his index
finger and thumb into the small tin, grabbing a pinch of some
brownish substance. I asked if the substance was snuff. "Yep,"
he said, "I'm trying to quit." He chuckled out loud, and contin-

Diners at Bea's Café. (l–r) Woodrow Simmons, Investigator; Mike Middleton, Sheriff; Calvin Cox, Texas Ranger. Standing: Gerald Baldwin. Photo: Nancy Scanlan.

ued, "It's mint! It's got 2 percent snuff and mints; it's something to kind of appease you," and he chuckled again. Hornsby put the pinch of snuff between his gum and his left cheek.

He had been cooking nearly all his life. His mother had once owned several restaurants in Anson and other nearby towns, and Jack had been a shipboard cook while serving in the Navy. He conjured up cooking stories as only people with an unusual devotion to something can.

"This story is funny," Jack said, "but it wasn't funny at *all* then. It was serious. For years and years I cooked chili for the fire department benefit. When you cook in one of those big pots, grease cooks up to the top, you know, and you get the grease out. And we'd have four or five drums of grease over there. And we'd stir that chili with boat oars! And ol' Knoxie Pittard, he come in here and got a 'Plumber's Friend' and walked over to that grease and got it all over it and then set it up there right by that big pot of chili." Jack let out a hearty laugh, and then continued: "And some guy come in and took a picture of that. When they had the chili deal they had a bunch of pictures made and they put one on a stand there by the chili that said that's what I'd used to stir the chili with. I walked in and I was mad— really hot! And ol' Knoxie just died laughing." Jack laughed again, a heavy, sincere laugh. It was clear that a great deal of personal satisfaction was tied to his career as a café man. When his mother retired from the restaurant business, Jack opened his own place.

FREE CHRISTMAS DINNER FOR ALL

In 1984, shortly after his mother's death, Jack vowed to make a wish of hers come true: to give the town a free meal on Christmas day. Two days before Christmas of 1989, Jack was preparing for an anticipated 600 people to take him up on his offer. The front page of the *The Western Observer* headlined its story: "Jack and Bea Want to Share Christmas Meal." "Once a year I just open the doors and let them have it," Jack told me.

A *partial* grocery list, according to the *Observer,* included 14 hams, 14 turkeys, an anticipated 280 to 300 pounds of dressing, 250 pounds of corn bread, 100 pounds of fruit for a fruit salad, 250 cans of cranberry sauce, 75 pounds of celery, more than 100 cans of yams, 50 pounds of onions, 60 boiled eggs for the giblet gravy, 2 1/2 gallons of half-and-half for a squash dish and 6 pounds of butter for the squash.

"We run it in the paper," Jack said. "This week it will come out in the front page of the Anson paper, and then the TV stations in Abilene will run it. I think we had 296 people last year, and this year it'll be a bigger crowd." On Christmas Eve, "The Eyes of Texas," a state-wide television program celebrating life in small-town Texas, aired the story about Jack and Bea and their free Christmas dinner.

Jack and I sat at the "community table" in the café, a long, white formica-topped table that seats some twenty people. As we talked, Jack received several calls from elderly widows who could not make it out of the house, asking to be put on Jack's "will-deliver" list for Christmas dinner. At one o'clock the temperature outside was still only twelve degrees Fahrenheit, and the forecast did not promise much improvement, but the café was toasty warm, and coffee was flowing quite freely. Each entering customer had his own story of winter woe to tell the others seated at the community table.

Knoxie Pittard, with his wide-brimmed black hat, could have been an actor in a Hollywood western except he was the real thing—a Texas cowboy/rancher. As he blew into his cupped hands, Knoxie told us of his tribulations in getting his pickup started that morning. Then he mumbled something about coon hunting to Dave Reves, who was seated next to me. Reves replied that "coons, like most people with any sense, would be pretty well denned up in this weather." Several of the other men seated around the table nodded their heads in agreement. Everyone seemed to defer to Reves, who was regarded as the ultimate hunting authority.

Jack received one call from an old woman he'd known since he was a boy. "That's Janie Stevens. She and I went to school together," Jack said with concern, "and for Christmas dinner she needs two meals. They can't get out. It's awful. We have a list of 'em. Ten or fifteen people."

I asked Jack about his motivation for doing his Christmas dinner. The Hornsbys were not wealthy by any stretch of the imagination. "I owe it to them," Jack replied, "Look how good the town's been to me."

When others tried to donate to the Christmas dinner, Jack steadfastly refused, explaining, "This is mine and I want to keep it that way. You get people in it and then first thing you know you haven't got it, somebody else's got it. Just like Meals on Wheels, they want to pay for it and I said no, because I'm doing it and I'm doing it for everybody. I feed all of them on Christmas Day so the Meals on Wheels volunteers can get off. None of them will have to be there," Jack said proudly.

Jack Hornsby loved to feed people. The café was set up with an open buffet. Customers entering the line served themselves.

The sign over the buffet hot plates and steamers read: "Take All You Want, But Eat All You Take." Jack's "hands," as he referred to the hired help, mostly his in-laws, dished out dessert, iced tea or coffee, with refills throughout the meal. His pleasure in being a bountiful provider was unabashed. When I commented on how tasty his Irish stew was (which came in a very large bowl, at least twice the serving I had anticipated), Jack replied, "That's one thing about it here, *idn'it* Dave? [He pointed to Dave Reves to verify his testimony.] When you come in here to eat you *get to eat!*" Hornsby laughed heartily, and then paused to give emphasis before continuing in his inimitable, vintage West Texas drawl: "All *yeu whont!* About three weeks ago we had a special lunch. We had ten different meats, and we had about 110 pounds of catfish, and I told the girls to get out from behind the counter. All l wanted them to do was to pour tea. Anybody who wanted to eat could eat about all they wanted, *anything* they wanted." Jack laughed again. "We had more fun that day!"

At 74 Jack had begun to show his age. Dressed in a white western shirt with brown pinstripes (he had taken off his ever-present white apron to sit down for our interview), his thin frame appeared a bit frail. Jack told me that he had quit drinking a couple of years ago: "Man! I used to drink a lot! I was drinking four and one-half or five cases of beer a week. You know, I was about half-tied the whole time. And after I quit drinking and quit smoking, I've been sick ever since!"

Jack laughed at the irony of the situation. "No kidding! That's not the way it's supposed to be! I've been to all kinds of doctors, and one of them told me, 'Jack, you been drinkin' all your life.' And I said, 'That's right, since I was 6 years old I've been drinking beer.' And I said, 'Because my mother was a full-blood German and that's the way I was raised.' And I said, 'I smoked since I was 12 years old.' And he said, 'And you quit all of that at one time.' And I said, 'That's right.' And he said, 'Your system cain't stand it.' And I really believe that's what's happened, because I've come up with sugar diabetic [sic] and everything else, and I've never had any problems my whole life."

A story from the May 14, 1989 *Dallas Morning News* carried
the following headline: "Restaurant Doors Always Open: Owner
Doesn't Lock Up, Invites Hungry to Help Themselves." A five-
by-six inch photograph featured Jack and Bea standing in front
of the "One Trip Only" sign by the buffet. Bea, clearly younger
than Jack, was standing slightly in front of him, smiling broadly.
Jack's look was a bit more pensive and stiff, not particularly
comfortable in front of the camera. The article reported that
Jack had "adopted a serious open-door policy at his restaurant.
He's so serious, in fact, that he hasn't locked the doors to Bea's
Café in 30 years."

When the café closed officially at about one-thirty in the afternoon the doors were left unlocked. "After that, those who need
a meal—whether they can pay for it or not—are welcome to come
in and prepare it," the newspaper article continued. "If a man
is hungry, he should eat," the article quoted Jack. "Nobody is
going to miss a sandwich if a hungry person needs it."

Nearly *everybody* is an early riser in a farming community
and some came into the café and fixed the first pot of coffee, but
Jack had also found lettuce, bread, and other sandwich *"fixins"*
out overnight, sometimes with payment, other times without.
"All my friends think I'm crazy for doing this," Jack was quoted
as saying, "but I've never had a problem."

A similar article in *The National Inquirer* was headed "Restaurant Never Locks Doors—So People Can Cook Own Meals
When the Staff Is Gone." The story had probably been picked
up from the Associated Press but added some different photographs: Jack and Bea at the community table with other customers, Jack's hand resting warmly on Bea's shoulder, and Jack
and Bea standing in front of the café, Jack still somewhat formal
and awkward, Bea still smiling broadly. The undated *National
Inquirer* story was framed and hung prominently along the dining room's main wall. Jack had brought *The Dallas Morning
News* article out of the kitchen for me to see.

Guests flowed in and out of the restaurant, greeting Jack with
affection. When Jack was sitting among the customers, the

banter was continuous, warm, and friendly. As the restaurant's patrons started clearing, I asked Jack how he and Bea, who was running an errand in Abilene on that particular day, had met. Jack smiled the thin, ironic kind of smile I had come to recognize as his hallmark.

"You know, my first wife was a sweet, wonderful person," Jack said as he leaned toward me with elbows on the table. "At one time I had four restaurants, when me and my wife were together, and I was making good money. Big money. And I was gettin' wild," and he laughed out loud. "All evil is money," Jack said with sudden seriousness, "but anyway, there were good-looking girls and I got to messin' around. And I went home one night about ten o'clock and my wife was waiting for me, and I thought 'What's she doing up?' I'd just closed up the restaurant. And I went to the bathroom, and I always carried a money box with me and a gun, and I set the money box and the gun down in the bathroom, and the bathroom door opened, and she said, 'Well I'm going to fix you up where you'll quit running around!'" Jack laughed again, this time somewhat anxiously. "And she shot me," Jack said, pointing to his crotch, "with a 20-gauge shotgun! And I thought, 'Oh my God!' But she missed them!" Jack laughed nervously again, and continued: "And that's what I told her when I went by the door. I patted her on the shoulder and I said, 'Honey, you missed them.'"

Jack took a deep breath. It was obvious that this story did not come as easily as the ones about cooking. "Well I just went on out to the hospital, and I was going to go on down to Stamford [a neighboring town with a larger hospital], but I got out here near the edge of town and I knew I was going to pass out. So I just turned around and come back to this hospital in Anson. Oh! Man! The blood was hittin' up the top of the pickup," and with real emotion he went on: "Dave Reves [who was sheriff at the time] was out there at the hospital; my wife had called him, and Dave wanted to go out to pick her up, and I just said, 'No, I deserved just exactly what I got, just leave her alone.' She was a good woman. She *is* a good woman. . . . She never bothers me and I never bother

her now. And I have three boys and they all think a lot of Bea, every one of them . . . but anyway, I could not say a bad thing about that woman. Even after she shot me. She's wonderful, but I just couldn't live with her, and I knew it and I told her I couldn't."

"I stayed thirty-two days in the hospital and she wanted me to move back home. And so I went back home after the hospital for about an hour and I told her I couldn't do it. I just couldn't do it. I had absolutely no love at all. It was completely gone. And now I think of her as a good friend, that's it," Jack said as he concluded the story.

He divorced his wife and left Anson with twenty-five dollars in his pocket to take a job near Houston working in construction for Brown and Root, the company that had bankrolled LBJ's political career. The company sent Hornsby to Louisiana where they had a major contract laying a pipeline. "Can you see me doing something like that?" Jack asked incredulously, "a café man like me?"

He laughed heartily again. Laying pipes was too much against his grain. Jack loved the restaurant business too much; he loved cooking and serving up those special lunches. But most of all, Jack Hornsby loved leaning back in his chair and bantering with his customers, many of whom he had known all his life.

Bea was the woman Jack had been involved with, but not the woman whom Jack's wife had suspected. Indeed, Jack's wife had suspected nearly every other woman in town, but not Bea. Bea was 16 and Jack was 54 at the time. Furthermore, Bea was Mexican-American. "She was washing dishes for me," Jack recalled, leaning back again in his chair, "and that was the prettiest li'l Mexican girl I ever looked at. She weighed ninety-four pounds and now look at her!" Jack laughed heartily. Bea's sister, Ann, was working the other end of the table, visiting with a few lingering customers.

"She's not here," Ann said, looking up from her cup of coffee. It seemed that Ann was both protecting Bea in a good-natured way and deflecting the implication of being overweight herself by making sure I knew she was not Bea.

"Ann," Jack added, "I'm going to tell him what you called me, and this is on TV too! [referring to my tape recorder]. She said, 'Jack you are a sorry S. O. B.'" That statement sent everybody in the café into fits of laughter.

That was twenty years ago. Jack had married Bea and opened a new restaurant, which he named after her: "I said, 'Well, if I'm going to have to make her a living, I'm going to have to make her responsible for somethin.' So she takes care of the book work, pays all the taxes, and when I can get her to work, she helps . . ." Jack paused for effect: " . . . a little." He got serious again. "No, she comes to work every morning at five-thirty and works till we close at one-thirty," he said.

Jack's marriage to Bea was as unlikely a union as one could have imagined in Anson. The discrepancy in their ages approached a whole lifetime—nearly forty years. But more important, he had once had a firmly established reputation in Anson as a racist. There were many Mexican-Americans in Anson who could recall, with bitterness, having to wait out back to get something to eat at Jack's restaurant in the old days. In fact, Bea's own father had been refused service. At the time Bea was washing dishes there the large sign on the front door announcing that this was a "Whites Only" eating establishment had been gone for only two or three years.

WHITES ONLY!

The legacy of those days lingered. Jack had few Mexican-American or black customers. "I'd say 95 percent of my business is white, all white," Jack noted. It was clear to Hornsby that the minority community of Anson had never forgotten, and this seemed to weigh on him. Most of the racist venom appeared to be gone from him now, leaving him perplexed as to why others might not have forgotten too:

"There used to be a sign right there that said 'Whites Only,'" Jack said, pointing toward the door. "And my wife's daddy, I didn't know who he was, well it wouldn't have made any difference anyway, they come in and sit down right over there, and I asked them to leave. And I think to this day there's a lot of bearing on that because as old as I am, they still remember that, and there's not a Spanish person in this town who won't holler at me [meaning to greet in the friendly Texas sense], and speak to me and do anything in the world to help me, but they do *not* trade with me. And I think that's part of it, way back there.

"And it's just like with the colored people, they will *not* come in here. And, this is funny. This boy worked for me, and about six months ago I was sitting at this table and this colored boy looked in the door, like that," Jack cupped his hands around his eyes and leaned forward as if peering into a window. "I didn't think anything about it. I thought he was looking for somebody. Well, this boy used to work for me when he was just a kid. He walked around behind the building and come in. And Gloria, the dishwasher, come in and she tells me, 'Jack, there's a man back here says he wants to see you.' So I went back there and he said, 'Mr. Jack, you don't remember me, do you?' And I said, 'No, I don't believe I do.' And he said, 'Do you remember Ray who used to work for you?' And I said, 'I sure do.' And he said, 'Well I'm Ray.' And I couldn't believe it. He'd gotten old. And so I said, 'Well, why didn't you just come in the door a while ago when you looked in?' And he said, 'I remembered what you'd told me.' And I said, 'What'd I tell you Ray?' And he said, 'You told me I was a nigger and I was always gonna be a nigger and to always have respect for a white man.' And he said, 'and I still got it.'"

Jack looked at me pensively. The silence felt thick. He seemed to be reflecting on the many implications that resonated in his story. He was clearly troubled by it. "And you know, that has a lot of bearing on what's happening," Hornsby noted sadly. "I don't think I'll ever have any colored business and I'll never have much Spanish business. And I'm not proud of that, but back then, that's the way it was. You know, if I wanted to keep the white business, I wasn't going to mix them. And I was one of those, you know, I didn't care who he was or what he was. As a matter of fact, some governor from Old Mexico or whatever he was, he was in here, and I got *him* out of here. And they took pictures of me, and they took pictures of the café and everything else, and I thought I was going to get into trouble over it, but I didn't. I said, 'We do not feed colored people or Spanish people.' They didn't like it. They left and I followed him to the door, and there was a big sign up there said 'Whites Only,' and they took pictures of me at the door, that was just before that law come in [the Civil Rights Act of 1964]."

"So you had a reputation for being a racist in town in those days," I said, observing the obvious. "Yep. I did. Bad. Real bad," was his reply. It was apparent that Jack found it difficult to reflect upon this contradiction in himself. He found it difficult to reconcile his past and his present. He had grown up in a world in which racial divisions constituted one of the fundamental truths, an irreducible element of reality. The world in which Jack Hornsby grew up was, unquestionably, a southern world in which whites and blacks and Mexican-Americans were assigned rigid places within the social order.

On a summer day in 1987 Dave Reves and I pulled into the parking lot behind Bea's Steak House. He had taken me to an abandoned house in the middle of a field to show me how to shoot his "snake gun." It seemed to be a kind of mission for Reves, as if at last my life might be realigned and put back on track if I could acquire a proficiency that any elementary school boy in West Texas already took for granted. It turned out I wasn't a bad shot. But the highlight of the morning had been when Reves had pulled out his 45-caliber pistol and repeatedly shot after a beer can that seemed to skip through the air like a rabbit.

We went into Bea's through the back door, passing the mops, broken chairs, boxes of paper towels and napkins, and boxes of vegetables that were stacked on a table. We also walked by the café's bathroom with its scuffed up door and a dangling hook that served as a lock. I thought of Knoxie Pittard's prank and the plumber's helper, which no doubt still sat propped against some nearby wall.

"How do you say five by five in Spanish?" Reves suddenly asked me.

I was taken by surprise. "What?"

"Five by five, how do you say that in Spanish? I want to tease ol' Bea." Dave Reves had a nickname for virtually everyone he knew. Like a caricaturist, he had a talent for picking out some distinctive feature in a person and anchoring a name to it. For example, earlier that morning he had introduced me to the man fixing the air-conditioning at the Opera House as "Windy." He designated Heidenhammer's Department Store as "Heidenskinner's" to reflect his disapproval of their high prices. He introduced me to O. B. Cox, a retired rancher, as "horse trader" Cox. (Cox was amused, despite the fact that he'd heard it hundreds of times.) Other friends and acquaintances Reves simply called "goofus" so-and-so, if they were men, or "bluesy" so-and-so if they were women. No one that Dave Reves had any affection for eluded being called some honorific other than their actual name.

"Cinco por cinco," I answered as we approached the longer-than-usual line for lunch. Jack and Bea were doing a brisk business on this particular day. The menu offered southern-fried chicken, one of Jack's specialties, or catfish, with mashed potatoes, canned string beans, rice, salad, and a few other options. I chose the fried chicken.

As always, Bea was at the cash register. I had pulled out my billfold to pay when Dave blurted out "Hey, que pasa cinco por cinco?" Bea started laughing. "Where'd you learn that?" she asked him in a tone that suggested his Spanish was plainly absurd. "It's getting to the point where we'll serve just about anybody around here," Bea added with a large dollop of good humor. The exchange was ripe with symbolism—Dave Reves speaking Spanish while Bea's retort invoked the "whites only" days at the restaurant.

After the lunch crowd had cleared out, Bea and I sat at a table and talked. She had a pretty, rounded face with thick, dark brown bangs that stopped just short of her eyebrows. Her eyes were large and receptive and she had an easy smile.

When Bea and Jack began seeing one another, she was 16 and already the mother of a child. Jack legally adopted Bea's daughter, Laurie, to whom he became absolutely devoted. Laurie and Jack's relationship was a source of great satisfaction for Bea, whose relationship to her own father was conflicted. She was pleased by the interest that Jack took in Laurie, especially since she was not his biological child.

Laurie became Jack's constant companion. He taught her to hunt and fish, and when she was still in elementary school, to drive his old pickup truck. Once, while they were fishing at a remote spot on a friend's ranch, Jack suffered a stroke. He managed to get himself to the truck, but was too weak to do anything else. Maintaining her wits, 9-year-old Laurie drove the two of them back to town, which Jack's physician said had saved him from sustaining significant damage and, indeed, may have saved his life. Jack and Laurie were almost inseparable.

When Laurie was 16, Jack gave her a shotgun for Christmas. It was a beautiful gun, and she was quite pleased. However, it was a turbulent time for the Hornsby family. Laurie was dating a black boy from nearby Stamford. If Jack had succeeded in transcending his prejudice toward Mexican-Americans, the thought of his daughter dating a black man was unbearable. He tried to prevent the courtship, but was unsuccessful.

In the summer of 1987, Laurie died under mysterious circumstances that suggested suicide. One night, when Laurie returned from a date with the boy from Stamford, Jack became furious and went after him in his pickup truck. Laurie was distressed, went into the house, and got the shotgun Jack had given her. Joe Ramos, Bea's brother-in-law, found Laurie out in the front yard, her face blown away by a shotgun blast.

Bea found it almost impossible to talk to me about this tragedy. Tearfully, she told me that it must have been God's will. She had to have faith in that, she said. All things happen for a reason, she added. In fact, following Laurie's death, Bea had been "born again." Finding Jesus changed her life, and her faith was the most important thing in her world, she told me. Maybe

Laurie's death was meant to be for reasons only He could comprehend.

At another time, Jack tearfully recounted the events of that night and his conviction that Laurie had not intended to kill herself, but rather had been the victim of an accident while handling her prized shotgun.

"I have never been convinced that she done it," Jack said, his voice breaking. "I think the little girl was so disturbed at me that night that she went out and she grabbed her gun and I think she went out there, well there's an ol' tree out there, and I think she was going to destroy that gun. And I think when she come back like that [Jack gestured as if raising the shotgun over his head] she hit the tree and it went off and got her." Jack grew increasingly upset. This was clearly the most painful experience of his life. "But the police went down and investigated it and said it was self-inflicted," Jack went on after an emotion-filled pause. "Ain't *no* way! There's *no* way!"

Laurie had lived for three days before succumbing to her wounds. The hospital bill had come to $36,000, but the police determination that Laurie's gunshot was self-inflicted voided Jack and Bea's insurance, which normally would have paid her medical expenses.

All of the painful emotions of that nightmarish experience returned to Jack. He excused himself and went back to the kitchen ostensibly to get more coffee, but it was clear that he was overwhelmed talking about Laurie's death. It was late afternoon, and the café was almost empty. Joe Ramos had been talking to Bea's sister, Ann, at the other end of the community table. Seeing Jack leave, he came over. It was evident that he had overheard our conversation.

"There's no way Laurie could have reached that trigger," Joe told me. It was clear that this was a family trauma that had been examined and reexamined. "Plus, Laurie was wearing boots that night," he added. "There's no way she could have pulled the trigger with her toe or something. It was definitely an accident."

How to understand Jack Hornsby? He was renowned for his generosity all over the "Big Country," yet he was also a man who had once taken pride in his uncompromising segregationist stance. He was a man who had seemingly become the model of racial tolerance, yet his most prized and meaningful attachment was destroyed, apparently at her own hand, over her father's refusal to let her date a boy of a different race.

RACIAL ANXIETY

In his autobiography, Malcolm X says that "most white men's hearts and guts will turn over inside out of them . . . whenever they see a negro man on close terms with a white woman" (p. 94). The suggestion, clearly, is that such an interracial relationship activates the deepest, most primitive anxieties. Perhaps what was released in Jack Hornsby was a dreaded fear. He must have felt that he had to save his daughter from some kind of indescribable ruin.

A circumstance such as this is full of unknowable complexity. There are elements of human nature that will forever remain beyond our grasp no matter what the facts are. Whatever the origins, the pain suffered by Jack Hornsby was incalculably greater than the shotgun blast aimed at his genitals. It was a deep and permanent wound on his heart. For Bea, it was an event that seemed to strike endlessly upon the sides of a sound-proofed enclosure deep within her. She was mute in the face of it, except for the tears that flowed immediately at the slightest reference to her only daughter. Finally, there was also the pain of the young man from Stamford whose life, too, would be forever marked by his girlfriend's apparent suicide, an act wrapped in the confusing, primitive emotions that accompany the breaking of social taboos regarding ethnic boundaries.

Cultures, and the subcultures with which individuals become fundamentally identified, organize identity every bit as much as the social ecology that reigns within one's particular family. They provide the markers for the broad array of experiences that identify the I/We and delineate them from the Not We/Other. Such cultural markers permeate one's sense of self, though they are difficult to circumscribe or localize. Several years ago, while visiting a Civil War site in Georgia, I was struck by the spontaneous eruption of emotion occasioned by a trio playing "Dixie." Many of the whites in attendance, apparently southerners, flocked to the source of the music and joined in the singing, after which there were loud and extended whoops of solidarity. That simple, and, to the uninitiated, not particularly remarkable tune carried for many of these white southerners the emotional resonances that "We Shall Overcome" carries for African-Americans. Each of these songs has been infused with particular meaning linked to collective histories from which individuals cannot simply disconnect themselves without being dislocated from the very source of what makes them who they are. At the same time that these songs have been appropriated to carry the meaning of individual and collective histories, they simultaneously act as reference to these histories. They are both receptacles and pointers, passive and active cultural artifacts. And it is the unfortunate fate of mankind that this musical illustration of how cultural artifacts define identity is repeated in countless others like it that exist in every culture. Unfortunate because these two cultural signifiers point in different, potentially irreconcilable directions. Irreconcilable, that is, unless one is willing to mourn the loss of a part of the self. For southern whites, this means one thing, for African-Americans it means something else.

Tractenberg, in his discussion of anti-Semitism (1989), speaks of the extent to which political and religious ideologies form a part of the self. They are extensions of an individual's identity. Commitments and beliefs form a kind of ever-present twin, "a second self to which great narcissistic value is attached" (p. 468). Pinderhughes (1970) puts the same idea somewhat differently when he states that "important cultural elements are clung to by adults with the intensity with which children cling to mothers . . . " (p. 598). In other words, cultural beliefs (social, politi-

cal, religious) form an important part of who we are. Such beliefs also have the cognitive rigidity or fixity of Allport's (1954)
categories or schemas (though for that reason not always negative). Jack Hornsby was defined by a certain cultural world, a
café man born and raised in a rural, southern, Jim Crow tradition, where to a degree which few can appreciate today, segregation was not simply a legal structure. It was a way of life that
defined reality for those who lived within it, whether they were
white, black, or Mexican-American. As was true of everyone
living in the South, a segregationist mind-set had saturated
Hornsby's experience for fifty years before Congress outlawed
segregation. Hornsby's views toward African-Americans had
changed to some degree, if we are to believe (which I did) his
response to the young black man who came to greet him at the
café that afternoon. They had not changed enough to prevent a
tragedy from which he would never recover.

Pao, in a discussion on the role of hatred in the ego (1965),
suggests that hatred establishes a continuity between the present
and the past and may therefore be used as an ego-syntonic defense, as a basis for relating, and as the core of a person's identity (p. 258). To the extent that it plays an ego-organizing and
defensive role, hatred can help establish a sense of continuity
and identity. In a world in which such feelings had been pervasive and an accepted part of the culture, ethnic hatred is difficult to relinquish without a significant shift in an individual's
ego organization. According to Pinderhughes (1970), "Each group
structures the projection employed by its members, by which
the members will be identified" (p. 597). Thus, one's identity
within the group requires, at least partially, participation in the
group's projections. Projective and splitting mechanisms, as well
as other defensive processes, play an important role in the evolution of particular cultural identity variants. When human
groups designate groups or cultural practices as Other, such
designations serve a psychological function, namely, the opportunity to manage internal psychodynamics via one's relation to
the Other. This circumstance makes changes in group interre-

lations difficult. This is partly why racism and anti-Semitism are so intractable. For many, they are a facet of personal and collective identity, an identity formed, in part, by the group's characterological ways of managing intrapsychic conflict. Such collective psychological habits are partly what define a culture, giving it a unique stamp.

Pinderhughes (1970) offers a compelling portrait of the stakes when projective and other collective defensive processes cannot be resolved. In particular, he suggests that America missed an opportunity at the peak of the civil rights era when Dr. Martin Luther King Jr. and Malcolm X represented two poles within the black community, one integrationist, the other separatist. Pinderhughes believes that the verbal onslaughts of Malcolm X represented, in the unconscious of whites, the facets of the integration movement that "seemed like a threatening, dangerous, intrusive, invasion—an attack" (p. 604). At the same time, Malcolm X portrayed whites as "exploitative and destructive to black men, as some kind of devils who had altered them, destroying their families, groups, culture, morality, and basic humanity" (p. 604). Thus, kernels of truth notwithstanding, the circumstance lent itself to a mutually engaged paranoid process. The Other could be increasingly seen as the repository of all evil to be purged from the (personal and collective) self via a segregationist entrenchment. This became the strategy for managing the multiple stresses and regressive complexities of evolving ethnic relations in the context of a changing culture.

This circumstance interfered with the opportunities to resolve the ambivalence whites and blacks experienced with regard to one another, if for different reasons. The assassination of Martin Luther King Jr., the chief spokesperson and symbol for the integrationist impulse, tilted the balance of social forces in favor of the paranoid process between whites and blacks. The result was further polarization and an accentuation of collective splitting. For this reason, in Pinderhughes's view the Black Power movement was jointly created by whites and blacks. According to some contemporary sociologists, whites and blacks

are politically more estranged from one another and less trust-
ing of one another than at any point since the era of the civil
rights movement (see the work of UCLA's Melvin Oliver), notwithstanding the many social, political, and economic advances
made by blacks since that time.

Subjectively, within the phenomenology of Jack Hornsby's
experience, Laurie, Bea, Bea's relatives, perhaps Mexican-
Americans more generally, had become "white" in the sense that
"white," in this context, was shorthand for the known, the
familiar. White, for Hornsby, was that which had become part
of the "we" with which one identifies part of the ego, a part of
the universe accepted as an extension of the self. How this was
effected in Jack's case we can only conjecture. In part, I suspect
it was born out of the shock and trauma of a shotgun blast that
nearly took his life. Bea, a Mexican-American adolescent, an
unwed mother, played a central role in a circumstance that
brought him face to face with death. She also played a central
role in his emotional recovery. Like the whale and the dolphin
trapped in shallow waters and relieved of their otherwise ances-
tral animosity, Jack emerged from this traumatic experience
an altered man with more temperate views toward Mexican-
Americans. Our challenge as a society, of course, is to create collective experiences more analogous to that of the dog and the
cat—who are able to transcend their instinctual responses of
animosity when each naturally becomes part of the other's social world—than the traumatized whale and dolphin—who must
experience considerably more anguish and conflict in coming to
grips with the reality of the Other.

After Laurie Hornsby's death, the entire community of Anson
endeavored to help Jack and Bea pay the medical bills incurred
trying to save Laurie's life. Prominent among these efforts was
Mercy Torres and the Footloose Club, who organized a benefit
dance for the Hornsbys. The city of Anson also sponsored a Fun
Day to raise money. Nothing, of course, could relieve the lingering doubts and sorrow that Jack and Bea felt. Shortly thereafter, Bea joined the First Baptist Church of Anson, where she

sang in the choir. Although she was the only Mexican-American member of the church, she said it did not bother her: "I get a tremendous amount of support from them." She told me her religious involvement made it possible for her to go on.

Jack and Bea Hornsby had rebuilt their lives. His transcendence of racial prejudice was, perhaps like everyone's, incomplete. Yet Jack and Bea, in their own way, represented how much some things had changed in their community. In Anson, marriages between Mexican-Americans and whites were up sharply, much to the consternation of some of the local gentry. Sometimes it was their sons, but, more typically, their daughters, who were dating and marrying Mexican-Americans. Despite the strong racial prejudice that permeated rural Texas, Jack, a would-be Lester Maddox, had taken down his "Whites Only" sign. Bea's relatives took an active part in the restaurant, with Bea at the cash register while Jack made his special southern fried chicken—or whatever else he was inspired to cook—back in the kitchen.

7

The Garcia Family:
"He told them, in a manner of speaking, 'drink from the same glass.'"

In Anson, following the passage of the Civil Rights Act in the mid-1960's, Mexican-Americans started moving into town at an accelerated pace, in part propelled by the mechanization of cotton farming, which all but eliminated the need for hired hands and migrant labor. When I started conducting interviews there in 1987, a little more than twenty years after the passage of the Civil Rights Act, almost a third of Anson's population was Mexican-American. Further, as the children of Anson's white families moved to larger urban centers, Mexican-Americans increasingly filled positions that formerly had been beyond their reach. Anson witnessed its first Mexican-American farmer, sheriff's deputy, high school cheerleader, and bank teller, not to mention the clerks in the local stores. The Garcia family was a Mexican-American family who had determined to take full advantage of the new opportunities. For this reason, they provide an exceptional view of the psychological complexities inherent in social change, even when such change would seem to follow an ideal course.

Agustín and Fidela Garcia live in an aging house on the eastern rim of Anson, just before the town plays itself out into the dusty cotton fields. The house, of pier and beam construction, is small and weathered. The paved street ends about a quar-

Agustín and Fidela Garcia, lifelong Jones County residents. Photo:
Nancy Scanlan.

ter-mile back toward town, making the collection of houses here
look especially dusty.

A short wire fence runs the width of the house along the front,
with a gate at the center. Pairs of cinder blocks, arranged a
comfortable stride apart, run the distance between the gate and
the front porch—some thirty feet or so. The day I arrived for
the first interview, in the dead of summer, the cinder blocks
seemed odd, each standing alone some eight inches above the
dusty ground. But on the occasion of a good rainfall, those cinder blocks were clearly the only way to get into the house without sinking ankle-deep into mud.

When I entered the Garcias' dirt drive, Agustín Garcia came
out to greet me. He is a somewhat diminutive, stocky man. The
patrones (bosses) had always called him "Shorty." He is robust
in the way you would expect in a man who has worked the fields
for nearly sixty years. Agustín's thick, neatly trimmed, black
mustache was beginning to gray. His shirt sleeves were rolled

Veronica Garcia at the First National Bank of Anson. Photo: Nancy Scanlan.

up to his elbows, and he wore Levis and work boots. *"Pásele"* (come on in), he said, as he motioned me through the screen door.

Inside, the house was dark, especially to unadjusted eyes coming in from the bright, mid-afternoon sun. Fidela, Agustín's wife, waited just inside the door to greet me. She was small and somewhat square in her proportions. *"Pásele, pásele,"* she repeated, smiling broadly. She sported a pair of '50s style silver-rimmed glasses that complemented her silver-gray hair, and gave her a stately, attractive appearance.

The front door opened into the living room of the Garcias' home. An old console television was tuned to a Spanish-language station airing a show about youth gangs in East Los Angeles. Fidela turned the volume down and motioned me to sit. The living room furniture, two well-worn lazy boys and a sofa, was arranged in a semicircle around the television, which clearly was the family's main source of entertainment. The sofa was draped with a bedspread to cover its years of wear. Similarly, the armchair in which I sat had towels covering arm rests that had been worn to the cotton stuffing. Though shabby by middle-class standards, the room actually felt quite warm and comfortable. Despite their poverty, the Garcia household was dense with the rich feeling of a living, working home that reflected the family's investment in it.

Above the television were many framed photographs of the Garcia children and grandchildren. The Garcias were proud of their children and with good reason—all had graduated from high school (in Texas the high school dropout rate for Hispanic children is 50 percent), three had graduated from college, two from post-high school technical schools, and one was currently enrolled in college.

As my eyes slowly became acclimated to the light, I noticed a plastic bust of Jesus on one of the walls, a cheaply framed depiction of the Last Supper, and numerous other icons. This was a religious family.

THE FAMILY'S ORIGINS

Agustín was born and raised on the farmlands surrounding Anson. He and Fidela met when her family, migrant farm laborers, came to Anson following *la pisca* (the harvest) from South Texas. Agustín never attended school and does not read or write. A prominent childhood memory is of his mother's death when he was 6 years old. He stood beside her deathbed, scared, asking her if she was feeling better, looking for some glimmer of hope in her ashen face. No doubt sensing his fear that he might lose her, she had sought to reassure him: "Yes, I think I'm feeling better." But her weakened body was unable to muster the strength to fight off the pneumonia that gripped her, and she died shortly thereafter. "We were too timid in those days to even go to the doctor," Agustín recollected, still feeling his sadness. He and his brothers and sisters were sent off to live with their maternal grandmother.

"I have always worked in agriculture," Agustín told me. "I started working with *los Americanos* when I was 8 years old. It was pretty hard work. Me and Fidela have always maintained ourselves just by our work, what we earned in one week is what we had to live on. Now that we're *viejos* [old], things are a little easier, but in the old days it was a constant struggle."

I asked the Garcias to describe the changes that they had witnessed in Anson.

Fidela: "Well, it started more or less when President Kennedy took that bad law away, he told them, in a manner of speaking, 'drink from the same glass' because the truth is that it was very hard . . . and when I had my own family . . . I said to myself, 'Even if I feel embarrassed sometimes, I'm going to show my children to *emparejarse* [to be equals] with these people that feel that they're the only ones who can do anything—so all of my children have finished school."

Agustín: "That was my only ambition, that *they* finish school so that tomorrow, or after that, they would grow up and be hard working, but that they wouldn't have to go through what we went through. And look, it's paid off. Because now, three are teachers, and like I told my *Señora,* when our *chiquillo* [littlest one] finishes, then we're going to go to high school and we'll finish college, too!"

Fidela and Agustín both burst into laughter, but beneath the laughter I sensed that Agustín had revealed a point of vulnerability. His lack of education was a source of deep embarrassment.

This was clearly a conversation that could have taken place in countless American immigrant homes, across several centuries. But scholars and social scientists have argued that racial prejudice has made the Mexican, as well as the African-American experience different from that of many immigrant groups, complicating their pursuit of the American Dream, for color constitutes a kind of indelible marker that rising social status and income can at best only fade, not erase.

Fidela recalled the drugstore owned by a group of doctors in town. "They sold everything, medicines, lotions, everything. But if you sat down, immediately they'd be on you, 'You can't sit there, you have to go out.'"

Agustín: "Ice cream, coke, *lonches,* whatever it was, but you couldn't sit down in there. You just bought what you needed, and they grabbed the money, but you couldn't sit down there for anything."

THEY THOUGHT THEY OWNED YOU

Like the rest of the South did with blacks, Texas, especially rural Texas, retained a near feudal system well into the 1960s for blacks and people of Mexican ancestry. "The *patrón* sort of owned you," Agustín recalled, "and there were lots of men, *Americanos,* who'd say that they were good. 'No *hombre, cállate!* This *hombre* is real good. He'll help you when you need it, you just go and he'll help you.' Yes, but they didn't know why. . . . They helped you because that way when the day came that you wanted to go somewhere else they'd say, 'Oh? You're leaving? After all I've given you?' It's sort of like they had you bought . . . and I still know people that were born and raised on a *rancho,* like José. He's over 60 now. He was raised on that *rancho,* he got married there, and he still lives there to this day, but now he's retired. He's too old to work now."

Agustín and Fidela reflected on the fact that the law was always on the side of the *Americanos:* "The law was all turned around," Fidela said. "They didn't want to hear anything from a Mexican. Whenever a Mexican complained about something, the *bolillo* always came out in the right. They'd take the right away from the Mexican and give it to the *bolillo,* regardless of whether he was right or wrong."

Dave Reves who had been the Jones County sheriff during the 1960s, I learned from the Garcias, was an exception. "Dave Reves was a good '*sherife,*'" Agustín recalled. "He was more on the level with the rich and the poor, Mexicans, blacks, everyone. So some of the *Americanos* didn't like him, because he'd lock up *hombres* with money, see, the children of the *hombres* with money, and they didn't like it . . . Now, the sheriffs are afraid, because if they do something that people don't like they take the position away from them, because the town votes on them . . . I may be old-fashioned about this, but I think that if a guy's going to be an employee, even if he's from your family, he should do what's just. For example, I've got nephews and cousins in the Highway Patrol, and if I don't stop at a stop sign, and my nephew sees me, and he lets me go, well I'm breaking the law, and just because he's my nephew doesn't mean that he ceases to be Highway Patrol, so that's why I say, that's the way the law's got to be."

Fidela recalled a time that Agustín had a major run-in with the law. He was sharecropping a man's land, and the work in the fields was finished. The cotton was harvested and taken to the cotton gin. With that job finished, the Garcia family had no other income for the remainder of the winter. For seven years, at the end of the harvest, Agustín had taken a job on the night shift at the local cotton gin to keep his family afloat until the next cotton season. "We had four in school," Fidela remembered. "Where else were we going to get money?"

The owner of the local gin liked Agustín and called him each year when business picked up sufficiently to start a night crew. One year Agustín grew impatient. "I knew that they were ginning," he said. "Aren't you going to start up the night shift? Don't I have my job?" Agustín asked.

"No," the gin owner answered, "I don't know what arrangements you have with your *patrón*."

"Look," Agustín answered, "I told the *patrón* when I made my arrangements with him, I told him clearly that I work at the gin when it starts nights. The man at the cotton gin told me, 'No, that's not what he told me, he told me that you were working for him and what was I doing giving you work?'"

Agustín was incensed. "If that's the way it is, forget it, you keep his cotton," he told the gin owner. "Because he said, 'Shorty, if I give you the job the *patrón* will get mad and take his cotton elsewhere.' He preferred losing me, after all those years I'd worked there, than lose the customer with the cotton because it was a lot of cotton that he was going to lose."

I was puzzled: "What did the *patrón* have to lose, if you had already finished his fields for that season?" I asked him.

"No, it's like I'm telling you," he responded. "They say, 'You work with *me*, and you do what *I* tell you.'"

Agustín found a job at another cotton gin in a neighboring town, but the *patrón*, a prominent farmer and member of the Anson Church of Christ, was still not satisfied. Typically, the sharecropper worked the land, and the landowner paid for the expenses associated with the production of the crop. In addition, because the sharecropper and his family needed money to live on during the growing season, the *patrón* advanced a share of the anticipated earnings. Once the cotton was sold, the sharecropper and the *patrón* would share the profits according to a preset agreement, usually two-thirds for the *patrón,* and one-third for the sharecropper. The farmer and Agustín had yet to meet to go over the figures for this year's crop, as was usual at the end of the season once the cotton was sold.

Farming typically proceeds as an act of faith. The farmer must borrow significant sums of money from a local bank in order to purchase seed, fertilizer, herbicide, and fuel, pay labor costs, and buy equipment. Additionally, he has to pay his leases on rented farmland, taxes on whatever land he owns, and the mortgage on his own home. Of course he must also keep his family fed and clothed. The typical cotton farmer incurs substantial debt at the beginning of the season. The act of faith revolves around the question of whether this year's crop, vulnerable as it is to weather, insects, and price vagaries, will cover his indebtedness. Such circumstances put the best of men to the test, creating enormous tension and pressure. At times, such pressure manifests itself in clearly irrational acts.

Perhaps it was just such pressure that prompted the farmer to lose his bearings in response to Agustín's success in finding work that was not directly under the *patrón's* control. When he learned that Agustín was working at another gin, the farmer came to the Garcias with another *Americano* and started to hook up Agustín's half-ton pickup truck to tow it away. The pickup belonged to the *patrón,* but part of their sharecropping agreement included Agustín's use of it.

The dogs were making their usual ruckus, which brought Fidela to the window, where she saw the *patrón* trying to hook the towline. She came out of the house and asked him what he thought he was doing. Without the courtesy of an explanation, the farmer tried to tie the bumpers of the two pickup trucks so that he could tow it. Nearly hysterical, Fidela told him in no uncertain terms that what he was doing was unjust. The farmer claimed that Agustín owed him money, which was true, but the cotton had just been delivered to the gin and had yet to be ginned and sold. Typically that was the point at which the *patrón* and Agustín would have settled their accounts. The real issue was that Agustín had the gall to go work for someone else and not submit to the feudal arrangement inherent in the sharecropper's existence. Fidela jumped into the pickup and, before the farmer and his friend could stop her, drove off to the gin where Agustín was now working, with the *Americanos* following close behind her.

At the gin, Agustín was working a difficult job—he was a baler. Cotton gins are unbearably noisy, dusty, and hot. The cotton is wheeled up to the building in carts from which it is sucked into the gin by enormous vacuum hoses. The ginning process cleans impurities from the cotton, such as stalks, leaves, seed, insects, and field dirt. But the process transforms the cotton gin into a swirl of cotton dust, prolonged exposure to which increases one's risk of serious lung damage. The thin, sheetmetal structure that constitutes the cotton gin absorbs, traps, and then amplifies the sun's heat. It is a veritable oven on a warm day.

When the cotton has been ginned, it is baled, weighed, and tested for quality. This information is then affixed to each bale. Most cotton bales weigh approximately 400–500 pounds. The baling operation is dangerous. In addition to the dust, noise, and heat that act as constant strains on a man's senses, the machine that bales up the cotton, whipping metal strands of wire around the compacted bale with lightning speed, requires close concentration if the worker is to avoid severe injury. Agustín and another man, using large grappling hooks, were responsible for positioning the bales, sampling the cotton, and then pushing them out a chute, where other workers loaded them onto a truck for transport to a storage facility. Like a job on a conveyor belt, as soon as one bale was out the chute the next was in position to be wired.

It was at this point that Fidela, very upset, ran into the gin. "The *patrón* wants to take the pickup and he says he's harvested the cotton and we don't have anything coming," she said. While she was explaining what had happened at the house, the *patrón* entered the gin and shouted that he wanted to talk to him. The situation was ripe for an explosive encounter.

As Agustín reflected on it years later from the easy chair in his living room, what had most angered him was that the *patrón* had gone to his house and upset his *señora* without coming to deal with him directly. This was a serious misjudgment of Mexican sensibility on the grower's part. He had backed Agustín into a corner from which he had no alternative but to confront the *patrón*, whatever the consequences, in order to keep his own pride and dignity intact. To Agustín this was the foremost consideration. Years of injustice had taught him that there was no assurance that he would be dealt a fair hand, but he had never permitted that reality to subvert his pride in himself and his family. People in the community, *Mexicanos* and *Americanos* alike, recognized this and respected Agustín for it.

At that moment the *patrón* from the *rancho* opened the door and he yelled, "You! I want to talk to you." I told him I couldn't talk until I had the *paca* of cotton baled. And I don't know why, but in those times I was really strong, and we had these big hooks that we used to pick up the cotton

bales, and I could grab a bale and stand it up and shove it
out to the trailer, and so I picked up the bale with the hook,
and when I threw it he grabbed me by the shoulder and
said again, "I want to talk to you." And when he said that
to me, I did this with my hand [motions as if pushing]. I
thought I had just *pushado* him, but I was real angry, I
was enraged . . . But Fidela told me that I'd actually hit
him. "You hit him and you made him fall back," she said.
And the wrong thing that I did, which I shouldn't have
done, is that I jumped on him right away, and the truth is
that I was thinking I wanted to kill him, he'd angered me
so much. I was especially angry that he'd gone and bothered my *señora*, which he had no right to do. And then I
grabbed the hook and he thought that I was going to get
him in the face, but really I was going for his shoulder
blade, I was going to rip his shoulder blade with it, and
when I raised my arm like this to get him, at that moment
the other *Mexicano* grabbed me, and he talked to me good.
"Look, you have a family and he has a family, think about
it." I told him to move out of the way, and the *patrón* just
stayed there, his eyes were immense, and I told the other
Mexicano, "*Quítate* [get away], let me kill him," and then
the others arrived and stopped us, and the owner of the
gin came and told the *patrón* to get out of there.

Agustín's problems were far from over. The farmer went into
Anson and reported the incident to then-sheriff Dave Reves who
came looking for Agustín at the gin. Agustín remembers that
"Dave Reves was always joking in a friendly way with the Mexicans. And when he got to the gin he said, 'Shorty, I've come to
pick you up, and if you don't want to go, [he had a 12-gauge
shotgun with him] I've got this baby right here.' So I said to him,
'Mr. Reves, as a law-man I've got a lot of respect for you, but
man to man, if you're going to use that thing you'd better think
twice.' I told him . . . 'I'm not kidding, you're big but I'm not
scared of you.'" It was also an important point of pride for Agustín

that he did not want to be treated like a common criminal. Reves seemed to sense that and put his shotgun back in the patrol car. With this, Agustín stepped out of the gin and into the sheriff's car.

Agustín was confined in the county jail, next door to the courthouse, in the heart of Anson. When Fidela asked the old judge if he would be let out, the judge made it clear that Agustín might be in for the long haul. A Mexican attacking a white man was no small matter in West Texas. Fidela panicked. There was not enough money to feed the family, much less to make bail. "I thought they were just going to make barbeque out of me," said Agustín.

For reasons that are probably only comprehensible within the mindset of a small town, where all lives are intertwined, two men, Frank Johnson, who was on the board of the local bank, and P. B. McNair, a leading farmer, came to the jail. "Look," the two men said to Agustín, "we're here to get you out of jail. You need to be with your family. This isn't a place for you, you aren't a drinker or a troublemaker. But we just want you to assure us of one thing: that when you get out you won't do *anything* to anybody. We don't want you even to spank your kids. And if you'll agree to that, we'll sign the bond and we'll get you out of here. You don't need to be in here."

The county offices were closed by the time Agustín agreed to the conditions the two men had set. Johnson and McNair tried to get one of the jailers to release Agustín. As leading citizens of the community, they had the jailer's ear. 'Well, you can just open it," they told the jailer. "Go ahead and do it. You're going to get the peace bond papers and we'll sign 'em," they said.

I asked Agustín how he understood their motivation to come to his aid. Had he worked for Johnson or McNair? "No," was his response, "but they knew me, they knew who I was and what I was like."

The peace bond under which Agustín was released from jail ordered him to have absolutely no contact with the farmer nor go near his home or farm for one year. The night before the peace bond was to expire Agustín could not sleep. He was still enraged. The next morning he awoke early, loaded his shotgun, and drove to the *patrón's* house. On not finding him, he drove out to the the man's fields, and then all through town, but he was nowhere to be found. "What really bothered me, what I couldn't shake, was that he had *no* reason or justification to come out here and throw himself on top of my *señora* that way," Agustín said. His wording reflected a psychological experience of castration, of violation, which the Mexican pride will not tolerate passively. "Because if he had a problem with me . . . he should have come to me. I've never liked that someone will bother my *señora or los chamacos* [the kids]." But Agustín's anger was mostly spent, and he gradually allowed those events to recede.

A few months later, as fate would have it, Agustín's son ended up on the same Pony League team as the farmer's son. "I would watch those kids and, *mire,* they were like brothers, they liked each other so much. And me and that old man were all puffed up and full of anger at each other [Fidela laughed hard]. And then I thought, and I thought. It was very hard for me, and then I said, 'God is the one that does it all, so I'll forget what happened and let God forgive him if he wants to.' But my anger lasted all that time." Fidela interposed, "Then that man lost his mind and he killed himself. . . . " (The farmer had subsequently shot himself in downtown Anson, as a result of severe marital discord.)

Agustín reflected on the implications of his conflicts with the farmer for how others, especially the *Americanos,* saw him. He felt that he was accorded greater respect for having stood up for himself and his family. But that respect, in turn, had nourished a more positive attitude in Agustín toward the *Americanos.* "Since that time, all the *hombres* wherever I went, the situation changed. Wherever I went they treated me well, they talk well to me, and they treat my family and my *señora* well. I don't have any problems . . . and there are lots [among the local Mexican-Americans] who say that '*No,* the *bolillos* are this and that.' And I tell them, 'I'm sure it's because you don't look for a way to raise yourself up, to find a way to build *amistad* [friendship] with them."

It is evident that Agustín and Fidela have fought a hard battle, a battle from which they seem to have emerged victorious, at least in personal terms. Agustín was clearly proud as he reenacted the morality play of his confrontation with the abusive *patrón*. For the *Mexicano*, so the truism goes, maintaining one's pride and self-respect is essential. Virtually any adversity can be faced and accepted as long as one's dignity remains intact. Agustín's struggle with the farmer reflected the importance of that value. Here was a hard-working, law-abiding man, whose labors mainly profited the *patrón*. Agustín did not rebel against this inequity. On the contrary, he had delivered his life into it, provided there was hope of a future for his children, that they could attend school, and that the privacy of his family was not violated. The *patrón's* arrogant intrusion into Agustín's home to tow away the pickup, an impulsive act by a man who, himself, felt desperate in the face of a thin crop and pressing personal concerns, represented an assault on what Agustín most valued in his life: his family and the dignity with which he managed his life in the face of pervasive poverty.

CONFLICT BETWEEN THE GENERATIONS

Between each generation, there is a cultural breach. This circumstance creates fertile ground for familial conflicts embedded in the fact that the reality of the younger generation has shifted from that of the parents. During one of my interviews with Agustín and Fidela the discussion turned to their concerns about young people. In the Garcias' view, the younger generation just did not seem to have the same values and sense of right and wrong.

"This happened with our youngest, Veronica, the one that works as a teller at the bank," Fidela said. Veronica was the first Mexican-American to assume a white-collar position at the bank. In her mid-twenties, Veronica had moved out of the house a few years ago.

"Veronica didn't like for us to be telling her anything," Fidela went on. "Our other daughters grew up poor, poor, poor. They worked. They worked hoeing cotton and later, as they were growing up, whatever we gave to them—and we didn't have enough to give them much—they were satisfied. And when they went out, I went out with them. They were never of the *muchachas locas* [crazy girls] who'd just go out whenever they felt like it. They went out at my side. But Veronica started working, and she started getting her own money, and then 'This is *my* life' started."

Fidela became upset. "And her being the youngest we wanted her to date in the way I was just describing to you [chaperoned]. And she had everything. She had a car, the others never had a car. She had her own money. Her own job. She had everything. And then it wasn't enough, she wasn't satisfied, she wanted her freedom, see, without knowing that that freedom was going to cost her someday. So then I said to her: 'Fine, you can move out, but remember one thing. Don't come running back here when you get into difficulties, because we aren't throwing you out. We've given you everything. . . .' She was already free to come and go as she pleased, what more did she want?"

There was deep consternation in Fidela's voice. What to a white family would have seemed like a sign of good progress along a normal post-adolescent developmental trajectory—getting a job and living a responsible, independent life—to the Garcias represented a personal rejection and abandonment. They were clearly hurt.

"That's what I just can't understand," Fidela went on. "It's like they've gotten too much freedom. And then you don't dare say anything to them about it because they get mad at you. They think they know more than you do. I try to tell them, 'Look, you're just starting out. You haven't had to do what we've had to do, and if life gets hard on you, you're going to suffer a lot, you just don't know, like if you don't have water you'll die of thirst, or if you don't have food you'll die of hunger.' They don't understand."

Fidela grew pensive. It was evident that she was thinking
about specific things from her past, times when she had faced
real adversity as a young child—perhaps the very adversities
(thirst, hunger) she was now invoking:

I haven't forgotten that when I was a little girl, my father
went out to the jobs, to *la pisca*, I was 7 or 8 years old, and
my mother had a baby of 6 months, and we lived in a little
room. I don't even remember if it was hot or cold (meaning summer or winter), but the baby was very little and *la
niña* got sick, and they didn't take her to the doctor because
people in those days were very timid and they didn't want
to go to see doctors. They were afraid, you see, and my little
sister got sick and I would stay with her. It was about 1935.
Mamá would leave me with the baby. Me and another of
my sisters. And I remember that my baby sister would get
real hot, the fever would hit her hard, and my mother was
pisceando [picking crops], and then when she got home in
the afternoons, she'd ask me how the baby was. And so one
night, I was asleep, and the baby took a turn for the worse,
my parents went out to get help, and the *patrón* lived
nearby and they went for the *Americanos*, and they left us
asleep. And when she came back, I woke up because I could
hear someone sobbing. And when I woke up I saw her
standing at the door, and the *Americana*, the *patrón's* wife,
had my baby sister in her arms. . . .

Fidela started to cry. The tears slid out from under her silver-
rimmed glasses onto her brown cheeks. More than fifty years
later, the memory of that traumatic night was still raw and painful. "That's why I tell them," she went on. 'You haven't seen anything. These are *hard* things.' I say to Veronica, "Look *m'ija*
(affectionate for daughter) You haven't suffered what we suffered, that's why everything seems so easy to you.' I remember
my mother sobbing and sobbing and sobbing, and I got up and
touched my baby sister, and she was dead. And my mother was
just saying 'The baby's dead.'"

The meaning of this association was painfully obvious. She experienced the estrangment between herself and her daughter, Veronica, as a very deep personal loss. This was an estrangement manifested in a conflict between traditional and contemporary values, a gulf played out in the patterning of how one finds a mate in contemporary culture, or how and when the boundary is drawn between family and self. Fidela's sense of loss was so painful that it resurrected an image of another painful and devastating memory—the loss of her baby sister. The connection was probably unconscious to Fidela, but it could not have been clearer: beneath her anger and disappointment in her daughter's contemporary rebellion against the Garcias' traditional values was a deep sadness. To Fidela, Veronica's successful assimilation was like losing a second baby.

THE INFLUENCE OF CULTURE

In his 1926 address to the Society of B'nai B'rith in Vienna, Freud gave one of his most incisive descriptions of what constitutes the essence of cultural experience:

What bound me to Jewry was [I am ashamed to admit] neither faith nor national pride, for I had always been an unbeliever and was brought up without any religion though not without respect for what are called the "ethical" standards of human civilization . . . [But] plenty of other things remained over to make the attraction of Jewry and Jews irresistible—many obscure emotional forces, which were the more powerful the less they could be expressed in words, as well as a clear consciousness of inner identity, the safe privacy of a common mental construction. [p. 273]

The psychological mechanisms through which culture absorbs and holds individual lives, as Freud so aptly states, reflect powerful forces, irresistible as they are obscure and elusive when it comes to clear articulation. Winnicott (1953) observed that culture is created out of that realm of experience situated between the infant's desire and the mother's response, or what he termed the *potential space*. The first experience of culture is bound by the realities governing that relationship. It is created within that dyadic matrix and is defined by it. While the mother is the representative, the instantiator, of the cultural universe that exists beyond the infant's capacity to perceive and know, Winnicott's idea centers on the notion that the infant is not merely a passive recipient of that culture, but an active participant in its construction.

Thus conceived, culture is created in the interplay between the individual and reality as objectified by the mother in the region that so fascinated Winnicott, where the child's creative construction of reality could not be separated from the facilitating maternal environment. For Winnicott, this is the zone of experience that forms the basis for those shared and interrelated illusions: aesthetic and cultural experience. This is where the subjective experience of culture originates. It would seem that an appreciation of this origin should facilitate a discourse incorporating both the intrapsychic and the social facets of human experience.

Framed within Winnicott's thesis, it should be apparent that cultural change almost always represents a rupture with that primordial "holding environment" (Modell 1976). To the extent that culture evolves and is transformed, the assimilation of a new cultural vision taxes and strains ties to old objects (internalized and otherwise). Hence we see the generational conflicts we have come to view as normative in Western societies, but less so in those (increasingly few) societies that are premodern and more stable. In the latter societies, traditions still represent viable sustaining structures providing meaningful mechanisms for ushering individuals from one phase of life into the next.

When a child ceases to participate in aspects of the cultural universe that a parent has helped to define and create (as when a person marries outside of his or her religion, race, nationality, or social class, but also, in Western societies, when a child engages the generational subcultures that are normative while "countercultural") such ruptures may represent a developmentally prescribed break in the mutually sustaining potential space. In other circumstances, such ruptures may also signal an acting out that is secondary to a faulty holding environment. In either circumstance, however, such transformations represent losses to be absorbed by both parents and their offspring, although probably in different ways.

If social currents often require that adolescents and young adults disidentify from their parents, at least in circumscribed and transient ways, there is another force at work here as well. I am referring to the near universal fact that parents often wish for their children what they cannot or did not attain for themselves. Notwithstanding the fact that such ambitions may be partly governed by narcissistic considerations and the vicarious gratification that parents derive from their childrens' successes (Kohut 1971), these successes, as I will illustrate, may also bring about a sense of rupture. At least temporarily, we sometimes lose what we most love when our children succeed in the ways we have urged them.

This is especially observable in the experience of immigrant families who see their children become successful in a culture alien to the parents (Modell 1991), a success partly predicated on the fracturing of that "common mental construction" to which Freud alluded. Immigrant children often face an impossible choice: they can remain tied to the culture of their parents, at the expense of effective engagement with the broader culture in which they now live, or they can assimilate, threatening the earlier, original ties that had sustained their parents.

For the immigrant child a disjunture is often experienced in which the facilitating maternal environment becomes less usable. As the child enters the world beyond the immediate maternal envelope, there is a potential for excessive conflict and dislocation. Presumably children of successful immigrant families have received enough as infants to be creative, to be able to "play," in Winnicott's sense, and to engage the environment from which the mother has protected the child up to now in a constructive, meaningful manner (Modell 1991). An obvious variant of these same processes can be found in the experiences of ethnic minorities who, like members of immigrant groups, live in a cultural universe embedded within, but substantively different from that of mainstream American culture. Children of minority families develop within a particular niche that defines certain features of experience.

Both immigrant and minority children, especially those who become successful in mainstream terms, must experience the kind of disjuncture and attendant loss just described. Modell notes, in reference to such children, that they will begin to observe the differences between their own construction of the world and that of their parents, an awareness with profound consequences for further development. Thus, cultural transformation and cultural change imply a kind of object loss, at least a temporary break in that common mental construction for both parents and children. Even in the most successful of circumstances, assimilation has profound intrapsychic costs, whether or not such assimilation represents an adaptive engagement with a new social reality (Hartmann 1939).

Individuals engage cultural elements and put them in the service of intrapsychic conflicts (Volkan 1988). To the extent that an individual's experience of culture is an extension of the primordial relationship that originally and fundamentally defined subjective experience, culture itself becomes more readily conceivable as a medium for the enactment of intrapsychic conflicts and needs. Culture not only resides within us, shaping and defining us, it also represents a social artifact to be appropriated, manipulated, and engaged in ways that tap the most central elements of our psychological experience. This is partly what Volkan means when he speaks of "targets of opportunity." This suggests that cultural elements, like any facet of reality, can be appropriated to intrapsychic purposes.

Just as the child uses the parent as a medium for organizing internal experience by projecting, identifying, playing out aggressive and libidinal impulses, or for acting out any number of other developmental issues around which primary, organizing experiences become crystalized, so individuals can utilize cultural forms more generally for similar purposes. Culture is the medium for expressing intrapsychic conflict, just as readily available for this purpose as is the individual's body or his relationships.

It is evident from Agustín and Fidela Garcia's story that, in their experience, Veronica's successful assimilation represented a loss. The interviews with Veronica illustrate a different perspective and reflect the themes of gratitude and reparation, but also guilt regarding her strivings.

THE CHILD OF IMMIGRANTS

In Anson, as in most American communities, social and economic realities partly shape destinies by clustering the haves with the haves, and the have-nots with the have-nots. Veronica Garcia lives in a small house on the west side of Commercial Street where the successful farmers and small business owners live, not far from Mercy Torres's home. The houses are more neatly manicured on this side of town, the cars and pickup trucks of more recent vintage.

Like the other houses on her block, Veronica's was neatly kept. Her living room held a couch, a couple of end tables, and a stereo in a cabinet, but the room was clearly under-furnished, giving it an open feeling. Along the back wall of the dining room was a bookcase full Veronica's trophies. She was a talented softball player, and had a true passion for the sport. (Her team had made it to the state semi-finals one year, she told me with pride.) The refrigerator door held a picture of George Strait, the well-known country western singer, which had been cut from the cover of *Texas Monthly* magazine.

Veronica, an attractive woman of 25, exemplified the values of middle-class American culture in many respects. She also reflected the cultural transformation countless immigrants to

America have experienced: while Agustín and Fidela spoke limited English and felt awkward in doing so, Veronica clearly lived and worked in English. English was the language with which she was most comfortable when talking about her life, her work, her hopes, and aspirations. However, the clearest index of the social ground traversed by this family was reflected in the fact that her parents were janitors at the bank where Veronica was the only Mexican-American teller.

At our initial interview, Veronica had invited four of her closest Mexican-American friends to meet with me to talk about their experiences growing up in Anson. Both of the young men were involved with law enforcement; one (Veronica's cousin), was with the Highway Patrol, and the other was a Jones County sheriff's deputy (the son of Y. Z. Jimenez, the only Mexican-American farmer in Jones County). The men's wives talked of staying home, raising their children, and excursions into the shopping mall of Abilene. They obviously represented part of Anson's emerging Mexican-American middle class. The parents of every one of them had been agricultural workers all their lives.

Later, as I listened to our interviews, I was struck by the thought that someone listening to Veronica's taped voice would have sworn that she was a blue-eyed blonde, Texas farm girl. Only the fact that she occasionally sprinkled her conversation with Spanish words revealed her Mexican ancestry, but this feature primarily connected her to her companions that evening. It was a way of invoking a bit of solidarity. In a white crowd, Veronica's English was textbook perfect.

During one of our interviews, Veronica described the conflict with her parents and her decision to move out. From her perspective these events were structured quite differently. "I respect my parents in every way, and I appreciate the things they do for me," she said, "but it got to the point where I was growing and I was maturing, and I needed a little bit more, not so much freedom as to use it or abuse it, but . . . they were overriding my privacy a little bit. . . . I had reached a point in my life where I felt I could carry on myself, but they wouldn't let me accept responsibility for myself. A lot of that was because they were my parents and they felt they always had to protect me and I didn't want to be protected anymore."

From a contemporary American vantage, Veronica's plight was clear: here was a young woman who had made her own life, who had a good job, who wanted a little independence, who wanted to be able to date whom she wanted, and come and go as she wanted. Veronica was 23 years old at the time. She had been working at the bank for four years and was tired of having to ask her parents for permission every time she wanted to go out.

Unconsciously, Veronica was living out an acute cultural conflict. She was the medium for a clash between two world views. Veronica could not fit in with contemporary America as a bright young woman while still living at home under tight parental direction and supervision. She could not fulfill the expectations for achievement and success that her own family promulgated without abandoning some of the traditional frameworks for living that had sustained them. This framework was a rich and vibrant source of life-meaning that allowed the Garcias to survive generations of poverty and struggle against overwhelming adversity with their sense of dignity and human respect intact. For Veronica's parents, her abandonment of those mores could only engender the deepest fears and sense of desperation regarding their daughter's future. Mrs. Garcia felt, quite literally, that her daughter was dying, spiritually if not physically.

For Veronica, on the other hand, these values seemed to have become an obstruction to her quest for a meaningful life. She no longer lived in a rural and Mexican world as her parents and their ancestors had known it. The very sociocultural structures that had saved her family from a life of deprivation and rootlessness now posed a threat to Veronica's effective engagement with contemporary realities.

Veronica's associations led to a recollection of her sophomore year in high school, when she decided to try out for cheerleader.

No Mexican-American had ever served on the high school cheer-leading squad. In West Texas, high school football is serious business and serious politics determine which daughters of the community's leading families are selected for the highly coveted spots on the cheerleading squad. When Veronica became the first Hispanic in the school's history to win a cheerleading slot, she was ecstatic with pride and excitement. "It was a break-through for all of us," Veronica recalled. It still made her smile to remember that heady moment. "It was a breakthrough for the *Mexicanos*, because, being the first *Mexicana*, I think they felt they really had a sense of belonging then, like they were going to have somebody from *our* group in there."

Her family, also excited and proud of Veronica, had no idea, however, of the financial commitment required of a high school cheerleader. The price tag for Veronica's cheerleading outfits (only expensive Nikes were permitted), pompoms, megaphones (which had to be custom painted with the school colors and logo), and the compulsory cheerleading camp the squad would have to attend in San Antonio, exceeded $2,000.

The cost stunned the Garcias. Student body votes were clearly not the only factor that had kept the cheerleading squad as a private reserve of the wealthier white families in town. It was a somber gathering at the Garcia home that met to reflect on Veronica's predicament. "Look, *m'ija*," Agustín said, "*Hacemos lo que tenemos que hacer* [We'll do what we have to do], but I don't want you to give up. We're not going to let them do that to you." The entire Garcia family pitched in to cover the cost and it was no small sacrifice.

"They did it," Veronica said tearfully. "I don't know how we paid for all that stuff, because I mean, we were *poor*. My brothers helped. But it was hard. And that's why I just, you know, Mom and Dad, I'll just do anything for them. They're my parents and they've always been there and they always will be. And what-ever I did, I didn't mean to hurt them in any way. I hope that they understand that. I've always tried to do them proud, or at least right, you know, that if anybody ever said something to them about their kids, it would have been something good, not anything bad or shameful."

These reflections led Veronica headlong into powerful conflicts concerning her family—the deep sense of gratitude and indebtedness to them, as well as her guilt and worry that her struggles for individuation represented aggressive, hurtful attacks on them.

The tensions between Veronica and her parents reflected two irreconcilable forces at work: tradition and continuity versus transformation and change. Veronica's parents wanted her to be "good" in the traditional Mexican sense, yet they had poured themselves into helping her assimilate and become successful in the new southern reality. They wanted all those things for her that they had been denied, yet they failed to see that this dream also required Veronica to be different from them in ways that were threatening and painful. Similarly, while she deeply appreciated those sacrifices, she found her parents unacceptably binding and their values discordant with what success required of her.

Veronica's election to the cheerleading squad was a victory of multilayered meanings. A seemingly trivial event betrayed a complexity of forces latently at work. Anson High School's cheerleader election, laced with petty considerations of transient popularity and adolescent cliquishness, was in reality a manifestation of a fundamental transformation in the social structures that organized the community. For Veronica and her family, it was a sign that they had arrived, that they had won at a strange life-game of which their daily suffering only permitted an episodic awareness. It was worth the $2,000 price. The family understood that at some level the issue was not really cheerleading. This was about the struggle for advancement and the powerful wish to be part of the American Dream. But at the same time, the Garcias had sown the seeds of their own consternation and sadness, as their daughter separated from them, psychologically and culturally, moving along the very path they had cleared for her.

Cultural change, because it always activates developmentally early, intrapsychic processes, including primitive defense mechanisms, ego ideals, and identifications (Volkan 1988), is almost always conflictual. This is the case even in those families where the challenge of coming to grips with a hostile environment has had a significant measure of success. Indeed, the presence of these conflicts in the context of a highly adaptive family only serves to underscore the ubiquitous nature of such intrapsychic stresses. In a family with less cohesion, buckling under the multiple traumas of prejudice, poverty, and cultural dislocation, such intrapsychic conflicts are frequently played out less adaptively.

8

Marta: Dwellers
of the Dark Bottom

Marta (because of the nature of the material contained in this chapter, all names have been changed) was not as fortunate as Veronica Garcia. Marta was a product of Anson's permanent underclass. She had grown up in pervasive, entrenched poverty, with a chaotic and destructive family life characterized by neglect and indifference. Unlike the Garcias, Marta's family had been completely incapable of extricating itself from that vortex of personal and social forces that undermine the capacity for happiness and fulfillment. They seemed trapped in a deep, dark hole of complex origins.

Culture is a series of enclosures—a collection of social-psychological structures that hold and possess us as we possess them, at once sustentative and suspensory. As Winnicott (1953) indicates, culture runs in a straight line from the earliest, most intimate engagements between mother and child, increasingly becoming influenced by complex signifiers such as language, ethnicity, and religion, which give culture its hue. All of those things that ring through with a sense of the familiar, that hold us psychologically, are seeded within the family. Thus, it is within family structures that we find the conditions that facilitate a network of holding cultural experiences, or, on the other hand, the conditions that lend themselves to experiences so fractured and anemic that healthy development is undermined and deeply stunted.

Marta and I sat at one of the back booths at the Hatahoe drive-in. The best hamburgers in Anson were served here, a block south of the Church of Christ on Commercial Street. Marta was an attractive 14-year-old Mexican-American, with shoulder-length, thick dark hair and nearly black eyes. She wore a plain turquoise T-shirt, stone-washed denim jeans, and well-worn tennis shoes to this first interview. An inexpensive chain with three medallions, a treble clef, a musical note, and the happy/sad faces of Greek tragedy, hung around her neck. Today, her own emotions appeared consonant with the happy face as she smiled easily and talked readily after an initial period of self-consciousness. However, beneath this affable exterior, one could discern the traces of a somewhat muted affect that suggested an ample share of sad times, too.

"He won't bite you," her friend, Jean, told Marta as she dropped her off at the Hatahoe. Jean, a teacher at the local middle school, had set up the interview. She had been impressed with Marta's intelligence, her attractiveness, and her potential. Yet Jean had also been witness to the painful stresses affecting Marta that had gradually eroded her youthful, innocent optimism, grinding her down and bringing her to the brink of emotional collapse.

Typically, such emotional stresses begin to crystallize early in adolescence (Blos 1968), hardening into a character style that acts as protection against the raw vulnerability and pain of past experience. Unfortunately, this psychological strategy carries the very seeds of the conflicts and relationships that have brought despair in the first place. It sets the stage for lifelong reenactments of troubled relationships that ultimately undermine the effort to leave one's past behind and construct a more coherent, reasonable life in the present. Knowing what I did about Marta, I was prepared to meet a very troubled young girl who might not be able to talk with me. Instead, I could readily see the contours of the qualities that had impressed Marta's teacher. In clinical lore, adolescents are renowned for their reticence. Typically, their parents are clearer about adolescents' need for professional help than they are. Thus, I was surprised by the ease with which Marta candidly described some of the troubles she'd already faced.

At the age of 11, Marta had been introduced to drugs by some friends. Experimentation with marijuana came first, but in very short order, she started using an assortment of pills of various colors and shapes (only vaguely identified in terms of effect, "uppers," "downers," or the sardonically termed "black beauties"). Finally, Marta took drugs intravenously. The full course of this decline, from latency-aged infielder on the softball team to pre-pubescent drug addict, took only one year. On her 12th birthday, Marta had allowed a friend from Abilene to tie a tourniquet around her left arm and inject heroin into her vein.

Now, at 14, this child of rural America had experienced all the problems typically associated with inner city ghetto life—poverty, drugs, and a chaotic, unstable family life. Marta's father had left the family prior to her birth. Her earliest memories were of her mother Carmen bringing numerous boyfriends home. "This is your daddy," Marta remembers her mother saying as she faced yet another unfamiliar man.

This unintended cruel tease reflected Carmen's hopes for a better, more settled life. But the strategy that Carmen had adopted to transform herself lacked the kind of emotional foundation that allows an individual to tolerate the imperfections in real relationships. A healthy emotional foundation gradually helps quell the ubiquitous, intense, even desperate needs of the young child, in favor of a more measured internal pressure to be loved and comforted and respected, a pressure which, because of its lessened intensity, can actually elicit a more realistic response. As Kohut has noted (1971, 1977) the failure to establish such a foundation facilitates the erection of ethereal, unrealistic fantasies around people believed capable of washing away

the emotional pain and suffering that one has experienced. Such
people typically cannot. Instead they reenact the very damaging relationships they are attempting to flee.

This is precisely the course that Carmen's life took. She was
14 when she had her first baby, Tony. Soon, she was pregnant
again, this time with Marta. Abandoned by her teenage husband
during this second pregnancy, Carmen was grasping for someone with whom to share a life and fashion some kind of future.
But the men she brought into her life were no more capable of
filling those desperate needs than was Carmen herself. As a
young adolescent, she was still a child. This was even more the
case in the sense that an individual growing up with significant conflict and emotional deprivation comes to experience life
against a permanent backdrop of developmentally early needs
and wishes that a maturing physical body cannot undo. Such
histories result in a peculiar discordance between physical maturity and inner immaturity. Carmen increasingly turned to
sexual relationships in an effort to temporarily satisfy and transiently create an illusory feeling of hope and succor. But these
fleeting islands of possibility do not sustain, and soon one slides
back into contorted efforts to get what has been missed but of
what one is only vaguely and sporadically aware. The *un-thought
known*, as Bollas (1987) terms it.

Then one day Marta came home to find a new stranger: "The
first time I met my dad I was really scared, because he came up
to me and asked, 'What's your name?' And I told him, and my
mom told me that that was my *real* dad. and [he] was really
horrible looking—a long beard and long hair, with the smell of
beer, and very dirty clothes, like he hadn't changed for three or
four days." Marta's first reunion with her father was an ambivalent one, and it set the tone for their relationship for years to
come.

We have grown accustomed to questioning the assumptions
that underlie middle-class values and habits of family organization. From a psychological point of view, what is most important is a network of relationships that safeguard a child's need

for a sense of continuity and stability in the experienced world within a "good enough" caregiving matrix (Winnicott 1953). It is also true that the young child, lacking sufficient ego development to adequately perceive and understand self, others, and reality, is easily overwhelmed by chaotic instability and traumatizing unempathic experiences at the hands of those upon whom the child depends for survival (Kohut 1971). For Marta, such instability was commonplace throughout her young, tender years.

THE RETURN OF THE FATHER

Once her real father returned from South Texas where he had been living with his parents, the parade of other would-be fathers stopped. The return of her husband, Francisco, gave Carmen the hope of rebuilding a real family, but Francisco's return brought more chaos, not less. Poignantly, Marta described her excitement and hopes for her newfound relationship with her father: "I was really curious about what he was like. . . . we were trying to get along." But the burdens of the already depleted lives each of her parents had brought to their adolescent marriage were too much to be transcended by such hopes. Instead, family life at Marta's rapidly broke down into a painful cycle of conflict and emotional abuse. "My father and mother would come home from work and they'd get into big arguments about every little detail. And if the dishes weren't washed they'd scream at me or at my brother. If their room was a mess, they would scream at us or gripe at each other. They were always arguing."

In addition to the conflicts between her parents, Marta encountered significant difficulties in her relationship with her father that persisted for a long time. "We would try to hug him and he would tell us to get away from him, that we were dirty, and that we weren't really his kids. He would tell me that I wasn't really his daughter, that Tony was his son but I wasn't his daughter. And he would call me names. He'd call me a little bitch, or a little dog. . . . and he was always pushing me away."

Abruptly, Marta's feelings toward her father changed. A conflict between Francisco and Carmen's parents, with whom they were living, precipitated Francisco's leaving Anson again. "He didn't know my mother was pregnant. And he was gone for about a year," Marta said. It was during his absence that Marta's feelings for him changed. "I guess something happened when he was gone and I started missing him. I didn't want anything to do with my mother. I started calling her 'Carmen,' and I'd call my grandfather 'John' and my grandmother 'Mom' and when he came back, it wasn't too long before my mother had the baby, he would hug me and everything, and tell me that I was his baby, but he wouldn't look at me, or act like he meant it, and him and my grandfather didn't get along very well, because my father would get a job and he would work two to three weeks and they would either fire him or he would quit."

It is difficult to grasp how such experiences feel to a young child. Marta's life consisted of an emotional panorama in which the subjective categories of "mother" and "father" consistently shifted, and hence could not provide the psychological mooring that every child needs. Marta's childhood and her longing for a father in her most vulnerable, impressionable years made her fall, repeatedly, for the sadistic tease of momentarily believing that each stranger that Carmen brought home might truly be him. When Francisco finally returned, the knight in shining armor turned out to be a marginally functioning man who could not keep a job and who eventually turned on Marta, denying that she was his child. This is the kind of confusion that undermines a child's emotional core. Then there was Carmen, a child herself, trying to cope with adult problems. This strain ultimately led Marta to calling her mother "Carmen," demoting her because of her failure to perform competently as a mother. It was a desperate attempt to repair a confusing state of affairs. In point of fact, psychologically, Marta wasn't sure who her father *or* her mother were. She hardly felt that she had parents at all.

Marta's extensive family problems, serious as they were, were not the only trauma she had to manage. She had witnessed the horrifying death of her aunt in a house fire. "We came back to Anson from South Texas . . . it was on my birthday . . . and we were going to see our grandparents, because mom said she wanted to live back here. . . . and when we arrived, we had all our clothes and stuff in the back of the car, and when we got there, we found the house on fire, and I had an aunt that died in that fire."

Marta's maternal grandmother lives a few blocks east of the Hatahoe, in a small, two-story house with a gnarly mesquite tree in front. Inside, a large console television provided constant background noise for the adolescent girl who talked on the telephone while she paced up and down the staircase, stretching the telephone cord to its limit on her way up, and then slowly on her way down, bouncing on the balls of her feet at each step. She waved me into the kitchen, which was just behind her, without a hello. In the kitchen, Mrs. Martinez was feverishly cleaning the kitchen table.

"*Siéntese, siéntese* (sit down)," she said, "Carmen told me she'd talked to you." The kitchen chairs were 50s-style, with aquamarine seat and back cushions on stainless steel frames. They were still sturdy and comfortable. Mrs. Martinez was missing a front tooth, and she seemed softer than I had expected. A gaggle of grandchildren peered at me through the torn screen of the side door. There were five children, four girls and a boy, all under the age of 6.

I assumed that Mrs. Martinez was babysitting, but it turned out that a couple of the children were actually living with her. I remembered Marta telling me of a time that her brother Tony had gone to live with their grandmother, and of Marta's decision to call Mrs. Martinez "Mom." As is not uncommon among Mexican-American families, especially poorer ones, generational boundaries and roles typical of middle class America were blurred.

"I've got lots of grandchildren," Mrs. Martinez said with pride. "Just this year, we finally got our twentieth grandchild." She smiled, invoking a universally understood and obvious benchmark of success. She started naming her five children, and how many grandchildren each had given her. One of her daughters had five children by four different men. Carmen, Mrs. Martinez's oldest child, had four children by two men. It was Carmen who had just given Mrs. Martinez her twentieth, a child born out of wedlock. Another daughter had been married three times, once to a *bolillo,* and had four children. The remaining eight grandchildren came from her two sons, although here Mrs. Martinez did not specify whether from multiple unions or just one. For some reason it seemed more important for her to pin down the paternal line of her grandchildren.

Mrs. Martinez grew somewhat defensive when I asked about Marta's drug problems. *"Sí, tuvo muchos problemas,"* she said, "but I don't know much about it." However, she recalled vividly the big fire that had claimed Marta's aunt. It was a cold night in January, and the family was going to a brother's house to celebrate their anniversary (Marta had recalled the special occasion as her birthday). Mr. Martinez's brother and sister-in-law had prepared a big meal for them. *"La tía"* (the great aunt) had been left behind. She was an older woman, and it was not uncommon for her to refuse commitments that required her to leave the house.

That same night, Carmen and the children had arrived in Anson, with all their possessions stuffed into the back of the car. Marta's recollection on this point had been accurate. As Carmen and the children pulled up to the house, it was already engulfed in flames. They ran to a neighbor's home and called Carmen's parents at her uncle's.

Seeing me talk with their grandmother gave courage to the youngsters who had been playing outside. The screen door was flung open, and they marched into the kitchen, announcing that they were hungry. But first they gathered around me. The oldest asked coyly what we were doing. *"Nomás estamos hablando*

[We're just talking]," Mrs. Martinez responded matter-of factly. I asked each of the children their names and how old they were. Only the oldest, the 6-year-old, gave me her age in words; the rest used fingers.

"Mire nomas," Mrs. Martinez said. "They know their names, how old they are, and the names of their mothers and fathers. I didn't know those things when I was their age. It wasn't until I went into the second grade that my teacher taught me what my last name was and how to say my name in English. From the second grade on, I had to use my name in English on all my school work and that's what everybody started calling me. These kids learn it all real early now. *Mire nomas!"* The two oldest girls spoke perfect English. The younger children spoke little and also in English. But all of the children appeared to understand Spanish, which is the language that Mrs. Martinez spoke to them.

It was apparent that the children were used to taking care of themselves. In short order, there was a loaf of bread on the table, a jar of grape jelly, and a large, government-issue can of peanut butter. They were making their own sandwiches without consultation.

The 5-year-old girl looked up, smiled, and simply said, "peanut butter and jelly," as she tried to spread an uncooperative glob of peanut butter over her white bread. It just balled up and refused to spread. There was greater success with the more cooperative grape jelly. The older girls helped the youngest boy make his sandwich.

There was laughter and the children seemed happy except for the boy, who was whiny. Families can undergo a gradual transformation, which means that over time children's lives are affected differently within the context of the same family. The chronic conflict that seemed to characterize Marta's life as a young girl seemed different from what I could see of these children during my brief visit with Mrs. Martinez. Perhaps their mothers or fathers were more responsive than Marta's had been, although judging from Mrs. Martinez's brief sketch of her grandchildren's parentage, stability was not its hallmark. Or perhaps the Martinezes, now a retired, aging couple with grandchildren as the main focus of their lives, could give these children a bit more than they could when Marta, their second grandchild, was growing up. They had problems of their own at that time, contending with their children who were still at home. Perhaps, too, these little children feeding themselves around the kitchen table also experienced tensions and conflicts in their lives that would gradually undermine their futures. It was hard to tell what lay in store for them.

MARTA'S TROUBLES

After the death of her aunt in the house fire, Marta became quite anxious and acutely symptomatic. The consequences spilled into the rest of her life and overwhelmed her fragile ego. She became paranoid and fearful of her mother, somehow associating her with the aunt's death.

"I didn't want to be with my mother after the fire. I was afraid something was going to happen to me if I stayed with her, like we would get into an accident. I had this thought that my mother was bad luck for me, because of what had happened in the fire," Marta told me on another afternoon at the Hatahoe.

I asked her if she remembered her actual fears from that time. "God!" Marta exclaimed as if the events had transpired just a few days ago. "It was . . . my brother was telling me that my mom said she didn't love me anymore, because he hated me. He still hates me. And he was saying that mom was going to make me die in a fire too. And that she didn't love me, because *he* was her baby, and that that wasn't our daddy, and I was adopted! All these things! That I wasn't his sister. And he was always telling me that one of these days Mom was going to leave me at home and something was going to go wrong and I was going to die."

Marta's mother went into labor around this time. Marta recalls going to the hospital with her and several relatives. Somehow, in the confusion of Carmen's labor, Marta was apparently left alone in the car where she quickly regressed into a paranoid state. In her imagination she believed that somehow her brother's threats were coming to fruition, that all of the awful and scary things that he had told her would happen were coming true.

When Marta's aunt came back to the car some time later she found Marta in a near panic. "I was mad, *really* mad, and I asked, 'Why did they want me to die? Why did they leave me alone?' and I remember my Aunt Maria asking me, 'What are you talking about?' And I told her the stuff that Tony had told me, and she said, 'Well, your mom would never let anything bad happen to you. She would *never* let anything like that happen to you.'"

Marta's fear that she might die as her aunt had reflected a child's symptomatic reaction to a traumatic, overwhelming event. Grafted onto this specific symptom, however, were the broader concerns derived from her anxieties and conflicts in relation to her parents and her family. Marta felt an intense fear of abandonment, and feared that the animosity she felt from her mother and brother (as well as the anger *she* felt toward them) would find expression in a fratricidal or parental act of revenge. The panic she experienced in the car at the hospital was intense and nearly overwhelming. She momentarily believed that "it was happening." The ego of 8-year-old Marta temporarily dissolved into an acute fear that "they" wanted her to die.

By the age of 9 or 10, Marta had lived in numerous homes in and around Anson, had twice moved to South Texas and back, missing months of school because no one had the time or interest to register her at a new school. Worse, however, was the pathetic effort by Marta's mother to invent a family, to bring men home who would assume the role or function of a father and husband, efforts that failed repeatedly, and left Marta very perplexed and confused. The return of her real father only fueled her emotional distress. Here was a strange man with all the markings of a loser; yet she was supposed to love him. For his part, he rejected Marta's efforts to get close to him, viciously calling her a "bitch" and a "dog," but, most hurtfully, telling her that she was not really his daughter.

Marta took another sip of her cherry-lime soda and leaned back in her seat. She was drawing at least as much air into her straw as she was soda, but she took some pleasure in the challenge of getting every last drop of liquid from the bottom of the cup. I offered to buy her another, but she politely declined. She continued to describe significant episodes from her childhood:

In sixth grade that's when things really started getting bad, because my parents kept getting together and then separating. They'd argue in front of us. I remember one time we were at my grandfather's house and we were supposed to have gone to Abilene to go out to eat with my grandparents. And me and my brother were there and we had been asleep in the living room, and my mom and dad started arguing and he was wearing his wedding ring around his neck, because it wouldn't fit on his finger. And they had started arguing and they took it into the living room and they woke us up. And Johnnie [her younger brother] started crying . . . asking why they were fighting, and I remember my mother grabbing the ring and tearing it off of my father's neck and telling him that he wasn't her husband anymore and that we weren't his kids as far as she was concerned. And my brother started crying more. And all I did was I walked outside. And they dragged me back inside and told me that they were going to get divorced. And I told them that I didn't really care as long as I could be with Dad if they did get divorced. And my mother told me that it wasn't up to me where I went. That it was up to her. And until I was old enough to move out and get my own place, that's how it was going to be. Two days later, my father moved to Abilene, and that was the first time I ever started doing drugs.

It has become somewhat fashionable to look at drug addiction primarily in biological, genetic terms, rather than in social terms. Addicts and alcoholics are taught that they have a disease and their only recourse is abstinence. Further, they are taught not to look back, to take one day at a time, and pray they will have the strength to fend off the temptations that will lead them to renewed use of the substances that have wreaked havoc upon their lives. Such a framework has been helpful to many in their efforts to lead better lives. However, if pragmatic, such a framework can also do a disservice in its implicit fostering of a certain kind of self-alienation. For example, in many instances, the relationship between the realities of people's lives and their substance abuse is also very clear. Such links are important and meaningful in making intelligible the devastation the substance abuser has brought upon him- or herself. In Marta's case, the reality of her substance abuse was probably not embedded in the activation of some vague genetic defect, but rather it manifested an emotional buckling under the cumulative weight of life circumstances too painful and confusing for her brittle ego to withstand.

"There was always a problem," Marta went on, "because if it didn't have something to do with my mom, it had something to do with my dad, or something involving me and my family, and I didn't want to get all hooked up in it." Instead, Marta got "all hooked up" with something even more damaging. Her desperate efforts to escape the ravages of the chronic conflicts and disappointments in her family life only added fuel to what was already an inferno.

It is clear that the final unraveling of her family, always tenuously held together, was the last straw for Marta. The timing of her turning to drugs following the final rupture of her parents' marriage and her father's departure was no coincidence. With all hopes dashed, a rapid downward spiral began in her life. Most of the arduously garnered outer trappings of a normal childhood—relative success in school, success in sports, social success—quickly evaporated, to be replaced by a very different, drug-laden world.

"The summer I was 11," Marta recalled, "I had gone to a real bad party in Abilene. My mother knew I was going, but she didn't know there would be drugs there. And that was the first time that I tried hash and acid. After that, it just kept getting heavier and heavier. I would try different drugs and I wouldn't want to stop. I thought people were telling me, 'If you only smoke pot then you're not cool.' And so I kept getting heavier and heavier into drugs."

I asked Marta about the first time she started using drugs intravenously. She laughed nervously and said, "It was on my twelfth birthday. My mom was working and my grandparents had gone out, and a friend from Abilene and his brother came down and they brought one of their friends. He was 28- or 29-years-old. I was asleep when they came in, and they walked into the house and started playing some heavy music, and we were drinking and eating and smoking and popping pills and everything, and they told me they had a surprise they were going to give me. They knew it was my birthday and they wanted to give me a gift. They tied my arm and found my vein and shot me up. After they left, I was really tired, and I kept trying to go to sleep but I couldn't, and my mom and everybody came in and they thought I was asleep, but that whole night I didn't sleep."

A quiet desperation pervaded Marta's life, all alone on her twelfth birthday. She had already endured so much. Later, she continued shooting up on her own: "I had a younger cousin, and I would have her tie something around my arm. She didn't know what I was doing and I would shoot up in the bathroom."

Marta reflected that she was only 11 when she started doing drugs. She saw with painful clarity the extent to which she had ravaged herself: "If I could do it all over again, I would have said 'no' and left that first party."

Drug use brought even more chaos in Marta's life:

I would get into terrible moods when I was shooting up. The slightest word, if I heard someone say anything about my father, I would start cussing at everybody and tell them

that if they wanted to talk about my father don't do it while
he wasn't there, and one of my aunts was pregnant, and
she said something about my father and we got into a fight,
and she broke my arm. . . . I knocked her into the tub, we
were fighting in the bathroom, and she caught my arm
between her legs and when she turned over she broke my
wrist. And every time if I heard my father's name or even
my aunts' and uncles' from my father's side, I would
get really upset and I would go crazy. And they didn't
know what was wrong with me, and so they never tried to
help me.

Things went from bad to worse for Marta. One afternoon an
argument between Marta and Carmen escalated into a violent
fight. It started when Marta confronted her mother about having
thrown her out of the house. Carmen denied having done so,
but when Marta pressed the point, Carmen hit her:

She slapped me and told me that I was lying and it went
on for two or three more times, and my brother and
his friends walked out of the house, and she started telling me some more things about my father and I got really
upset. . . . She said he was no good and if he really loved
me he would be here with me instead of in South Texas.
And I got upset and I knew that something was going to
go wrong and I started walking into my room, and she
grabbed a bat and hit me with it, and I turned around. I
was really mad. And I just dodged her and I hurt her arm
and her hip. I tackled her. And we started fighting and she
finally got me down, and I told her that I didn't want to
keep fighting the way we were and that I didn't want to
be with her when I was mad and that was why I was walking out of the room. And she said that I didn't need to be
lying to her. And she didn't know that I was using drugs
and I got up from underneath her and just walked into my
room and fell asleep. And my brother stayed with his friend

next door because his mother wouldn't let him come home
when they heard us fighting. And that next day at school,
it was the day before Christmas vacation two years ago,
she called my aunt and she had all my stuff ready by the
time that I got checked out of school. I didn't know anything about that. She called my aunt and my aunt came
down and I moved [to a neighboring town], and that's when
I really realized that I needed help with my drug problem.

Thus, at the age of 13, Marta's life was in shambles, but with
her aunt's intervention, she received some help at a county
mental health clinic for her drug use and her other concerns.
Now, she was only 14 and I wondered what lay in store for her—
how she would come to terms with all that had happened to her.
How could the immediate world in which she lived become a
more benign place or would she simply see more of what she
had already seen in her life?

Marta leaned forward and her hair fell over her face. She
brushed it back in the effortless movement she repeated countless times during the course of our interviews. When she looked
up, I asked what sorts of things she liked to do. "I like sports,
and parties, but . . . I don't like school too much," Marta answered, "but the classes I'm into are math and reading. I'm really good, especially at history, I love history. . . . Sometimes
my mom pushes me [Marta had stopped calling her mother
'Carmen' following her treatment] and tells me I can do better,
but she doesn't really try to tell me what to do with my school-
work."

I asked Marta what she wanted to do when she grew up, and
she said she would like to become a lawyer or pediatrician. "I
wanted to be a mechanic, until eighth grade, then I changed my
mind. When I got into eighth grade, I really didn't know what I
wanted to do, but my English teacher spent time with me and
talked with me a lot. . . . She was always telling me that I was
good, and that I could do things."

I asked Marta what it would take to accomplish some of these goals, to which she replied, "After high school, I'd go to a four-year college and then maybe I'll get married and probably have one or two kids, that's it."

Marta smiled. She had a pretty smile, with bright, white teeth so neatly arranged that one could have easily, but incorrectly, guessed that she had been under the care of an orthodontist for years. Her aspirations were all-American but so poignant when contrasted with the ugly, debilitating realities of her childhood. Her father was gone again, and her mother was seeing another man with whom she now had a child. Marta was still estranged from her mother. They spoke only with some difficulty. I wondered who would help usher Marta toward fulfilling her dreams.

SIMILAR . . . YET DIFFERENT

Marta and her family inhabited the dark bottoms of Anson's social waters. Poverty and the turbulent, destructive relationships, the staple of her family circumstances, were formidable adversaries to overcome. My thoughts went back to the Garcias. Marta's and Veronica's families were comparable in terms of their origins: both were poor and Mexican-American. Both had endured the pernicious prejudice that assaulted them economically, psychologically, and spiritually at every turn. Both families had spent generations working in the fields, under the same hot sun, for the same meager wages, with the same lack of education.

Yet, the two families could not have been more different. Veronica's family was a stable one with a deep commitment to its children. Marta's, by contrast, was characterized by an ever-changing chaos that took an immense toll. Veronica's mother could articulate her awareness of the impact of racism and her committment to overcome it ("to be treated as equals"). Marta's family, a porous, feeble structure, could not manage even its more immediate survival needs. A palpable sense of pride, which the Garcias manifested in their family, was entirely absent from Marta's life. The Garcias had suffered greatly, there were deaths of parents and siblings and untold hardships from a life of heavy toil, but they had found the psychological fiber to persevere in the face of those challenges. One of the structures that supported the Garcias was their deep religious beliefs, an enclosure that "held" the Garcia family through their travails. Marta's family appeared to have no comparable resources to sustain them or to help them transcend the great adversities they had faced.

The holding environment is the medium which gives rise to what Edward Shils has called "primordial affinities" which have "ineffable significance" (Isaacs 1975). What we come to recognize as familiar, regardless of how much we share in common with others within our neighborhood, city, region, or country, is always idiosyncratic. The familiar is that layering of experience defined by psychological realities at play within our immediate family (hence the word "familiar"). Like a wren building a nest out of the material in its environment, families make use of cultural forms (social and psychological) that exist within their experience to fashion a (familial and familiar) culture. While this culture overlaps significantly with culture in the broader sense, it is never identical with it. Indeed, culture, in that broader sense, is perhaps only a mirage. The closer one gets to it, the more one attempts to grasp it, the more elusive it is as a collective reality. It is only in individual lives which uniquely instantiate culture that one has the opportunity to see it, and here it is always seen as a mixture of the intrapsychic and the social, never as an abstracted, pure form.

In Marta's family, cultural forms were defined by a Mexican-American, rural reality. They were poor; they had only known hard work in the fields, and they had only known the marginalized status of those who are appropriated or discarded by the needs of farmers and their crops. But these realities, harsh as they are, do not entirely account for the tragic disarray of Marta's life. They were filtered through the psychological structures that defined Marta's mother and father and the kind of holding environment they could create for their children. The psyches of Marta's parental objects (mother, father, grandparents) acted as filters and/or conduits, mediators of Marta's experience of that brute reality in which racism and poverty could have such ravaging effects. For it is *these* people whose psyches bore down directly on Marta and defined the immediacy of her world, depicting for her who she was meant to be.

Unlike the Garcias, who acted as a buffer for their children, shielding them from the harsher elements of the world, Marta's family offered very little protection. Her parents were themselves broken in mind and spirit, caught in a desperate labyrinth of darkness, suspended in a confusion of primitive need which, in turn, chronically destabilized Marta's world. At times Marta's life was reduced to fragmentary glimpses of hope—that her father would return, that her mother would be a mother, that they would get back together—reference points to the salvation for which she longed. With her family unable to insulate her, Marta would later attempt to create her own buffers in the drugs she took.

Marta's mother, herself only a child, did not have the emotional resources to give her daughter more. Carmen was herself lost in a vortex of pain and emptiness. She sought connection in libidinized experience that gave the illusion of momentary fulfillment or provided momentary distraction. While Carmen sought to satiate inchoate cravings, her daughter, seeking to satisfy her own cravings, silently sank into the murkiest depths known to humanity. It was a place with no moorings, no reliable reference points—a space devoid of memory or history from which she could only grasp fleeting, evanescent moments of gratification from a world as empty and lifeless as her mother's.

Experiences of this sort represent more than the specific, concrete instances of a caretaker's negligence, abuse, or other lapses. Rather, it is the totality of an emotional context that is important here, the subtle vicissitudes of a gradually unfolding phenomenology. The nuances of human experience, the sharp insistence of our most intimate thoughts and feelings, come to define our lives. A suitable holding environment is created by continuity, attention, affection, caring, and stability. It is the protected medium through which the "unthought known," aided by language, (Bollas 1987) is gradually transformed, into consciousness. It creates the threads from which a constructive life fabric might be woven. Development represents in every instance a delicate balance, an unstable alchemy, which over time can yield either an inner beacon that acts as a source and a resource if things go well, or an inner emptiness destined forever to grope for imitations if it does not. When the suitable holding environment is in place, it yields a capacity to engage others and to allow oneself to be engaged by them. The clearer that inner beacon, the greater one's availability for constructive participation in the human community. It is just such an inner beacon that is increasingly lacking within the fragmenting families of America's minority communities, creating a social conundrum that persistently eludes successful social intervention.

9

P. B. Middlebrook: "I was not even sure some of these people could be saved."

The narrow dirt and gravel parking lot was full so I parked in an adjacent patch of grass, really a patch of budding stickers still deep green and tender in this early spring. By midsummer this little stretch of ground would be a treacherous, dense cluster of dried and hardened stickers, waiting for unsuspecting passersby. A few people stood outside the one-room stone building, with a large sign above the door that simply read "Peanuts," which is why everyone in town called it the "Peanuts Building." It housed a preschool during the week, but on weekends the owners rented it out for special events, such as the wedding I was attending.

Inside, the bride's little sister and niece, no older than 9 or 10, had been assigned to the reception table, making sure the guestbook was signed, and handing out little rice bags to arriving guests. Tucked into each memento was a tag with the name of the bride and groom. Most of the guests had already arrived, and it was clear that the wedding was about to start.

A large, three-doored armoire decorated with lively pandas and lions and A-B-C's was the only reminder that it was a schoolroom. Otherwise, the arch at the front of the room, decorated with artificial flowers and vines, and the neatly arranged metal folding chairs in which the wedding guests were seated, success-

P. B. Middlebrook (second from right) and family in exile from the Anson Church of Christ. Photo: Nancy Scanlan.

fully transformed the room. Any preschooler who happened to enter the Peanuts Building that evening would have felt completely disoriented.

I had learned of the wedding only the day before, when P. B. Middlebrook, who would be presiding over the ceremony, invited me to come along. Middlebrook was the city council member who made the infamous pronouncement at the March meeting that on the spectrum of sin dancing lay somewhere between card-playing and prostitution. The bride's mother had called only a day or two earlier to ask if Middlebrook would be willing to conduct the ceremony. The affair had all of the markings of what in earlier times would have been called a "shotgun wedding," although Middlebrook himself was quite circumspect and discreet. To further complicate matters, the bride-to-be was white, the groom Mexican-American and it was evident which guests were the groom's and which the bride's. Mexican-Americans in the room outnumbered whites by a substantial margin.

The ceremony and festivities reflected the haste of the arrangements. Only minutes before the guests were due to arrive, the bridal party had been rehearsing the wedding. Now, the bride was sequestered in a large walk-in closet in the back of the room, ready for the procession to begin. The groom stood at the front of the hall next to Middlebrook, the only man wearing a coat and tie. He looked quite distinguished, particularly since I had never seen him in anything other than a jump suit in the three years I had known him.

Almost everyone was seated when the bride's mother signaled to a young man at the back of the hall to begin the processional music. He started up a cassette player with a tape of the Wedding March. The first sound was that of wedding bells accompanied by some birds chirping outside of the window. Again, at the mother's cue, the maid of honor, sister of the bride, took the best man's arm and started down the aisle between the two clusters of chairs. In her early twenties, the maid of honor was attractive, blue-eyed, and blonde—a classic Texas beauty. She masked a trace of anxiety by playfully gesturing with her artificial bouquet, as if she were posing for TV rather than her mother's instant camera. The best man, a young somewhat squat and overweight Mexican-American, was noticeably shorter than the maid of honor. He sported a thin moustache and nearly shoulder-length black hair. Unlike his partner, he found it difficult to mask his discomfort in the spotlight. He wore plain black slacks, a white shirt, and a tie.

As the Wedding March continued, the bride's mother gestured to the cassette player for more volume, and the procession continued toward the front of the room and the waiting groom. The groom was a handsome young man who held himself in an erect posture that gave him an air of pride.

At the cued moment, the bride emerged with her father from the darkened closet at the back of the room. She was also blonde but less attractive than her sister. On cue from the bride's mother, the Wedding March was brought to an abrupt halt.

Middlebrook started the service: "We are gathered today . . . I always hesitate for a moment when asked to perform a wedding ceremony because it seems like all too often nowadays people don't really take to heart that these are vows they are making before God. . . ." He had a way of speaking to the young couple and the assembled guests that made these often repeated phrases sound less hollow or cliched. His sincerity and warmth transcended the makeshift character of the occasion. It was as if Middlebrook was saying, "I don't care that you are not of the same race. I don't care that you may be pregnant. If you listen carefully, and if you take this to heart, everything will work out fine for the two of you and your anxious families."

This was not one of those weddings where the couple amends the traditional wedding vows to reflect some contemporary vision of sexual equality. On the contrary, Middlebrook instructed the bride to remember that she was to obey her husband, as he instructed the groom to remember that, as Eve was to Adam, so his bride was a part of him. Therefore, as God instructed Adam, so he must treat his bride as he would his own body. The bride grew tearful and her voice cracked as she repeated her vows, looking intently and earnestly into the groom's eyes as she held his hand with the wedding ring ready to be slipped over his finger. Middlebrook invited the newlyweds to kiss, and the assembled relatives and guests broke into polite applause.

The wedding ceremony was over. From the initial sound of the taped wedding bells to the final kiss, the entire event had probably lasted little more than ten minutes. The maid of honor signaled to the man at the tape player to turn it on again so the couple could walk back up the aisle. She could not get his attention because he was already in conversation. The couple walked back toward the front of the room without music. Family and friends gathered to congratulate, but also to introduce one another, for it was evident that numerous uncles and aunts were meeting the bride or the groom for the first time.

A foldout card table covered with an orange tablecloth held an assortment of finger foods. One dish contained carrots, broccoli, sweet pickles, butter pickles, and sour pickles. A basket next to it was filled with a variety of crackers, behind which sat Mixed Vegetable and Fresh Cheddar Country Crock dips still in their plastic containers. At another table, a young woman served what she described as "melted orange sherbet punch," which appeared to have a little ginger ale mixed in. The punch was non-alcoholic: the bride's family and Middlebrook were members of the nearby Truby Church of Christ, where smoking, dancing, and drinking were considered sinful.

After the cutting of the cake, the newlyweds became something of a backdrop for their guests who were socializing in small clusters. Jack Hornsby's brother-in-law, Joe Ramos, was with his wife Stacey, who is white. Joe walked up to Middlebrook and smiling warmly said that the only thing he had specified to his wife about his death was that he wanted P. B. Middlebrook to do his funeral. "He's one of the best men in this entire county," Joe told me. "Maybe the entire state!" Joe and Stacey laughed, while Middlebrook blushed.

The wedding formalized a mingling of families as well as races. Mexican-American and white embraced and shook hands over and over again, an action that for some was tentative at first, but gradually with less awkwardness and more warmth. A future generation was being established. These families, whatever their personal feelings about this union, were now related— an irreducible reality in their lives. Somehow they would have to forge a future together. They would have to find an accommodation to their differences in style, taste, custom, and habit. Out of the generations of disparity would hopefully come something new. Typically, white families had only known the Mexican-American as a laborer who toiled in the sun to help produce the crop, without whom they could not survive economically, but whom they could see only through the eyes of the *patrón* over the wide gulf of a different language and culture. Similarly, the Mexican-American, conditioned by generations of low status and vaporized hope, tended to view whites with ambivalence and mistrust. Now, these families would have to search for a common vision. The couple represented the irrefutable fact that life in Anson, as in the rest of America, was changing.

P. B. MIDDLEBROOK

P. B. Middlebrook lived in a simple ranch-style home in the more affluent west side of town. As I drove to his house for the first time in the summer of 1987, three years before this wedding, I wondered what kind of person could really harbor the view that dancing was sinful? What kind of life experiences could breed such a strict superego?

Few of the houses on Middlebrook's street had street numbers, and since most streets in Anson do not have street signs, the difficulty of finding someone's house is twice compounded. An outsider lacking specific directions typically had to inquire from neighbors to find a destination, which is what I did. I pulled under the wide carport extending over the portion of the circular driveway immediately outside Middlebrook's front door, and parked in the shade next to a white Cadillac, belonging to his wife, Dorothy. Middlebrook drove a pickup truck that was parked on the side of the house, in front of a two-car garage. The house was on the very periphery of Anson's west side, and bounded on two sides by cotton fields.

Middlebrook was at the screen door waving hello before I was out of my car. In his late fifties, with white hair and a ruddy complexion, he greeted me with a broad, open smile that caught me off guard. I had expected someone angular, thin-lipped, exuding harsh judgment from every pore; instead, I found a man who seemed to be friendly to a fault. His warmth and geniality were immediately discernable, although initially I did not entirely trust my perceptions. As we entered the house into an unusually large living room, Middlebrook offered me a glass of iced tea, which I declined. Dorothy Middlebrook was watching a game show on TV. The living room was lined with bookcases that housed an exquisite collection of Southwest Indian pottery, most of it from New Mexico and Utah. "A lot of those were given to us by the Indians we worked with when Dorothy and I were missionaries," Middlebrook said when I inquired about the collection.

He ushered me into his study, which doubled as a spare bed-room. Above a neatly organized wooden desk was a book shelf crammed with religious texts. Middlebrook pulled up a chair for me and sat at the desk. The man who had stood before his com-munity and the Abilene press to argue against the legalization of dancing accounted for his views in terms of his religious up-bringing. This background constituted a powerful cluster of be-liefs that had organized his life for as long as he could remember:

"It wasn't like I'd just been in a shell all my life," Middlebrook said of his life in the Church of Christ. "But we were still pro-tected, and we still were influenced by a set of morals that our mommas and daddies had been influenced by and we'd been taught. . . . It's tradition. It's something you've been told all your life. And, every one of us . . . Man, I was taught, *always*, you don't dance! Boys and girls don't dance together. I was even taught don't go swimming together."

There were many things on the list of do's and don'ts that Middlebrook had firmly internalized and lived by, as a boy and later as a young man, growing up within the fold of his church. "I've never had a drink in my life, you know. . . . I've never had even a drink of beer in my whole life! I've never had sex with anybody but my wife. I have smoked about that much," he said as he gestured to the first joint of his little finger, "on one ciga-rette in my life. I *have* slipped off and gone to a few dances, when I was younger. . . . "

Middlebrook stopped momentarily to reflect on the intensity with which this scheme of the moral universe had been incul-cated. These were thoughts and ideas that fundamentalist churches deeply ingrained in their members from the very youngest on. "They used to teach us that these things were wrong, you know, they taught us that *hard!*"

He surprised me. He seemed too genial to also be the kind of fire-breathing fundamentalist who would try to squash a group of civic-minded parents wanting a well-chaperoned prom dance for their teenagers. In Middlebrook's view, Anson, the little rural community he had known all his life, was changing, becoming more like the rest of America: lax in its attitudes toward morality. "The world's kind of caught up with us," he lamented, and viewed the media as a key culprit in the breakdown of the nation's moral fabric. "I think that television and books and the glorification of sex have a lot to do with it," he went on. "This 'good life' that people hear about has been glorified to the extent that everyone's trying to live it." Middlebrook paused. He felt that it was important to underscore that point. "I think it's a mirage," he continued. "I think it's a terrible mirage. But boy! There's not anybody totally immune to it, you know, not anybody."

His world was slipping away from him and he felt he had to draw the line somewhere. In Anson's dancing controversy, fate had given him an opportunity to take a stand and he had taken it, media lights or no. "There are moral issues being fought all over the world," he said. "Most of them have been so subtle and we give up on so many points that when something like this dancing thing [comes along], that in most people's eyes is relatively innocent . . . they say 'Well, Oh boy! If they think *this is* wrong!' . . . " Middlebrook could see that the entire scenario might appear ludicrous to some, but for him there was a context for it. It was a part of a larger struggle and the time had come to stand up and be counted.

"I kinda put my foot in my mouth," he said of his infamous pronouncement linking dancing with prostitution. It had been sparked by the remarks of Paul Davidson, the Footloose Vice President. Middlebrook summarized what he remembered of Davidson's moment before the city council that night in the spring of 1987: "He said 'This is a personal issue. It's a moral issue that is to be decided by me. Nobody can legislate morality!'"

"'Well, I'll tell you,'" Middlebrook recalled. "I told him, 'You know, in a sense you've got a point.' And I said, 'There are people right here in Anson that think playing cards is wrong. There are probably really only a few, but some do.' And I said, 'Some others, you know, you've got to go all the way maybe to prostitution before they get riled up and say it's wrong.' And I said, 'We do, in that area, we do try to legislate morality. We have laws against prostitution.' So I said, 'I suppose in the minds of the people of Anson dancing falls somewhere on a scale between playing cards and prostitution.'"

Middlebrook broke into a laugh as he remembered the electrifying tension of that meeting, and the stand-off between Davidson had himself. He continued his narration of the events. "I won't say *how* close to prostitution or *how* close to playing cards, but in the minds of most of the people in Anson, we've been taught all of our lives that this is wrong. So maybe we don't have any business trying to legislate morality, and I know it's never been successful, you know, look at Prohibition, and prostitution is still rampant in our country. . . ."

"Anyway," Middlebrook continued, "that got picked up on pretty good! And some people here in town even came up to me and said, 'I heard you said going to a dance is as bad as going to a prostitute!' And I said, 'No, I didn't say that!'" Middlebrook was laughing again. "But I think from that point on, we all started being a little more careful and we began to take Footloose more seriously."

"The media had a tremendous influence," Middlebrook recalled of that meeting. "We didn't know how to react to it. And I guess the media tends to make you look foolish, really." However he had appeared before the world, Middlebrook was unrepentant. "If I had my way I would forbid dancing. I would forbid divorce. I would forbid pregnancy in the schools. I would forbid a lot of stuff. . . . " Middlebrook seemed to become almost mournful as he reflected on what he viewed as the many sources of distress in people's lives. "But I know I can't do that. And it's really only through an understanding, somewhere we've got to get back to the basis of what's right and what's wrong. I remember when I was a kid we had an old man in the church up here and every prayer he'd say, 'Father help our young people to know the difference between right and wrong' And, you know, I'd think, 'Well, why is he praying that I know what's right and wrong?'" Middlebrook started laughing again. "I may have known better then than I do now."

It was clear that for Middlebrook the entire controversy was wrapped up in the complex motives that govern people's behavior. If understanding failed, Middlebrook seemed to be saying, then perhaps legalisms could take over to make people lead good lives. But he was also voicing a definite cynicism for the very approach he had apparently championed at the city council meeting. There was a sense of inner conflict that gave Middlebrook an element of complexity I found appealing.

He also rationalized his stand in terms of the City Charter that stated the city council "shall be able to enact ordinances to protect the morality of the city." But the more I got to know Middlebrook, the more perplexed I became by his stand. In spite of his background, steeped as it was in Church of Christ mores, there seemed something incongruent between the rigidity of his stance at the city council meeting and much that I was to learn about him as our interviews unfolded.

Middlebrook was a near mythic figure in Anson. Over the years he had held numerous positions in city government, including mayor and city councilman. At one time, he had also been a leading businessman in the community. Middlebrook was an Anson blueblood of sorts since his grandparents had come to Jones County shortly after the turn of the century. However, his family had been far from well-off. On the contrary, he was the son of a man who was a mechanic when hunting and fishing did not interfere. His father had once left the city's only ambulance on blocks while he went fishing, much to the mayor's consternation. P. B. started to work at the local dairy when he was only 9 years old. When he finished his work at the dairy, he delivered papers so that he had already worked two jobs by the time he went off to school most mornings.

As a high school student Middlebrook discovered his knack for salesmanship when he outsold his adult co-workers at an Anson furniture store. He went on to sell automobiles at a local dealership, and by his late thirties he was owner or part-owner of numerous dealerships throughout Texas.

He was a model Christian in the eyes of his contemporaries

and became the youngest person ever elected as a church elder—
a powerful and influential position within the church.

Although Middlebrook was extremely generous with others,
his own approach to life was characterized by frugality and
abstinence. For example, while he was generous with his
children—each got a new car as soon as he got a driver's license
—he refused to move from the family's low-rent home until he
could buy a new one for cash. The thought of owing so much
money to a bank sparked unbearable anxiety. He could buy each
of his children a new set of golf clubs, but could only buy a used
set for himself.

Middlebrook had never felt comfortable with his affluence.
His partners in the car business urged him to dress in well-
tailored suits and invited him and Dorothy to expensive weekends in Dallas. However, P. B. could never feel at ease with the
alligator-shoed, ostentatious lifestyle. It ran counter to a deep-
seated personal reality, the poverty-stricken reality he had
known so well and the self-denial that it had instilled. He was
anything but comfortable in the expensive fashions of the
Neiman Marcus department store in Dallas.

Then, when P. B. was in his early forties, his economic success at its zenith, a major change occurred. A last-minute hitch
in a major business deal left Middlebrook with a great deal of
cash and a moment to reflect on his life: "It seemed like destiny
almost that I not go back to the car business. And I had always
wanted to do something. . . . I had always wanted to be a minister. . . . and a fellow came by, a friend of a man I knew very
well, and he said, 'Man, I know the place. You need to go to
Española, New Mexico. Hey! Let's preach up there! You won't
have to pay them much to come and preach.'" Middlebrook broke
out into another hearty laugh. In a decision that would forever
change his life, he tucked away his investments, packed some
belongings, and moved with Dorothy to Española.

Middlebrook traded in his comfortable niche within the
American Dream to become a missionary for his church. When
he arrived in Española to begin ministering to the Mexican-

Americans and Native Americans, Middlebrook had a definite, specific image of what constituted right and wrong, of what was sinful and what was not. Middlebrook's views were almost immediately challenged as he started to work with people whose lives differed from his in almost every respect.

WHY MISSIONARIES?

Missionary work, which derives its name from the extensive efforts of the Spanish priests in the New World to convert the native inhabitants, is a very particular kind of calling. It is work that takes place at the edges, where cultural visions scrape against one another. It is work that begins with the consciousness of the Other, within that zone in which the "we" engages the "not-we." Almost by definition, therefore, it is an ambivalent enterprise in which the "otherness" of the other is what we wish to restructure so that it conforms to the "we" of ourselves. For this reason, missionary work is ripe for all of the psychological processes at play in questions of ethnic prejudice, or the complexities of engaging cultural difference and change.

Because religion is an expression of our deepest values, it is irrevocably entwined with our culture. Thus, Christian missionary work has always been bedeviled by this essential ambiguity: Where are the boundaries between Christian and cultural conversion? In numerous articles in *Practical Anthropology,* a Christian publication that addresses the theoretical and practical problems associated with missionary work, contributors frequently grapple with this very question. "The Armenian Evangelical Church," says one article (Nida 1965), " . . . is not making significant advance, for it is so tied to its ethnic origins, both in language and culture, that *it can only assimilate* [my emphasis] those who have grown up within the framework of Armenian life" (p. 29).

Kraft (1963) in another article in the same publication suggests that "[attitudes reflecting an identification with Western culture] provide a primary hindrance to effective cross-cultural communication of the Christian message, since they generally lead to a definition of 'conversion to Christianity' which is concerned primarily with purely cultural issues. . . . this type of attitude toward conversion aims more at promoting Western moral and spiritual ends than at the demonstration of the acceptability of any culture as a vehicle of God's interaction with man" (p. 18). In a sense these reflections, and the tradition within which they are embedded, miss the point. The spirit behind them is laudatory insofar as it speaks to a wish to give, rather than impose. However, there is no avoiding the fact that to convert means to change, and thus it is a process tied to those deep tensions we experience with respect to the existence of the Other.

Difference poses a ubiquitous problem for human beings. Missionary work is but one version of our perpetual efforts to meet this universal challenge, an instance of broader social processes through which we consistently seek to make others more like ourselves. Missionary work can be an expression of the sublime in human nature, a hopeful element, notwithstanding the prevalent views that it is inherently ethnocentric and a form of cultural imperialism. Of course it is. However, the term "cultural imperialism" simply reflects the perspective of those who do not wish their culture and beliefs to be changed.

It may be that humans are, by nature, "cultural imperialists." Whether the setting is religious, political, theoretical, social, or professional, people are perpetually offering a personal vision they seek the Other to embrace or at least acknowledge. This human proclivity thus reflects the best and the worst of us. Missionary work, to return to the present example, begins within a framework of the most noble aims. In its truest form missionary work entails immense self-sacrifice in the effort to bring what one loves, what one believes is good, to another. In this context missionary work is profoundly charitable and ultimately communitarian. At the same time, because difference is so troubling to us, what we conceive as charitable efforts toward others may mask a more dehumanizing process. The Span-

ish conquest of the New World is but one example among countless others.

It was after P. B. Middlebrook's move from New Mexico to
the Indian reservation at Moctezuma Creek, Utah, that he really
began to examine his own beliefs and assumptions. The Church
of Christ missionary who arrived at the Indian reservation still
thought he knew exactly what he would require of the Indians
to make them good Christians: "My first inclination was 'I've
got to teach these people about morality first before they can
even *think* about being saved.' And I devoted a lot of time to
that," Middlebrook told me in his study one afternoon. "And,
finally, I had to reach some conclusions. I was not even sure that
some of these people *could* be saved. . . . That's a hard statement. It's something I had to deal with, you know, *really* had to
deal with. Maybe these people are hopeless. And then I finally
turned. I decided that nobody is beyond the love of God."

One conflict for Middlebrook centered on Indian mores regarding marriage:

> I've been taught all my life that if you were in a second
> marriage and you didn't have a scriptural reason—and the
> only scriptural reason being the unfaithfulness of your
> partner—if you engaged in another marriage you were
> living in adultery. . . . And if you were the innocent party,
> I had always been taught that you probably could be mar-
> ried again. And if you married the right person, and they
> were not guilty of adultery, then you could be acceptable
> to the Lord. But, I got out on the reservation . . . in the
> first place they really didn't marry like I'd been accustomed
> to people marrying. But they considered it marriage, so I
> had to work that out. . . . Most of them didn't have a cer-
> emony. They had an agreement, you know, sometimes it
> was with family consent, sometimes it was with tribal con-
> sent and a tribal ceremony. Sometimes they had a conven-
> tional type of marriage. . . . I finally decided that in order
> to make any of them acceptable to God, if they were living

in an adulterous union, they would have to separate, you know, give up the present husband or wife.

This was standard Church of Christ fare. In the church's view, only the "innocent" party to a divorce could ever marry again. It is obvious that Middlebrook was struggling with the cultural and religious differences between the structures that made up his world and those that made up the world of the Native Americans on the reservation. "That's what I'd been taught all my life," Middlebrook continued. "But it seemed that everybody I talked to on the reservation, you know, was living in that kind of situation. And they were not interested in giving up a husband or a wife unless they were real mad at them! And so that kind of an appeal was not acceptable at all." Middlebrook broke into his characteristic laugh. He could now see how ludicrous it was in safe hindsight.

"And so I thought, 'I better find out in the Bible where it says you gotta do that; see how many times an apostle or somebody says you gotta give up a mate . . . and it's *not* there, you know," Middlebrook chuckled again. "Nobody was ever told, 'You're gonna have to give up a husband or wife in order to be a Christian.' And so I finally dealt with it, and decided to take them to the water, and tell them about the Lord. Tell them what I thought they needed to do to be saved . . . and let the Lord cleanse them at that point and go from there. I decided that I was trying to bind them to some things that were the traditions that I'd been taught."

A CENTURIES-OLD CALLING

When P. B. Middlebrook first set out to be a missionary in Española, New Mexico, and later in Moctezuma Creek, Utah, he was plunging into a centuries-old calling in which he sought to bring his understanding of Christianity to the lives of those who, from his reference point, constituted a version of the Other. In his book *Aristotle and the American Indians: A Study of Race*

Prejudice in the Modern World, Lewis Hanke (1959), citing Juan Comas, suggests that European expansion into Africa, America, and the East fundamentally changed European conceptions about race: "Generally speaking, there was no true racial prejudice before the fifteenth century, for mankind was divided not so much into antagonistic races as into 'Christians and infidels'" (p. ix). The conquest of the New World, in particular, created a radical dilemma for the Spaniards who were simultaneously charged with an economic/political task and a religious one: how to regard the peoples of the Americas. Were they semi-human creatures closer to beasts of burden than to true humans? And if they were humans, how ought Christians to conduct themselves toward them, who were so different in color, culture, and religion?

At no time in history has missionary work been more central to a church's self-understanding than it was to the Roman Catholic Church under Spain's Carlos V who ruled Spain between 1516 and 1556. While Protestant Christians engaged in ecclesiastic warfare with Catholic Christians in the rest of Europe, in Spain there seemed to be a clarity and unity of purpose: to extend Christianity to the heathen peoples of the New World. Spanish priests accompanied the *conquistadores* or quickly moved in behind them spreading the Christian word into the Spanish and Indian villages and communities.

The Spaniards struggled to find a means of defining the peoples they were encountering for the first time. Some of these native peoples lived in splendid cities like Tenochtitlán, described by Bernal Díaz del Castillo in his *Historia de la Conquista de la Nueva España* (1980) as more magnificent than any city in all of Spain, with its ornate temples, magnificent avenues, and immense markets, while other peoples the Spaniards encountered had no discernable social organization, went unclothed, lived in caves, and engaged in cannibalistic practices. Further, all practiced idol worship, which to the Spaniards, in the context of the purifying zeal of the Holy Inquisition, represented the most objectionable and heathen of practices. (In Spain, the

Inquisition was put under state control in 1480 and carried out vigorously throughout the sixteenth century.)

The human propensity for splitting carried into various arenas. There was clearly a capacity for the most primitive forms of aggression against the Native Americans, as reflected in numerous accounts written by the Spaniards themselves, alternating with genuine concern embodied in their Christianizing efforts.

We see in the life of Bartolomé de Las Casas an example of what happens when the defenses that facilitate the viewing of persons or groups as Other, in the profoundly alien sense, begin to break down. Early in the sixteenth century, when the priest arrived in the New World at Hispañiola, what he found gouged his senses—a nightmarish, truly genocidal process at work, in which masses of native peoples were succumbing to unspeakable cruelty, being starved and worked to death, or being decimated by disease (Tannenbaum, cited in Hanke 1965). He was deeply affected by what he saw. Whether his transformation was immediate or gradual we can never know with certainty. What we do know is that those whom the conquistadores saw as semi-human creatures, Las Casas came to see as truly human. And with that transformation, his mission began in earnest, for Las Casas became the defender of the native peoples he encountered. He made numerous journeys back to Spain to advocate against the killing or enslavement of indigenous groups, culminating in the famous debate in 1550 with Juan Geinés de Sepúlveda, another Spanish priest, in Valladolid. They debated whether the American natives were human, with salvageable souls, who could learn to live autonomously, who could learn to live among the Spanish as productive contributors to "civilization."

This history is a fascinating study of the complexities of cultural difference and ethnic integration. Las Casas advocated the full inclusion of native peoples within the Spanish communities of the New World. And, interestingly, he championed four social experiments, with the support of the Spanish crown, in which the American natives were permitted to live among the

Spaniards, working mines and farm lands on their own, as long as they paid the requisite tribute to the king that Spaniards were obligated to pay. Three hundred years before the American Civil War, the Spaniards became engaged in deep debate about the ethics of slavery and how to integrate those who were currently slaves into a New World society that was economically structured around their labor.

The Valladolid debates were some of the most pointed and, perhaps, honest explorations of these issues the world has ever witnessed. Indeed, in 1550, the King of Spain went so far as to suspend all new expeditions to the New World until the questions could be resolved by Spain's leading theologians and academics, a deliberation Hanke (1965) lauds by noting that "No other European people, before or since the conquest of America, plunged into such a struggle for justice as developed among Spaniards shortly after the discovery of America. . . . [it was] one of the greatest attempts the world has seen to make Christian precepts prevail in relations between peoples" (p. 1).

We can only speculate on Bartolomé de Las Casas's motivations. Many in Spain came to regard him as a traitor to his culture. To see the native peoples as humans with salvageable souls, despite the hedonism ascribed to some of them, or the cruel rites and practices in which some of them engaged, cost Las Casas dearly among his compatriots. His pronouncement that "All the peoples of the world are men . . . " was a question hotly debated. Artistotle, after all, had stated that slavery was part of natural law (an argument adumbrated by Sepúlveda in the Valladolid debate).

Bartolomé de Las Casas had himself been converted. He became a champion of the indigenous Americans. In a manner in which some might find echoes to today's debates with regard to multiculturalism and its role in education, psychology, and any number of present pursuits, Las Casas argued that no priest was to be permitted into towns (Spanish or Indian) unless he was properly trained to preach correctly on Indian questions. He urged harsh punishment for Spaniards who mistreated Indians, that Indians not be moved from their homelands, and he suggested that what today might be termed "culturally sensitive," sympathetic books on "Indian questions . . . be printed and sent to the islands [Hispañola] so that Spaniards there may realize that Indians are men and are free and must be treated as such," (Hanke 1965, p. 57). These efforts on behalf of the native peoples no doubt influenced Pope Paul III's famous bull, *Sublimis Deus*, in which he stated that American natives were not to be treated as "dumb brutes created for our service" but "as truly men . . . capable of understanding the Catholic faith" (Hanke 1969, p. 73). In Mexico, a country where the conquest is still experienced with a most bitter taste, no statue or portrait of Hernán Cortez is permitted in any public government place, but Las Casas is revered.

And yet, as Jorge Luis Borges ironically notes in his *Historia Universal de la Infamia (1954)*, this noble humanist also proposed to the King of Spain that Africans be imported as slaves to replace the indigenous Americans working in the mines and sugar mills. Twenty "Negroes or other slaves" were to be placed in the mines in each community to replace the American natives working in them (Hanke 1965). Much backpeddling, or softpeddling has been done with regard to this fact. Las Casas subsequently recanted and, one suspects, repented. But the deed was done. He would later argue strenuously that "it is as unjust to enslave Negroes as it is to enslave Indians, and for the same reasons" (Borges 1954, p. 17). In both of his major treatments of Las Casas, Hanke stresses that the *Protector de los Indios*, as he came to be known, ultimately viewed all forms of slavery as odious. Yet, as late as 1544, Las Casas himself is reported to have had "several Negroe slaves" (Hanke 1959).

HISTORY REPEATS ITSELF

Perhaps derivatively paralleling their African ancestors' first experiences of the New World, in post-civil rights Anson, Texas, most of the evident changes in the social structure reflected gains made by Mexican-Americans, not African-Americans. True, blacks were no longer barred from entering restaurants, and they would have been allowed to sit anywhere they chose to if Anson still had a movie theater, but the rising middle class that I have described was virtually all Mexican-American. In many respects Anson's post-civil rights transformation reflected a shift from a two-tiered society, in which whites occupied one tier and Mexican-Americans and African-Americans occupied another, to a three-tiered society with blacks in the lowest tier. According to the 1990 census, there were only forty-eight black households in all of Jones County (compared with 1,306 white households and 178 Mexican-American households). The county's economic statistics, however, reveal that nearly 42 percent of blacks in Jones County were living below poverty level, compared with 24 percent of Mexican-Americans and 10 percent of whites, respectively. Similarly, the mean personal income for Jones County's blacks was a mere $8,454, as compared with $17,534 for whites. The mean income for Mexican-Americans, at $16,255, was near that of whites. As is clear from these statistics, blacks, continuing to occupy the terrain of the Other, were being left further and further behind. In African-American communities across the country, the awareness of similar circumstances in which Hispanics, Asian-Americans, and other minority groups appear to gradually succeed in "moving up," at least in relative terms, breeds an admixture of desperation and deepening resentment.

The problem of racial prejudice is a special instance of the problem of divergent cultures and how we respond to such differences. Thus, it is deeper and more complex than many contemporary treatments fathom. The need for clear-cut villains and victims may streamline and smooth out consciousness, but it undermines an appreciation of the intricacies, and, perhaps, the limitations of the human mind. Splitting as a defensive process is not a defense exclusively linked to primitive psychopathology (Kernberg 1975, 1976) . Our capacity to seal off facets of experience is immense and pervasive in circumstances where we find it necessary to avoid inner conflict. All peoples invoke it. Splitting is a psychological process that has both individual and collective manifestations. Groups of people and whole cultures resort to these mechanisms at a collective level as a means of managing intergroup tensions and hostilities. Volkan (1988) traces the capacity to engage in this kind of defensive process to our earliest developmental experiences, which become interwoven with broader cultural significations as development proceeds. But they are truly universal and manifest themselves collectively in a broad range of behaviors and attitudes that range from the prosaic to the perverse. The same psychological process that can make people, as a sociocultural group, develop unexamined and reflexive feelings of ethnic or racial prejudice, can make partisans of sports teams develop real, strongly felt antipathies for their team's opponents. (Indeed, this is part of the mass appeal of sporting events and may be part of a psychological function they serve—that is, as outlets for a variety of identificatory and subliminatory needs.) While the consequences of each of these forms of splitting differ substantially, the mechanisms differ only in degree.

Splitting is ever present in our lives. It is the key element at work in the development and maintenance of feelings of solidarity and belonging to those we hold dear, while simultaneously organizing all manner of prejudicial attitudes toward those we do not. It is the crucial mechanism behind Volkan's (1988) observations on the universal need for allies and enemies. However, like all defensive processes, splitting exists within an unconscious medium, and thus the phenomenology of splitting is like the air we breathe: it is ever present, but we never think about it. Living within that psychological process we do not typically experience the contradictions it covers. Thus, we carry the capacity to exhibit irreconcilable feelings and attitudes while not experiencing their disjuncture within ourselves, thereby maintaining intrapsychic equilibrium. This psychological process is one of the elements in our nature that makes life itself profoundly paradoxical. It is splitting that could allow a gen-

eration of devoutly Christian Spanish ship captains to promul-
gate and enforce strict laws against blasphemy and card playing while they carried their cargo of African slaves to bitter
destinies in the New World (Hanke 1965); or the Nuremberg
Trials, which revealed that it was perfectly ordinary, "good"
German citizens who participated in the systematic annihila-
tion of Jews and others during the Holocaust of the Second
World War.

Bartolomé de Las Casas, a man of immense moral courage,
was, alas, a mere human being. If Las Casas was capable of
deceiving himself to such an extent, even if only temporarily,
then we can only wonder about the rest of us. The Africans whom
the Spaniards imported were victims, as were the native peoples
who preceded them and, to a very large extent, followed them.
But all of us, perpetrators and victims alike (and we are all
potentially both depending on the historical moment), are
capable of and readily resort to the psychological mechanisms
that underlie prejudicial attitudes and related processes.

Missionary activity is a form of cultural influence, covert and
overt, conscious and unconscious, in which the subjects of the
missionary work are to be changed, culturally and spiritually,
into people similar to the missionary and his culture. The Other
must be transformed into an acceptable version of the self. In
this sense, Las Casas was unarguably a cultural imperialist. Yet,
as is characteristic of all people who evince compassion, he was
merely attempting to give to those he came to love the experiences that organized him and gave his life meaning. His intent
was to improve and care for, not to annihilate and vanquish. To
further complicate matters, one might argue that facets of the
New World's culture were clearly problematic, such as the pervasive practice of cannibalism. It is also true that the Americas
to which the Spanish came were already a cauldron of antipa-
thy and continuous warfare where native peoples perpetrated
upon each other forms of oppression that were as brutal and
virulent as those brought by the Spaniards. Obviously, this does

not exonerate the Spaniards, but these awkward facts about the human condition are repeated over and over again, across cultures and generations. What makes them awkward, in addition to the fact that they reflect poorly on us, is our desire to see the world in simple terms where good and evil can be neatly delineated. Unfortunately, existence is a perpetual struggle between these proclivities within ourselves. The Christian doctrine of original sin arises from this truth about the human condition, as do Freud's hypotheses regarding the ubiquitous presence of the id.

Given that Catholicism represents the worst kind of apostasy for members of the Church of Christ (because of its belief in a pope, because of its "unscriptural" practices, and for numerous other reasons), it is unlikely that P. B. Middlebrook ever considered himself a descendant of Bartolomé de Las Casas. But he was. When Las Casas came to the New World as a priest shortly after Cortez's fabled successes, he came as a man dedicated to the culture he knew; he came as a champion of the Spanish version of Western civilization. He came, for better or for worse, to bring the Word of God to those whom he considered heathens.

Middlebrook, a West Texas Bartolomé de Las Casas, came to see in his missionary efforts that the Mexican-Americans and Native Americans with whom he worked were people struggling with the kinds of human suffering that confuse and baffle on the Indian reservation no less than in Anson or New York. He came to feel genuine compassion for them. But the denouement of his missionary experience came only as he was preparing to leave the reservation. Harry Harvey, an old medicine man, sent his 9-year-old grandson to tell Middlebrook that he wanted to be baptized. Harry Harvey was 83 years old and did not speak English. In many respects, Middlebrook's views had changed a great deal in the ten years since he'd left Anson, but the idea of baptizing an Indian medicine man stretched his tolerance to its limits and so P. B. called a meeting at the church.

"Boy, I didn't know what to do! You know . . . he was a medicine man and they are *serious* about that! So I called the church
and called a meeting, and I said, 'Listen, ol' Harry Harvey wants
to be baptized, he wants to be a Christian!' And I asked, 'Can a
medicine man be a Christian if he doesn't quit being a medicine man?' And the assembled members of the congregation said,
'Absolutely not!'"

For Middlebrook this stance was entirely ironic in retrospect.
"*Every one* of them went to the medicine man themselves, you
know," he noted with a characteristic chuckle, "but they said,
'No, that's impossible. He calls on all kinds of evil spirits and
everything else. A medicine man can't be a Christian. He's got
to quit.' So I kind of refused. Well, I *did* refuse to baptize him."
Middlebrook continued:

And this went on for about three weeks, and there was a
little fellow who ran a gas station in a little trailer park
down there named Don Kimner. He was a rough and
worldly fellow in a lot of ways, but there's a lot of good in
everybody, you know. I didn't know he ever had a religious
thought. He cussed and then he'd say blankety-blank, "Excuse me!" It was so much a part of him. But anyway, I went
down there, just a day or two before we were to leave. And
he said, "P. B., when did you start playing God?" And I
asked, "What do you mean?" And he said, "I hear ol' Harry
Harvey wanted to become a Christian and you won't baptize him," he said. "The whole community is upset with you."

"Well Don," I said, "I had a meeting with the church and
they said unless he's gonna give up being a medicine man,
he can't be a Christian." And Don said, "Why don't you
leave that up to God?" So I talked to Dorothy and she said,
"That's what I've been trying to tell you . . . you always say
we should find a scripture. Well, find a scripture where
they refused somebody." "It's not there," I said, "Well, I
believe I'll go talk to ol' Harry and see if he still wants to
be baptized."

Middlebrook found the aging medicine man at home. With the medicine man's grandson serving as translator, Middlebrook told the old man of his change of heart and asked him if he was still interested in being baptized. It turned out that not only was the medicine man still eager, but his wife wanted to be baptized, too.

It was only a matter of days before the Middlebrooks were to leave the reservation and their replacement was due to arrive. Baptizing the medicine man and his wife would be Middlebrook's last official duty at the little reservation church. There was one problem, however. The old medicine man was almost unable to walk, much less go up the steps to the baptistry of the church. Middlebrook called Don Kimner and asked him to help put in a ramp at the church so that Harry Harvey could get to the church baptistry. The day before he was to leave the reservation, at the little log-walled church that the Middlebrooks had built, he baptized the medicine man and his wife as their grandson translated. The medicine man's conversion was tremendously satisfying to Middlebrook. He recalled with pleasure the simple ceremony and the convert's lingering smile that required no translation. Harry Harvey died three months later.

Middlebrook's change of heart regarding this baptism represented a final turning point in his religious education. But it was only in retrospect that he appreciated its full impact.

Middlebrook found considerable humor in his final days on the reservation, especially this incident, which he thought was hilarious:

The thing that amused me is that young fellow who came to replace us. I told him about ol' Harry Harvey and told him about the meeting we had and everything. And while we were moving out, he just sat at his desk and he was making a list. And I asked what kind of list he was making. And he said, "Oh, I'm making a list of what ol' Harry Harvey is gonna have to do and what he's gonna have to give up." And I said, "Why don't you just kinda leave that to God."

THE MISSIONARY RETURNS HOME

At their return in 1980, the Middlebrooks were welcomed as heroes by the Anson Church of Christ members. The congregation had subsidized the Middlebrooks' modest salary during their missionary work. In addition, the church ran a Vacation Bible School at the Utah Indian reservation, so communication between the Middlebrooks and various members of the church had been frequent. The Middlebrooks had also returned to Anson two or three times a year, since both had family in town. Most important, ten years of missionary work reflected an unusual dedication to their church and a substantial personal sacrifice, qualities nearly everyone in this small community recognized and valued. Middlebrook was reinstated as elder and started teaching Sunday School classes again.

Yet, the return to what should have been familiar territory had ultimately been harder than P. B. had anticipated. "I think that the culture shock we got when we came back home was greater than the shock of moving to the reservation," he recalled. "What I thought I had left and what I found when I got back was very different."

Evidence of the decline of the town since 1969 was everywhere. Nearly half the businesses that had once operated on Commercial Street had closed.

"It's gotten to the point where just about the only profitable business in Anson is car sales," Middlebrook observed. The Ford and Chevrolet dealerships could draw people out of Abilene because their relatively low overhead translated into better prices. Otherwise, Anson's balance of trade with Abilene made America's economic relations with the East seem heavenly by comparison.

However, while the economic plight of the community and of the friends he had known all his life was immediate and painful for P. B., it was the changes within the Church of Christ that hit him the hardest. It was no longer the same church in which he had grown up. It was not the same church in which he had played an essential role as a much loved and respected elder. "It seems like I was on a collision course all the time," Middlebrook would later remember. "A lot of things had changed. And I thought that everybody else had changed, but they said, 'No, *you've* changed.' And maybe *I* had."

It was not long before the halo of renewed friendships was tarnished by a series of serious disagreements between Middlebrook and some of his fellow elders. "I got into an argument right off with my best friends on some issues," Middlebrook recalled on one of the afternoons we sat in his study.

The church had been in the midst of an orchestrated attempt by some of the elders to purify it. They had decided that some members of the congregation had become too lax in their Christian standards. There were rumors that in the higher echelons of the church, including the deacons and perhaps the elders, there were individuals who were engaging in sinful activity.

The orthodoxy of the church reached a peak during this period of moral purification. Members of the congregation were subjected to surreptitious investigations into their backgrounds. Were their marriages really scriptural? Did they sneak over the county line to buy beer that might be kept in the garage refrigerator? Did they secretly smoke? Were they womanizers? An influential subset of the elders was determined to clean up the church and make it a more "Christian" place.

The group drew up a secret list of "approved" church members who could teach Sunday School or pass the plate during communion or perform a variety of other religious functions. Those who were found lacking in some way were removed from these coveted positions. One family, for example, was brought before the elders because their daughter had decided to be baptized at the First Baptist Church. They were admonished for allowing their daughter to stray from the flock. Despite the fact that the young woman was an adult and presumably capable of making her own decisions, spiritual or otherwise, her mother

was taken off the approved list and no longer allowed to teach
Sunday School. If she could not set a Christian example within
her own home, so the logic went, how could she possibly be viewed
as a Christian model by the rest of the congregation? "We wanted
a bunch of perfect people, and if you had any imperfection, you
could come to church up here, but we were not going to let you
take part," is the scornful way one church member put it.

At the same time in the early 1980s the church elders made
an infamous list of individuals who were about to be disfellow-
shipped (the Church of Christ version of excommunication) for
not attending church. One of the individuals on that list was
Shannon Middlebrook, one of P. B.'s brothers. When Shannon
was 3 years old, another brother was playing with a welding rod.
He had tied a string to the rod and was whirling it above his
head, when the rod broke loose. Shannon was struck directly
on the left side of the temple, and was permanently disabled.
Severely handicapped all his life, as an adult Shannon had at
times occasionally turned to alcohol in an effort to cope with his
difficulties. He now helped P. B. with home repair projects; he
no longer abused alcohol and he was again attending the Anson
Church of Christ. However, during the inquisition, Shannon's
past made him a prime candidate for the list of those who needed
"visiting."

The elders' activities also included the investigation of some
church members' marriages. According to one report, a church
member who had been married for nearly thirty-five years was
discovered to be in an "unscriptural" marriage. Immense pressure was brought to bear on the couple. They were instructed
to live "as brother and sister" for the sake of their children, but
eventually the couple separated. One night, feeling increasingly
that his life was collapsing around him, the husband went to
the home of a friend, a fellow member of the church and accused
the elders of trying to destroy his marriage. Still distraught
when he left his friend's home, he drove downtown and, sitting
in his car, shot himself to death. The man was the local farmer

with whom Agustín Garcia had had the near-fatal encounter at the cotton gin a year earlier.

The church was also reeling from the deep divisions surrounding a bus ministry, a piece of local missionary work to bring Mexican-American and African-American children into the church, as well as other outreach programs that had created immense conflicts, within the congregation (see Chapter 10).

Middlebrook's conflicts with some of his fellow elders were directly related to his experience as a missionary and his evolving views on the question of divorce and remarriage. A married couple had sought membership in the church. However, it was discovered during their interviews with the elders that the husband had divorced his first wife and years later married his current wife. Middlebrook had been impressed with the couple. "I believed they were good Christians," he later recalled.

A number of other elders held a different view on the matter, however. Given that the husband's first marriage had not been dissolved for a "scriptural" reason (adultery committed by one's spouse) they took the position that the couple was currently living in an adulterous relationship. For these elders, the only solution was for the previously divorced husband to return to his first wife (which was probably impossible in any event) and attempt a reconciliation. This would represent true repentance and thereby heal the sinful breach reflected in his divorce.

Fresh from the Indian reservation, Middlebrook saw things quite differently. After all, these were the questions over which he had agonized, which had kept him up late at night for months on end as he tried to figure the proper Christian approach to the men and women on the reservation. During that period of reflection and introspection, Middlebrook had gradually shifted his understanding of God's will, which he summarized as a shift in emphasis from the notion of repentance toward the idea of forgiveness.

The debates between Middlebrook and some of his fellow elders grew heated and acrimonious, and he was increasingly

viewed with suspicion. Like Bartolomé de Las Casas, he was a
changed man following his years of missionary work, and the
changes brought him into direct conflict with his compatriots
in his church.

One can only imagine the inner conflicts with which Middlebrook struggled at this time. His transformed views seemed to
have repercussions in virtually every facet of his religious life.
It became common knowledge among congregants that he and
some elders were in strong disagreement. Some of them demanded complete obedience; they were unaccustomed to being
challenged about any church matter. They were incensed at
Middlebrook's attitude but he remained steadfast.

Middlebrook's fellow elders now began to question his missionary work in New Mexico and Utah. His views seemed so
deviant that they wondered what kind of Christian work he had
carried out as a Church of Christ missionary. It was suggested
that the baptisms he had performed in Española and on the
Indian reservation were flawed and that he should go back and
let those who were living in "unscriptural" circumstances know
that they were not considered true Christians.

The Middlebrooks were in an agonizing quandary. The Anson
Church of Christ was the church they had known all their lives.
In a way that may be difficult to imagine for those who have
never known the extremely interwoven character of fundamentalist churches, this church was, quite literally, an extension
of family to the Middlebrooks. For the longest period of time,
Middlebrook could not fathom doing anything that would undermine his link to the most important fundamental element in
their lives. These were lifelong friends with whom he was feud-
ing. This was the church that had been his spiritual and social
home as far back as he could remember.

Middlebrook began to question himself. "I'm not an expert
in anything anymore!" he laughed, but it was a laugh that carried knowing conviction and a message. "I got over it," he said.
"I got over it!" He became unsure about his ability carry on the
fight against what he believed to be the dark forces of human

nature. His stance against the Footloose Club's efforts to legal-
ize dancing in Anson represented one side of this conflict, but
there was uncertainty in the air.

"You become influenced by so many things," Middlebrook said
after a pause. "And talking about my issue with my brothering
in the church on the marriage and divorce question . . . that was
black and white for me! Before I went to the mission field out
there and saw what was happening. And then I tried to adjust
to reality I guess. . . . Boy, I search for answers all the time."
His voice trailed off. It was as if the interview had brought him
face to face with a previously repressed reality. The insight
opened another flood of uncertainty. "My real inclination is to
quit," Middlebrook said. He was shaken by the awareness of how
all of a sudden everything seemed complicated. "That's the truth,
I'm telling you the truth!," he went on, as if needing to underscore his point.

Giving up the security of self-righteous certainty was difficult. It was much easier to sit back, as some of his fellow elders
had done, and render judgments about people's sins. Middlebrook had clearly taken the harder path and accepted the painful reality of human imperfection. He valued the human struggle
toward biblical ideals and tried to help individuals move toward
these, but did not badger them for their frailties and shortcom-
ings. Yet, this man who had engaged in so much introspection
regarding such self-righteousness was the same one who a few
years later would look out upon the assembled audience at the
Anson city council meeting and attempt to derail the desire of
a group of parents to have a high school prom because he continued to believe that dancing was either sinful or that it pro-
moted sin.

INFRINGEMENT OF PRIVACY

In the early 1980s a successful lawsuit against the elders of an
Oklahoma Church of Christ sent shock waves through fundamentalist religious groups across the country. A woman named

Marian Guinn had sued the elders of her former church for in-
fringement of her privacy, publication of private acts, and in-
tentional infliction of emotional distress when they had publicly
accused her of "the sin of fornication" after she had withdrawn
from the church. The elders had also written letters containing
the accusation to other nearby Churches of Christ. The jury
found the church elders guilty on all counts and awarded Guinn
$390,000 in damages ($205,000 in actual damages, $185,000 in
punitive damages). The verdict clearly communicated to elders
and preachers that they were personally liable for acts committed under their direction and that church doctrines and practices did not permit them to violate individual rights. In order
to protect themselves from similar litigation, fundamentalist
congregations across the country flocked to courthouses to in-
corporate as nonprofit organizations.

It was in the context of this case that four elders from the
Anson Church of Christ filed articles of incorporation with the
state of Texas on May 3, 1983. The corporation designated its
status as nonprofit and its period of duration as "perpetual." It
pledged the congregation's assets to be used exclusively toward
the performance of its religious functions.

For P. B. Middlebrook, the filing of incorporation papers had
been the last straw in his ongoing conflicts with some of his
fellow elders. He could see the wisdom of incorporating, although he had mixed feelings about it. But, it was the act of
deception that had been committed in the process. In a panic,
given the judgment in the Guinn case and the extensive controversy that had enveloped their own church during the inqui-
sitional effort to "purify" it, the elders had proceeded with the
incorporation process prior to bringing it before the congregation for a vote, according to Middlebrook. Bringing the question
before the congregation would have been typical for so important a step. This failure was egregious enough, but when the
matter of incorporation was brought for a vote, the fact that the
process was already underway was not divulged.

Middlebrook was livid. He went to one of the most influential elders, a man with a lead role in the incorporation process
and accused him of deceiving the congregation. "And they had,"
Middlebrook said. "They had sought the congregation's approval
after the fact. There was absolute out-and-out deception, you
know. And I said, 'This can't be! This is not the way that the
Lord's church ought to be or is intended to be; you are wrong in
this.' I found it almost impossible to go to church," Middlebrook
said ruefully.

He concluded that there was no alternative but to resign from
the church. Serendipitously, it was at this time that Middlebrook
was invited to preach at the little Church of Christ in Truby.
He seized upon this invitation as the public reason for leaving
the Anson Church of Christ. Privately, however, Middlebrook
acknowledged that he could not continue to accept the practices
and policies of some of his fellow elders.

"The point I'm trying to make is that I had been raised in this
community. I probably see it different from most of the people
you interview because I went away. I saw a different world. I
saw things that we had believed here all of my life that just
wouldn't fit. And then I came back, and it caused some conflict.
I'm being sort of cynical and I'm not normally that way. I'm a
happy guy most of the time, I'm real pleasant," Middlebrook said
with a characteristic chuckle. "I feel like a lot of our traditions
try to bind, and we kind of—so to speak—choke on a gnat and
swallow a camel. I've seen a lot of hypocrisy."

Middlebrook went on, musing about the fate of Anson. "I may
be misjudging it . . . but I see people who still say we are this
good, middle America, Bible Belt, fine salt-of-the-earth people.
But I see our kids having as many or more problems than others.
I see divorce among the people that I know and love. And I see
them hurt, and I realize that maybe we've made the transition
into this modern way of life and don't admit it."

These are the very concerns that made inevitable the confrontation between the Church of Christ and the forces of change,

forces that were ultimately embodied in the Footloose Club. As
a church, but also as the core of Anson's social and political
power, it confronted an elusive, multifaceted foe: Mexicanization
of their town, a few African-Americans, the crumbling economic
base of the community, the flight of their children to Texas's big
cities, and the transformation of the community's social values.
To be sure, this was an odd amalgamation of enemies. The issues facing the church surfaced and receded in an ever-changing configuration that made it virtually impossible to grasp the
true nature of their collective circumstance. They felt like prey
to a pack of hyenas, never knowing from where the next assault
might come, seeing monstrous presences in the dark constructed
from terrified imaginations.

When Middlebrook was elected to the Anson city council, he
had already been preaching at the Truby Church of Christ for
several years. Despite the changes in his own world view, Middlebrook remained a fundamentalist at heart. His opposition to the
Footloose Club was a function of his conviction that dancing, and
the atmosphere around such events, tended to incite the darker
side of human nature. Thus, he had joined arms with the other
fundamentalists on the city council in opposing Footloose's efforts. However, as I listened and relistened to his interviews, I
could never shake the impression that Middlebrook's stance was
an effort to extend an olive branch to his old but now estranged
friends on the eldership of the Church of Christ. Emotionally,
he was still doing missionary work, but he wanted to come home.

The truth was that he had engaged the Other and suffered
the cost. It is precisely this engagement that is so fundamentally threatening to the self. When the self changes, not only
are the moorings of one's identity threatened, but also one's
status within the tribe or social group is brought into question.
Middlebrook's tribe eventually extruded him.

His personal psychology was a kind of repository for conflicts
that were transforming his community. It was as if those tensions had adhered to his psyche.

By 1985, just two years before the dancing conflict, a new orthodoxy had retaken control of the Anson Church of Christ. The Middlebrooks and a number of other church members had either been driven out or had left of their own accord. The remaining elders had fired the old preacher as well, thus clearing the church of any dissenting voice. These steps represented an extension of their Holy Inquisition, a desperate effort to hold on to a world that had already ceased to exist.

10

**Doug Browning:
"I could see that if we
didn't change their ideas
toward us, then the time
would come when they
would change us."**

Late one afternoon, I interviewed Doug Browning, a former member of the Anson Church of Christ, at the Hatahoe Diner. Browning tried to be circumspect when it came to his views about Anson's dancing controversy:

"I never voiced an opinion for or against [dancing]," he told me as he reflected back on events from which he had tried to remain separated. "It was just one of them free-for-alls."

Browning had a reputation for being eccentric and wildly extroverted. In his mid-fifties, he was graying, but his high cheeks, ready smile, and flashing green eyes gave him a youthful, impish appearance. He spoke with a deep West Texas accent, punctuated by a wry sense of humor bred from years of being on the "outside looking in."

He seemed impatient with my questions about dancing. However, it wasn't because of his life-long association with the Church of Christ. Rather, it was because, in his view, the entire dancing controversy had been based on a misguided premise. "It's not *just* dancing," Browning noted. "When we moved to Anson we were suprised that they wouldn't allow dancing but they *would* allow boys and girls to go to the swimming pool together. In Roby [a nearby community from which the Brownings had moved] there was no such thing as mixed bathing. This

Doug Browning, owner of the Hatahoe Diner. Photo: Ricardo Ainslie.

was around 1972. Then they had a wet/dry election in Roby and we went all out, door to door, everything, it was a knock down-drag out fight. And we won that election and kept Roby dry."

However, Browning did not exude the pride of a victorious warrior. He tried to steer me closer to his view of why the issue in Anson had not simply been about dancing. "We [referring to his wife Bobbie and himself] feel like kids today are not afraid of the ultimate consequences of their behavior, or punishment for wrongdoing. They feel they can get away with anything. It's a like a *counter* culture, counter movement."

I asked him why he thought this was the case.

"Well, because they took morality out of the schools. When they took prayer out, morality was no longer taught in schools, so if they didn't go to jail, well, then they thought that whatever they did was fine, because they didn't believe that eventually there would be an ultimate judgment for whatever they did."

Browning was outlining a common assumption within fundamentalist circles as to why America and her youth are in a precarious state. This view holds that religious beliefs are an indispensable precondition to attaining moral values. Thus, to the fundamentalists, education that disavows a religious frame of reference is hollow, the spiritual analogue to feeding an infant watered-down milk. Eventually that infant will suffer the effects of malnourishment.

> Our generation believed that whether or not we got caught by the law, someday or other we would have to answer for our actions. But the kids today don't believe that. If the law doesn't get you, you're home free. And how this relates to the dancing thing is that the churches are seeing this thing go too far and so they're trying to put the brakes on every little thing. So they're trying to stop the dancing, trying to stop the swimming, trying to stop the drugs, and it's what's going on at the other end that they *should* be stopping. They should be *showing* these kids that it don't matter if they get away with it, *some day* they're going to be held accountable for what they do. But the churches are trying to legislate morality. They've got to go to the heart, to the conscience, and teach these kids conscience.

I wondered out loud what thoughts he had about how a child could be brought to this kind of understanding.

"You just teach," Browning came back matter-of-factly as if it were the most obvious thing in the world. "Bobbie and I taught a lot by example. We reached out. We got inside of them. We got inside their minds and their hearts. We let the kids know that we really cared about them."

Browning was pessimistic about strategies he saw people using today. Dr. Joycelyn Elders, then-U.S. Surgeon General, had just finished her testimony before the Senate Labor and Human Resources Committee, in which she had been queried about her pregnancy prevention policies that included handing out condoms.

"People are trying to get these kids back on the right track," Browning noted. "They're trying to help them out, but boy, passing out condoms is not going to solve it because that's like say-

ing 'Two plus two equals five' and you're telling them a lie.
You're saying, 'Well, don't do it, but, here . . . ' So what are they
going to do?" Browning trailed off as if to say the answer to that
question was obvious—any kid would take that as a wink that
gave the green light for sexual activity. A school handing out
condoms was implicitly licensing sex. Before I could ask him the
standard counter (If kids are having sex anyway, might it not
be better to ensure that they are safe?), Browning dove into his
next point.

"Why did I never drink any beer or whisky or anything, not
even in the army?" Browning asked me rhetorically. "Because
my daddy, when I was a little kid, never said, 'Don't drink', but
one day we were driving down the road and we were looking at
this guy and he said, 'Look at him, he's wasting his life drinking.' And he said, 'Man, that will really get you in trouble!'

"And it was that example of teaching me that really left an
impression and it was what you call a 'teachable moment.'
Everybody has these teachable moments, which is when you see
something happening, then you tell your children or your student and you relate a story to that. You can do it at funerals, or
weddings, or births, hardships or good times . . . fishing, I like
to do it fishing," Browning added with a laugh.

This was his trademark—throwing in an irreverent notion
when you least expected it.

"You know, you teach your kids that way and they remember it. That's when the student's mind is open." It was clear that
this was a pearl of wisdom. Browning concluded with a laugh:
"I never went to college but I'm smart!"

I brought him back to the question of dancing, asking him
why he never stated his views on the issue:

"The reason I never did is because where I went to high school,
in Sweetwater, we *had* a senior prom, we had a 4-H dance, and
I never did dance but I never did see much wrong with it. But I
saw things going on that were wrong. There were two groups of
kids at school, and one would go out and dance and they would

also drink with it and get drunk and party, and there was another group that wouldn't and I think the drinking was the devil in it."

"So what do you think dancing leads to?" I asked.

"Oh, it was an *attitude,*" Browning responded.

"What about a ballet?" I asked.

"Ballet? What about a burlesque!?" was Browning's retort. "What we argued about this dancing thing is—see, I've taught a lot of kids in church camp about morality, and so I'd say, 'OK. How many of y'all believe in dancing?' And they'd all raise their hands. And I'd say, 'OK. Here's a broom. Dance with a broom. Are you going to get any excitement out of it?' 'No.' Then I'd say, 'All right then, if we were to rub bellies,' and I'd say, 'OK. Now, would that be exciting?'" Browning laughed out loud again. "What do you do when you rub bellies? That's dancing isn't it? Now, ballet is different than rubbing bellies. What you're doing when you're dancing is stimulating yourself like you're having sex, that's really what it is."

"Why draw the line around dancing?" I asked Browning, suggesting that there were more pressing concerns about America's youth. "You probably know guys who have been drinking all their lives and never got drunk or who never became drunks,"

Browning said, "See, you *don't* draw the line. That's my view. You just let them know that this is where the path leads."

"Aren't you taking a more benevolent attitude than would be typical within the Church of Christ?"

"Yes," Browning answered without a moment's pause. "Because I believe in grace."

When I asked how he had come to believe in grace, Browning grew impatient with me again: "Oh, Man! I don't know," he said with exasperation. But then, after a moment's reflection: "Because I'm not perfect, I need forgiveness, and the more forgiveness I need, the more I see that others need too. I've always had lots of empathy or sympathy or pity or something for the lowly one, for the underdog. And I always thought that the sinner was the underdog. I think it came from my own despair. When I was a kid I was put down by everybody. And because we were so poor, I was always the underdog."

I asked him again about the differences between his views and those of some of his fellow church members. He seemed less dogmatic, more open. "A lot of the people that go to the Church of Christ go to that one building all of their life," Browning noted. "One of the guys, up here in Anson, he told me one time, he said, 'You know, I've never been anywhere else.' But I'd been to probably thirteen churches before we got married. I've been to Churches of Christ in Korea, Canada, Japan, everywhere! And *everybody* does it different. And when we'd go to camp, we'd have church out under the trees. And so I'd say, you know, 'In that *building,* well, that's not religion. That's an organization. The *real* church is in people's hearts. You can have it anywhere!'"

"What if you're not baptized?" I asked, trying to lead him into the center of fundamentalist beliefs. He wouldn't go for it. "Don't get into that!" he barked back good-naturedly. "That's an argument!"

If Doug Browning was something of a fundamentalist iconoclast, he was the product of years of bumping up against the church establishment. It had all started back in 1980 when the church decided that it could not sit idly by in the face of the changes transforming their community. They could see that many of Anson's minority children were not going to church and were getting into trouble instead. In response, the Church of Christ established two ministries aimed at Anson's minority population.

THE ANSON CHURCH OF CHRIST
BUS MINISTRY

There were multiple motivations for establishing these ministries. The church's own membership was steadily declining and increasingly elderly. In addition, the strong fundamentalist beliefs of the church placed important emphasis on bringing in new Christians as an indication that they were doing God's work. The Mexican-American community and Anson's handful of blacks were the only untapped pools for such evangelical efforts.

While some Mexican-Americans attended Anson's lone Catholic church, most had no religious affiliation whatsoever. The same was true for African-Americans, some of whom attended an all-black Baptist church in town. One of the ministries established by the Anson Church of Christ was aimed at Mexican-American adults. It was set up in a little church-owned building known as the Herndon Chapel, a few miles out of town with a "Spanish" preacher, E. L. Ortiz, who owned a fruit and vegetable stand on the outskirts of Anson. Brother Ortiz also preached in a Spanish-language radio ministry supported by the Church of Christ. A separate ministry, which came to be known as the Bus Ministry, was organized to bring Anson's minority children to the Church of Christ on Sundays.

It is probably no coincidence that the Bus Ministry was housed at the church on Commercial Street, while the Mexican-American ministry was housed outside city limits. Children were less threatening and their presence in the church more palatable. Bringing minority adults directly into the Church of Christ, on the other hand, would have posed all kinds of problems. Anson, after all, was a community in which racial delineation had long been one of the basic truths around which society was organized.

Doug Browning, then a deacon at the Anson Church of Christ, was put in charge of the Bus Ministry. He and his wife, Bobbie, had just moved to Anson from nearby Roby following the successful battle to keep Roby dry. Browning had grown up on a farm twenty-five miles west of Anson, where his family was part of the rural poor. "There was no electricity, no water, no nothin'. I mean it's *country!*" Browning said of his native Longworth. As a young child, Browning and his siblings helped

E. L. Ortiz—"Spanish" Church of Christ preacher at his fruit and vegetable stand. Photo: Nancy Scanlan.

their parents work their small farm. His grandfather had been
a member of the Texas Ku Klux Klan, and his grandmother still
had the robes and hood—the one possession of hers that Browning said he wanted nothing to do with.

When asked why he became interested in the Bus Ministry,
Browning cited a biblical passage: "'Go to the highways and
byways and get the sick and the lame and the blind and the poor
and bring them in.' And it said 'Bring them in,' and the reason
you bring them in is because the Lord's house is empty." Part
of Browning's original interest in the Bus Ministry had to do
with Anson's rapidly changing demography: "I could see what
was happening," Browning said in reference to the community's
minority population. "I'm no prophet, but I could see. If we didn't
change their ideas towards us, then the time would come when
they would change us, I guess."

He became particularly interested in trying to understand Mexican-American culture. He read books that purported to describe the Mexican-American's views toward religion and race. He tried to understand the effects of poverty on family organization. He spoke of one book that was especially important to him. He was not sure of its title, but it was about Spanish culture in South Texas. Browning enthusiastically summarized its thesis:

OK, it tells how the Mexican culture over here in Texas— You know, they were here first, and *we're* the intruders. But we don't look at it that way. Well, the book says that in their minds God is punishing them for their evil acts. You know, they get drunk and all this, so God's punishing them. And the white person is taking over because God is using the white man to punish them. So, the more the white man punishes them, the more God loves them, and someday, they will be at the top when they've been punished enough. When I had the Bus Ministry, I read this book, and I understood them. The Spanish young male hates his race *so* much that he will do anything to change it. Well, he can't change himself, so he will do anything to marry a white girl in order that his kids won't be completely brown. And you see that here just over and over again.

By his report, Browning had a significant learning disability and had not been to college, but he had tried his best to understand the children he was bringing into the church. His groping efforts to make sense of the social reality of these children and their families were noteworthy, although clearly not without significant problems.

"I would say that I have been in every Spanish person's house in this town at one time or another. Knocking on doors trying to get their kids to go to church," Browning said, arms crossed

on the white formica table at the Hatahoe. As a child, Doug had
attended a small country school that served all the children in
the county, including one who was so severely retarded that he
could hardly feed himself. "We couldn't afford the luxury of segregation," Browning noted wryly.

After serving in the army, he went to work managing a 1950s
drive-in restaurant in Waco. Now he was a fairly successful
business man, with his hand in a number of ventures in Anson
and the surrounding communities. The Hatahoe (as in "hate to
hoe" after Browning's aversion to chopping cotton on the family farm) had a marquee that boasted of "the best cherry lime
soda in Texas." Browning had once hoped to open a string of
these between Fort Worth and El Paso, but the vagaries of the
Texas economy had put a damper on such ambitions. He also
owned several successful video rental stores in Anson and
nearby towns.

"There was no dancing, no drinking, no nothin' in this town.
I chose this town because of it, and because of the water," Browning added after a pause in his characteristic humor. The latter
sentiment reflected one of those rudimentary anxieties felt by
people who have grown up on a marginal, drought-vulnerable
farm: Anson is the "first tap" on the reservoir that supplies a
number of nearby towns and the city of Abilene with water. The
Brownings purchased an attractive ranch-style house on a modest acreage a few miles outside of Anson and settled into the
community.

Doug and Bobbie Browning quickly became active in church
affairs, and within a short time, he was appointed deacon at the
Anson Church of Christ. Among his church-related activities,
he led a group of volunteers who visited a local retirement home
to sing and lead prayer. "Sometimes on Sunday morning we'd
go out there and sing to 'em, and coming back, about 9:30 or
10:30, kids were just everywhere on the street. They wasn't
going to church anywhere. And I said, 'Why don't we stop that?
Let's get us some buses and get them kids and put them in
church.'" Browning was also involved in a Saturday Night Bible

Club with the church's youth minister, when the idea struck. With the blessing of the church elders, the Bus Ministry was launched.

Immensely adept at engaging young kids, Browning was perfect for the recruiting efforts. When asked how he succeeded in bringing minority children to church on Sunday mornings, Browning laughed: "You mean how would I go into a Spanish person's house and say, 'We want to bring your kids to church?' All right, you met me. Am I bashful? I don't know what a stranger is! And I don't know what it is, but to me those folks are just like everybody else. I just as soon go into those folks' house as go into a rich person's house, and, frankly, I think they sense that."

Initially, the Brownings ferried children to and from church in their own van, but soon the Church of Christ purchased a van for the ministry and then an old school bus from Moctezuma Creek, where P. B. Middlebrook had done his missionary work. Traveling up and down country roads, the bus already had a good many miles on it and was in poor mechanical condition. In his garage, Doug made the necessary repairs and painted it a cheerful, bright red. He also attached a moveable spotlight he could direct from the driver's seat so that people would not hurt or injure themselves trying to get to or from the bus after dark.

Every Sunday morning, the Brownings drove the bus up and down the streets of the east side of town where virtually all of the minority families lived. Whenever they spotted a youngster out in the street, they stopped and talked to him about coming to church for their Sunday School program. When they had caught the child's interest, Doug would go to his or her home, knock on the door, and get permission from the parents for the child to come to Sunday School.

Once a few kids began coming on a regular basis, the Bus Ministry quickly picked up momentum. Kids would go home and tell their friends about it and the next Sunday, when the Brownings drove by in their bright red bus, there would be new kids out on the street interested in coming along to church. The

Brownings's Bus Ministry was an almost overnight success, expanding faster than the church's capacity to provide transportation. Some Sunday mornings several trips were necessary, the bus packed to capacity each time.

They also used the bus as a sort of moving school house. "We taught them on the bus and then they'd come to church and suffer!" Doug said with a laugh.

Above the windows of the bus he hung a strip of cardboard that served as backing onto which were attached posters of the letters of the alphabet in bright and vibrant colors, the names of the books of the Bible, and colorful pictures, the kind one sees in elementary schools, which marked the seasons for the children. Bobbie Browning taught the children vintage Christian Bible School songs, like "Do Lord" as they cruised the streets of Anson.

The Brownings also endeavored to teach social values and what they called "basic manners." Bobbie Browning showed me a picture of three children at a water fountain with the message: "You're next! Be considerate!" It was typical of the materials they had used on the bus. "This is the kind of stuff we'd hang up there, trying to teach them to be courteous," she said. "We were teaching them how they could get along with each other. Just the basic things that Christ wanted them to do," added Doug.

The Bus Ministry had an immense impact on the Church of Christ congregation. For many, it was their first involvement with members of the minority community. The children coming to Sunday School were sometimes matched with volunteers from the congregation who sat with them during services. For example, Bogus Lollar, a successful and influential cotton farmer who was also an elder, "adopted" four children from the Aguirre family and they sat with Bogus and his wife at church services. During the week the Lollars took them on outings, bought them clothes, school supplies, and other necessities. P. B. Middlebrook also participated in this program. He and Dorothy took ten African-American children from one family under their wing. Other church members donated money to sponsor Bus Ministry kids at Summer Vacation Bible School. They also contributed to the congregation's small-scale Goodwill industry that the Brownings and others put together on the outskirts of town at the Herndon Chapel where E. L. Ortiz was preaching.

The Goodwill idea was inspired by the circumstances of Dolores Fernandez, whose children participated in the Bus Ministry. When the Brownings found out that her utilities had been cut off in the middle of a summer heat wave, the church paid the utility bill, and the electric service was returned. (In 1988 an angry pastoral letter by the Hispanic Catholic bishops, reported in the *New York Times*, blamed "an aggressive and disrespectful proselytism" for the number of Hispanic defections from the Catholic church. Others accused Protestants of buying off poor Hispanics by offering them food, clothing, and housing.) This act of benevolence played an unwitting role in the ensuing tragedy. Not long after the electricity was restored, a fire started in the family's sole air conditioner, which rapidly engulfed the house in flames.

The Brownings arrived just as the firemen had finished extinguishing the blaze. Mrs. Fernandez was in a state of shock—dazed and disoriented. Her five children were equally traumatized. One was running around the charred remains of the house in his underwear, the only clothing he had left. Another approached the Brownings, speechless, holding his prized possession: a seared baseball glove, still hot from the fire. Miraculously, no one was injured in the blaze, but the family lost virtually everything they owned.

The Anson Church of Christ collected donations for the Fernandez family, and in relatively short order they had clothing and shelter. But the Brownings wanted to be prepared for the next time a calamity hit a needy family. The Herndon Chapel stood on the edge of a cotton field a few miles out of town, across from the Brownings' ranch house. It had once been a farmer's utility shed prior to being donated to the church. It had not been used in years, but now the Brownings and others cleaned out the cobwebs and drove out the rats to make the building serviceable again. In no time, the Herndon Chapel housed a full array of clothing, organized by sizes, as well as myriad household appliances and utensils, all donated by members of the congregation. In addition to housing E. L. Ortiz's "Spanish" ministry, the chapel was used by the Brownings for occasional youth group meetings, graduation parties, and other church-related activities.

In fact, this was one of the problems. The Brownings seemed to have no shortage of ideas for projects and ministering activities that often proved to be successful beyond anyone's wildest expectations. For example, there was the Wednesday Night Bible Study Class started by the Brownings and the youth minister for adolescents. This was the Church of Christ response to the same concerns the Footloose Club would subsequently attempt to address: to make inroads into the local drug culture, to keep adolescents from getting pregnant or from dropping out of school, increasingly pervasive problems. For the Brownings, the solution to these problems was religious, and the idea was to reach kids who would not ordinarily be willing to come to church. The Wednesday Night Bible Study Class was a low pressure affair at the Browning home.

"We didn't care if they had long hair, what they were wearing; we didn't care what they looked like or what their morals were as long as we could get them there so that we could teach them Jesus," Bobbie Browning said.

Doug was an exceptional teacher, with a knack for telling biblical stories so that they were meaningful to adolescents, who are notoriously hard to reach. He could make religion come alive for them. "Doug can teach the Bible better than anyone I know," said Bobbie. "He can *teach* that stuff, just like a story book, and those kids could see Jesus alive in there, and we'd have tears, laughing, emotions, loving each other up. It was good!"

It almost brought tears to her eyes to think of it again. Even some adolescents who were known as fairly hardened and wayward came to the Wednesday Night Bible Class at their house. Within a year, the Brownings and the youth minister had forty to fifty kids attending regularly.

In fairly short order, the Brownings's success created tensions within the congregation. Some feared that the Brownings were beginning to create a church-within-a-church through their various ministering activities. One night the elders met with Doug and voiced their concerns. They suggested that he hold the Wednesday Night Bible Class at the church rather than at his home, to which Doug readily agreed. However, this created other problems. His style was extroverted and a bit on the raucous side. He was even more so when mingling with a gaggle of teenagers. He endeavored to present his religious instruction in ways that were humorous and engaging to the adolescents, and this was probably a key to his success. The class came to be dubbed "Doug's laugh-in" because the kids were having such a good time, but all the while he plied them with his religious message, making it palatable via his sense of humor.

But this approach was frowned on by some church members. It seemed that the Brownings were having too much fun to be doing serious Christian work. His methods were questioned in other ways, too. Doug seemed to have a kind of sixth sense for what these kids needed. For example, some of them were reluctant to be seen at the church by anyone other than their peers. Browning would invite them to class, assuring them that he would not make them attend church in the big auditorium afterwards. He would release them fifteen minutes early so that they could slip out the back door and not be seen by any of the adults. Such simple tactics were remarkably successful in getting some adolescents to the Bible class who would not otherwise be caught dead anywhere near the church, except for its dimly lit parking lot late on a Friday or Saturday night. Browning figured that if he could get them to come to his Bible class, eventually he could get them to come to church, and, more important, eventually he could get them to begin reflecting on what they were doing to themselves or to others, whether their sins

were in the realm of drugs and alcohol, sex, or general delin-
quency. However, when word got out that he was letting kids
have an option about attending Wednesday night services, some
of the elders were annoyed.

The success of the Church of Christ Bus Ministry sparked
competitive feelings among the other churches in Anson. Browning noted, "The Baptists said, 'Man, we can't let the Church of
Christ get ahead of us. We'll get a bus too.' And the Catholic
Church said, 'Hey, man, they're getting all our kids.' So they
got them a bus. Christian Life got *them* a bus, and in two-and-
a-half years . . . the kids either went to church on Sunday morning or they went out back and hid!" Browning derived a measure of ironic satisfaction from having sparked this competitive
frenzy among Anson's churches.

As Browning met the children and families on the east side
of town, he was startled by what he discovered. Like a New
Yorker who walks past homeless people on a daily basis and
manages to insulate himself from experiencing them, Browning had been living in Anson for several years, but knew relatively little about the lives of its poor.

Browning told me:

We found all kinds of situations. Like a little girl, Lucy,
we never did know her last name. She didn't have a mama
or daddy. She lived with her grandparents and her grandparents didn't speak no English. And they lived down here
in a li'l ol' shanty thing. It was *terrible*. We'd bring her to
church, and bugs would crawl out of her coat. She'd have
mites. At that time, she wasn't going to school, so the school
didn't know anything about her. That's the kinds of messes
we'd have to clean up. . . . We started picking Lucy up when
she was about 5. And that's when we found this old black
woman. . . . I don't know how old she was. She said she
was about a hundred. There was no food, no clothes, no
running water in her house. We went out and found her
there. This is [starts laughing], this is right here in Anson!
And this is supposed to be civilization!

Such ironies and contradictions only seemed to amuse Doug Browning. Nevertheless, it was evident that the Bus Ministry had provided him with an education he had not anticipated. It was also evident that the Brownings were ferreting out a local reality that many of the established, elite members of the community, both inside the church and out, would rather forget: the real impact of poverty and race on many Anson inhabitants.

A CASE STUDY IN DESEGREGATION

By the end of 1980 the Bus Ministry was at its peak. Sixty to seventy minority children were coming to church on Sunday mornings. E. L. Ortiz was broadcasting his Spanish-language sermons on the radio every Sunday morning and many of the parents of the children participating in the Brownings' Bus Ministry were attending services at the Herndon Chapel. In their collectivity, these various efforts constituted a full-scale missionary effort in Anson's minority community.

However, the very success of these efforts began to generate ambivalence within the Anson Church of Christ. On one hand, people seemed excited about bringing in so many "new Christians." As with other fundamentalist churches, effective evangelical work was considered a sign of the church's success, an index of the extent to which they were doing the Lord's work. On the other hand, however, the Bus Ministry in particular created some special problems for the congregation. This was partly due to the fact that, of all the church's ministering efforts, only the Bus Ministry was actually bringing minority children to the church—to Sunday School classes and worship services. E. L. Ortiz's Spanish Ministry at the Herndon Chapel was at a safe remove beyond the city limits. It was one thing to help support a "Spanish" minister preaching to a small group of Mexican-Americans on the outskirts of town but something altogether different to have minority children mingling with their own kids at Sunday School and the Big Assembly for services.

The Bus Ministry might be considered as something of a case study in the complexities of integrating people who differ in culture, values, language, and economic resources. In this capacity it is reminiscent of the desegregation and busing controversies that racked America's educational systems following the landmark court decisions of the 1960s and 1970s. In 1968 nearly 65 percent of African-Americans attended segregated schools, which were defined as having 90 to 100 percent minority population (Hochschild 1984). By 1980 the average number of African-American students attending segregated schools in the United States had dropped to 33 percent. This change was even more dramatic in the south, where in 1968 nearly 78 percent of African-Americans attended segregated schools, and by 1980 that number had dropped below the national average to 23 percent. Interestingly, the northeast was the only region of the country that went counter to this trend. There, the percentage of blacks attending segregated schools actually increased during this same interval, from 43 percent to 49 percent (Hochschild 1984). The great bulk of these changes occurred quite rapidly, mostly between 1970 and 1975.

Such changes in the ethnic composition of America's schools did not, for the most part, come easily. By the early 1970s the Office for Civil Rights had investigated, negotiated with, and arm-twisted over 3,000 school districts in the South alone, and courts had handed down desegregation orders in over 150 districts (Hochschild 1984). In addition to these legal efforts, the Emergency School Aid Act (ESAA) provided funds (peaking in 1978 at $300.5 million) for schools implementing desegregation plans. Notwithstanding the occasional southern governor standing in front of a high school or university trying to bar a black from entering, desegregation efforts in the South were a cakewalk by the early 1970s compared with the explosive efforts to desegregate some Northeastern cities, of which Boston remains the most unsettling example.

For all its apparent success in significantly reducing the number of children attending segregated schools, there is considerable difference of opinion as to whether this social experiment has borne the kind of fruit once hoped for. For decades now, social scientists have differed markedly in their assessment of the impact of desegregation on minority children's educational achievement. For example, St. John, in a review of sixty-four studies, concluded that they did not provide strong, clear evidence that desegregation would rapidly close the black/white gap in achievement (1981). Other social scientists arrived at the opposite conclusion. Russell (1990), for example, argues that although the relationship is not perfectly linear, research results indicate that the greater the percentage of white students in a school, the greater the gains made by black children in that school. Indeed, Russell draws strong conclusions from her review of this literature, stating categorically that while there may be differences of opinion as to the size of this effect, the percentage of white children appears to be the "cause" of "the positive effects" of school desegregation. Similarly, Braddock and colleagues (1984), citing ten major studies that assess the social outcomes for minority adults who had a desegregated educational experience, note that all but two of the studies found that the higher the percentage of whites in school, the greater the likelihood that a black student would enroll in a white majority four-year university, have white friends, live in an integrated neighborhood, and have positive relationships with white co-workers.

Reflecting this difference of opinion among social scientists, and the stalemated consequences of it, in the Fall of 1981, before the U.S. Senate Subcommittee on the Separation of Powers, four academicians were invited to present evidence on the achievement effects of busing. Two of them testified to the positive effects of busing and two spoke of its negative effects. "It wasn't social science's best hour," commented E. Joseph Schneider, Executive Director of the Council for Educational Development. "As the hearing ended, the social scientists shook hands all around while exchanging copies of their testimony. None seemed particularly bothered by the fact that the testimony, contradictory as it was, essentially nullified any social science influence on the proposed legislation" (Scott 1981, p. 37).

278   No Dancin' in Anson

No doubt such conclusions reflect not only differences in in-
strumentation, methodology, sampling, and analysis but also
differences in ideology as these subtly infiltrate the guiding
assumptions and interests of social scientists who, as we have
just seen, at times draw opposite conclusions from the same
studies (Russell 1990). These ideological considerations are also
reflected in the shifting perspectives within minority communities on the value and desirability of desegregation. On the very
heels of the overall successes of the nation's desegregation efforts, primarily through busing and redistricting, ambivalence
about desegregation began to grow among minority constituencies. To take one illustration, in a conference report of the
National Institute of Education (1977) José Cardenas, then
director of the Intercultural Development Research Association,
argued against desegregation as the mechanism for bringing
the educational achievement of minority students up to that of
whites. Instead, he championed a shift in educational practices
that would make these compatible with the characteristics of
minority populations. The main reason for minority student lack
of performance, argued Cardenas, "is the inappropriateness of
instructional materials and methodologies for the characteristics of the minority students involved" (p. 60). "School programs
developed by and for white Anglo-Saxon, middle class, English-
speaking populations are incompatible with the non-white,
non-Anglo, non-middle class, non-English-speaking students.
Language, cultural, economic, class, mobility, and perceptual
characteristics of minority students demand a compatible educational effort" (p. 61).

In what was an expression of solidarity with Dr. Cardenas's
comments, Maria Cerda, then Executive Director of The Latino
Institute in Chicago, noted that in Chicago her organization had
been actively involved in *fighting* desegregation efforts:"We have
always been fighting for moving Hispanics together, rather than
fighting against segregation," she noted (Cardenas 1977, p. 65).

In short, just as desegregation has produced intense ambivalence within white communities, so it has within minority com-

munities. In the latter, for example, there is heightened awareness of, and sensitivity to "second generation discrimination"
reflected in such practices as tracking and different disciplin-
ary practices, which have raised the ire of minority parents. A
further question, of course, centers on the meaning of the extensive resegregation that characterizes social realities within most
contemporary American educational settings. A recent docu-
mentary film, *School Colors*, chronicles the extent to which
Berkeley High School, in California, in one of America's most
liberal communities, is rigidly and extensively ethnically segregated. In the 1960s, it was one of the first schools to desegre-
gate voluntarily. As Peter Torres noted in Chapter 5, in his
school Mexican-Americans sat on one side of the school cafeteria,
whites on another. Such facts point us in the same direction,
namely, the perpetual difficulties and complications inherent
in resolving the problem of difference.

TWO MODELS

Perhaps because there had been no way to predict the bus
program's success, since there had never been anything comparable, the Church of Christ had not anticipated how it would
manage the integration of minority children into its life. There
were different views on the matter. Some, including the Brownings, wanted to follow the same approach that Bartolomé de Las
Casas might have advocated, namely, they wanted the minority children kept in their own classes until their religious education and their socialization into the ways of the church were
sufficient for their integration into the main body of the congregation. The Brownings were aware that one of the biggest
Church of Christ congregations in Abilene had a very successful outreach program and used a similar approach. The other
faction at the Anson church felt that minority children should
be integrated immediately, not anticipating what such a
strategy would mean to the rest of the congregation. The latter
group was actually heeding one of the fundamental principles

of the Church of Christ that went back to the earliest teachings of the nineteenthcentury Restorationists, namely, that there should never be a congregation-within-a-congregation, for such an organizational structure would lead to divisiveness and undermine the Christian aims of the church.

Even at the most superficial level, there were problems with the immediate integration model. The minority children the Brownings were bringing to church did not get up on Sunday morning to a good breakfast, dress in their finest clothes, and leave for church. They often had a skimpy breakfast if they ate at all, and church clothes did not exist in their wardrobes. Typically, these children were picked up right off the street, as Browning recalled:

> They wanted to mingle them in with everybody else so we would bring them off the streets, stinking, poor, uneducated, definitely not of our culture, and we'd have to . . . get their kids with our kids to Bible class, and mix them all up in there. And what we wanted to do was have a class and teach them on their own level and then, as they learned, bring them in and integrate them. And the kids never did understand what was going on, because a lot of the old people didn't like them. They didn't like them messing up the floor, they didn't like them talking during church, they didn't like 'em crawling over seats. . . .
>
> I don't know *why* they didn't like that. It don't bother me! It was total chaos. The teachers that tried to teach them—see they were used to teaching four or five li'l ol' white kids that would sit there real still and not say nothin'. And then all at once we'd bring maybe twenty and put them in their class, and the Sunday School teachers would pull their own hair out!

Most of the minority children had never been to church and had no concept of what was expected. They often found it difficult to sit still during services because their attention spans were short. The Brownings and other families who participated in the Bus Ministry often brought candy or coloring books to entertain them, but some members of the congregation were unhappy because the children created too many distractions during services. Browning tried to defend them:

> I got up there one time and told them, "You expect these kids to be still in church. They're not going to do it. And the reason I know they're not is that one time I went deer hunting. I set up there in a tree in a blind, waitin' on them deer. And my feet were dangling and after a while I nearly died! My feet weren't touching the ground and when your feet don't touch the ground you *cain't* sit still. These kids, look at them! Their feet don't touch the floor! They're kids' feet. This church is not built for them."

One afternoon the Brownings and I sat at their kitchen table, while Bobbie wrapped trays of neatly arranged cookies she called "sandies." One of her friends was having a baby shower that evening, and the cookies were her contribution. Bobbie is a tall, slender brunette, who exudes integrity. Although Doug, as one of the church's deacons, had officially been in charge of the Bus Ministry, they had actually been full partners in this endeavor.

Bobbie Browning reminisced fondly: "During the week I'd go down to the Hatahoe and make up some ice cream cups and leave them in the freezer. And as we would come back from church on Sunday night, all in that hot bus, we'd just go by and pick up our ice cream, hand them out, and they could eat those on the way home. Well, you know what?" Bobbie's voice took on a feigned identification with her detractors, "The reason we was so successful in getting them coming to church was because we was *bribing* them." This reminded Doug of the time that Earl McCaleb, the most influential elder at the church, instructed him not to give the children any more treats. Browning still felt resentful about it.

"You know," added Bobbie, somewhat defensively, "Some Sundays we didn't. If we didn't have time, if I didn't have them made up, they didn't get their treat. Sometimes they did and sometimes they didn't, you know. And if they didn't they accepted it, but if they got one, well, they was pleased for it."

I speculated whether or not hugging the children would also have been considered a form of bribery, which really roused Doug Browning's cockles. "It's the same thing!" he said. "See, when McCaleb told me that, they had ten or twelve cases of cookies packed and ready to go to Moctezuma Creek for the Vacation Bible School [one of McCaleb's pet projects]. They told me not to give the kids here nothin', but they were going to carry the cookies out there for Vacation Bible School!"

Later, they recalled some other experiences with minority children. There was Juanita, the daughter of one of Anson's poorest families:

"Her mommy and daddy didn't speak no English either," Doug remembered. This posed a challenge for keeping her attention during the Sunday services. "To have her sit there and make her be quiet listening to the preacher for thirty minutes, that would be *dumb* wouldn't it?" Doug asked rhetorically. "We drew pictures," Bobbie added. "Juanita wasn't there to hear the preacher to begin with. She was there for the fellowship and the love that she was going to get being there." This reminded Bobbie of an infuriating incident:

When you run a bus program with kids you have lots of experiences . . . there was this boy—his name was Jimmy— that by all rightful means should never have been in church, because the life that he had at home there was no reason for him to even know who Jesus was. Jimmy was about 10 years old, and he was sitting by me, and it was getting right to the point, at the end of the sermon, where everybody's standing up, and the kid knows it's really time to go. Well, he's standing by me and he keeps going to the end of the pew, and I go and get him and I tell him, "Now come back

Jimmy, just wait a few more minutes and we'll be ready to go and you can get on the bus." He'd ease back down there and I'd go get him and bring him back, and he wasn't walking very far, and he wasn't doing anything wrong! And this ol' lady behind us, who never sat with a kid, never even spoke to one, and didn't want nothin' to do with them, she picks up her songbook, pops him on the head and says, "You listen to her! You get back over there and just mind!" I turned around and I just flared! I said "Listen! He's *my* guest and I'll take care of him!" It really made me mad.

She was 70 years old, and see, she resented those kids being there because that was *her* church. She'd gone there all her life, and you just don't bring kids into somebody's house if they don't want them in there, and that's what we did. And I think that's the reason we had so many problems because we were doing things that was against what they wanted done.... It was like two different worlds, and they expected these kids to act even better than their own kids!

"They would suffer anything for thirty minutes to be with someone that would put their arms around them," Doug added. "Did you see those pictures of some of those orphans in Romania? It showed that there was no reason for them to cry because there was nobody that ever came to take care of them and they was little zombies there? Well, I saw that right here! And the kids were just that sad and the people at church would just put their arms around them and they'd just come to *life!*"

A CLASH OF PERSONALITIES

The Bus Ministry considerably taxed both the physical and emotional resources of the Anson Church of Christ, whose members were not social planners or experts in race relations and cultural diversity. They were, for the most part, simply a group of well-intentioned individuals trying to do what they believed to be morally right. Whatever sentiments existed within some quarters in the church that disapproved of the Bus Ministry efforts on prejudicial grounds, the stresses that the program's success created even for its staunchest backers were substantial.

"This whole thing snowballed on us," Doug confessed. "See, they thought we would go out there and bring in ten or twelve kids. . . . " Not even the Brownings, in their most optimistic prognostications, thought that the bus program would attract such an overwhelming number of kids. "It got tiresome . . . ," Doug admitted. But in his view, some of the members of the congregation became concerned with the question of race: "They got afraid that if they kept this up, pretty soon those kids would marry our kids and then we'd have an interracial church. . . . It's just some excuses that started coming up."

One of the results of these problems is that Doug Browning had a head-on collision with Earl McCaleb, the influential elder. They never got along well and Browning considered McCaleb to be a person who put on airs of power and authority. There was a deep anti-authoritarian streak to Browning's personality. Although they had engaged in a series of minor skirmishes since Browning's arrival at the church, the Bus Ministry created a new arena for their antagonism. McCaleb's dour demeanor annoyed Browning, and at every opportunity Doug appeared intent on embarrassing McCaleb, countering him, or, at the very least, grabbing the spotlight and making a scene. McCaleb grew more and more tense around Browning, never quite sure how to handle him or what he might come up with next, a stance that only served to incite Browning into more acts of irreverence. The two were like oil and water, and Browning laughs as he recalls:

> McCaleb was the chief honcho, and my personality and his personality, Oooo! They were different! You talk about two that clashed! And I was young enough, and I was doing all of this good, and he was setting up there trying to keep control, and I'd antagonize him. I'd do it on purpose. I was outgoing, outspoken, laughed all the time, and he never

laughed. And I'd stick it to him 'cause he wouldn't laugh. I'd say, "If Christ can't make you happy, he can't make you anything!"

The Brownings' Bus Ministry was the biggest thorn in the side of Earl McCaleb, both because of the tensions it was producing within the church as well as the antagonisms it was creating between Browning and McCaleb. Some felt that McCaleb was worried that the influx of minority children into the church was antagonizing and alienating some of the more established church members and that Browning's success was experienced by McCaleb as competition.

"One night," Doug said, "I spoke at a devotional, and I told 'em that Christianity and dogs are a lot alike, except that when a dog quits wagging his tail and shows his teeth, you know he's fixin' to bite you. But a Christian, you don't. He shows his teeth, and you don't have a tail to watch. So I said, 'The only way you can tell on a Christian is if he's smiling. If he's not smiling, you better look out. He'll bite you.' Boy that made McCaleb mad."

On a night in June 1982, less than two years after the start of the Bus Ministry, Doug Browning received a call from one of the elders advising him that they wanted him to attend a meeting that evening. "Should I bring my Bible along?" Browning asked. "No, that won't be necessary," was the reply. Doug was excited. "They want to talk to me about teaching that class," he told Bobbie. He thought that perhaps the tensions had been resolved.

When Browning arrived for the meeting, he was brought into a room where McCaleb and three other elders were waiting for him. One of them started off by telling Browning that they had asked him to the meeting to inform him that he would no longer be permitted to teach. Despite the conflicts his ministering had sparked, Browning was nevertheless stunned. He had never imagined it would come to this. The elders told Doug that he had "lost his effectiveness," an odd comment when the problem was that the Brownings had been *too* effective. Worse, Browning was informed that he no longer had the respect or support of the congregation. "You've lost your influence and your esteem in the church," one of the elders said.

They implied that Browning's actions had been out of line: "You've done so much that nobody loves you anymore. Your effectiveness is no good. It's best for the church that you not teach that class or any other class," Browning remembers being told. Surprised at what he was hearing and intimidated at being alone and facing the four powerful elders in that small church room late in the evening, Browning felt his self-esteem crumbling. In order to regain the love he had lost, the elders went on, they wanted him to sit at the back of the church for the next two years.

"For the next two years," Browning said, "I was not to do nothin' and not say nothin'. And I was to go to the preacher's class and 'learn how to be a Christian.' Within three months the elders had even fired the preacher."

Bobbie was worried because it was late and she suspected something had gone wrong. She recalls that he came home, completely crushed, four hours later.

"I have never seen him so serious and so humble. He wasn't crying, but it was like he was empty . . . and when he told me what they said, I couldn't believe it!"

But it was true—their activities with the Anson Church of Christ were finished. They tried to go to church the next two weeks, but the feelings were almost overwhelming. "Every time I entered that building, tears would just start coming down my cheeks because I was so crushed," Bobbie remembered sadly. "I had never been hurt by family members like I was them, and even though they weren't my blood kin, they were family members. It was devastating to be divorced from the church!"

She became choked with emotion as she recalled the feelings she had not expressed to anyone in years. She seemed surprised by the intensity with which they came rushing in. "I guess it took me about eight months to get over it."

"Eight years!" Doug interjected.

THE DEMISE OF THE
OUTREACH PROGRAMS

Bobbie and Doug had poured themselves into the Bus Ministry and their Bible study classes. Nearly every day of the week they were involved in one activity or another, activities that had been the focal point for their lives, but now they were charged with seeking personal power and aggrandizement at the expense of the church. In Church of Christ vernacular, this was a significant transgression.

Doug described how the congregation then behaved toward the kids from the Bus Ministry. "You know, these kids are really sensitive, whether they want to admit it or not. They know. You can't fool them. And they started phasing out the ministry and making them feel unwelcome, and they quit coming to church. And when they quit coming other people quit coming. You're either reaching out or reaching in. And when they quit reaching out, they started devouring one another up, and then it just fell apart."

The removal of the Brownings was the first and most decisive step in the church's decision to dismantle the local programs aimed at bringing in the minority community. E. L. Ortiz's "Spanish" ministry was cancelled, as was his radio program. Finally, to add insult to injury, it was announced to the congregation that anyone wishing items stored out for needy families at the Herndon Chapel was welcome to go and take whatever he wanted. The church requested only that individuals make a donation to the church equal to the value of the items taken.

On a sunny summer day I drove out to Herndon Chapel, situated just three or four miles outside of Anson on a farm-to-market road. All that remained of the little building the Brownings had cleaned out—where E. L. Ortiz had done his preaching and where the Bible study kids had their movies and lock-ins, where the hand-me-down clothing had been neatly arranged by sizes, and the donated irons and toasters, dishes and utensils had been stored in boxes and on tables—were pieces of charred, rotting wood. The chapel had mysteriously burned down within a year after the ministry was ended. Like a perverted game of Clue, there were plenty of suspects, ranging from disgruntled Mexican-Americans to a group of adolescents who had partied there. Now, a weathered white sign that was nearly indecipherable was the only indication that the building had once been anything more than an abandoned utility shack at the edge of a cotton field.

Although the Church of Christ Bus Ministry had lasted only a year and a half, it had an effect on the lives of some who had attended. An early adolescent at the time of the program, Brenda Solis remained "an active Christian," taking people to Mexico every summer for vacation Bible classes and "converting people to Christ." Juanita Hinojosa, who did not speak English when she first started participating in the program, met Joe Garcia there. They were married at the Church of Christ after the Brownings left. But most of the children who had attended the program faded back into the world of Anson's underclass, where poverty, lack of education, and broken spirits were the main staples.

At her kitchen table, Bobbie Browning's emotions had become increasingly heavy as she reflected on these painful memories. There was something strong about her, a distinctly rural Texan dignity. "We moved over here to Anson and really got involved. And we were so excited about the things that we could see that could be done! I think we really just did too much too fast," she said sadly.

But Doug saw the limitations of such efforts in terms of racial prejudice: "It didn't work because the attitude among some church members was, you can do mission work in their house, but don't go bring them home to our house. . . . There's a cathedral in England that's got a leper's glitch, a little hole in the wall. They won't let the lepers in, but the lepers can come up and squint through that little hole in the wall and that's their religion. I think that's the way they were treating the people here.

We were letting them just squint in, saying 'You can't come in, but you can look in.'" Browning felt that his removal was at least partly a result of racial attitudes among some of the church's members:" It ended up having to do with bringing in too many of the wrong kind."

I was surprised to learn that Browning had baptized a good many of those kids, assuming that such religious rites were reserved for the local preacher, but that was not necessarily the case in the Church of Christ,.

"You could baptize people as a deacon?" I asked.

"Sure," he responded. "Just as a Christian. After we left the Anson church, I baptized two girls one afternoon in P. B. Middlebrook's swimming pool. I've baptized four or five out in a little ol' stock tank [pond] behind my house. I don't believe in distinguishing between laity and clergy. That's where I differ from a lot of people. I believe everybody is, well, I don't know, there's preachers and I'm sure there's preachers, but everybody does the work, don't they?"

After leaving the Anson Church of Christ, the Brownings attended church in Abilene on Sunday mornings, but on Sunday and Wednesday evenings, they went to a little country church in the nearby town of Truby, just a few miles down the farm-to-market road that ran past their house. Truby had only 500–600 inhabitants, but its Church of Christ was well attended, its ranks increasingly swelled by people from Anson who also had gone into spiritual exile in this neighboring community.

Doug Browning leaned back in his chair with a rueful expression on his face. He was reflecting on some of the most important years of his life. The events that he was recounting had totally absorbed him at the time; neither he nor Bobbie had quite gotten over them. He pushed his glasses back on his nose, and continued speaking softly: "We've been going out here to Truby, a little ol' country church where P. B. Middlebrook is preaching. . . . You might say we're a splinter group, too. . . . We've converted more people to Christ since we've left than all of Anson combined," he added, trying to dig up some nugget of positive emotion to counterbalance the depressive turn that the interview had taken.

They had few regrets about their activities with the children and teenagers of Anson. "If we could have taught these kids eight years ago," Browning mused, thinking about where those kids were today. "See, we started bringing these kids in when they was little bitty, and now the ones we were working with are in high school, and the teachers say that when we brought them to church and taught them to behave, when they started to school they were better kids."

Months later, when Doug, Bobbie, and I were sitting around their kitchen table, it became evident once again that the wounds from the events of those years were not entirely healed. "She buried the axe, but the handle's still there," Doug Browning said, nodding toward his wife. "She's like an old mama hen. They hurt her kids real bad up here," Browning said. "They treated them like dog meat."

Bobbie leaned closer to me: "We still have kids who come into the video store and we're still close," she said with sadness in her voice. "They want you to hug them. And I know that if we hadn't touched them like we did when they was little, that wouldn't be the case. They wouldn't go to a white person like that."

III

A
HOLLOW
VICTORY

11

Time Changes Everything and Everybody except Downright Honesty

Foreigner: a choked up rage deep down in my throat, a black angel clouding transparency, opaque, unfathomable spur. The image of hatred and of the other, a foreigner is neither the romantic victim of our clannish indolence nor the intruder responsible for all the ills of the polis. Neither the apocalypse 'on the move nor the instant adversary to be eliminated for the sake of appeasing the group. Strangely, the foreigner lives within us: he is the hidden face of our identity, the space that wrecks our abode, the time in which understanding and affinity founder. By recognizing him within our-selves, we are spared detesting him in himself. A symptom that precisely turns "we" into a problem, perhaps makes it impossible, The foreigner comes in when the consciousness of my difference arises, and he disappears when we all acknowledge ourselves as foreigners, unamenable to bonds and communities.

Julia Kristeva
Toccata and Fugue for the Foreigner,
Strangers to Ourselves

David Montejano concludes his (1987) book, *Anglos and Mexi-cans in the Making of Texas, 1836-1986,* on a hopeful note. In his examination of the threads of history governing the relations between these two ethnic groups, Montejano notes that despite the fact that the Mexican community of Texas lags far behind on all mainstream indicators in the areas of education, health,

income, and political influence, "several signs—increasing use
of English, intermarriage, upward mobility, for example—suggest a measure of integration for the Mexican-American." By
the mid-1970s the civil rights movement in Texas and the Southwest was spent, and the cultural nationalism that had governed
Mexican-American political aspirations as a means of organizing against the remnants of the old guard had given way to
internecine warfare within the Chicano movement as activists
now exchanged accusations of "selling out" and "opportunism"
(Montejano 1987).

As the Mexican-American experience became transformed by
the effects of the Civil Rights Act and the Voting Rights Act (the
latter had been extended to Mexican-Americans in the Southwest in 1975) a new set of circumstances prevailed. A weaken-
ing of racial divisions in Texas facilitated the emergence of class
interests. Community groups that once relied on the natural ties
of family, parish, and ethnicity to achieve their goals, eventually transcended these. "Once the segregationist framework had
been toppled, Mexican-Americans could press for 'previously
ethnic' issues in a 'nonethnic' manner" (Montejano 1987, p. 300).

Mercy Torres was emblematic of the developments noted by
Montejano. A woman with strong ties to her ethnic heritage and
a keen awareness of (and identification with) the civil rights
movement and the politics of ethnicity of the 1960s and 1970s,
her leadership of the Footloose Club reflected the transcendence
described by Montejano. Footloose as an organization had no
ethnic affiliation. On the contrary, it was characterized by a kind
of ethnic secularity despite the fact that Torres, with her social
activism, her dark brown skin, and her Mexican peasant dresses,
was an undeniable ethnic signifier.

It was not so much the ethnic composition of Footloose (predominantly "outsider" whites) that gave the group this transcendent quality as its vision. In their book, *Habits of the Heart,*
Bellah and colleagues (1985) note the ideals that governed Puri-
tan life: not material wealth, but the creation of a community
in which a genuinely ethical and spiritual life could be lived. As

I read this book, I remembered the afternoon when I sat in Mercy Torres's living room as she explained her "Variables Chart" to me. Her vision for Footloose was anything but narrow or parochial. She envisioned a kind of utopian social organization in which Footloose members and their children would engage their community's struggles and needs in a constructive participatory spirit. Cleaning up highways, sponsoring dances to raise funds to help the elderly, transforming the hospital basement into a tornado shelter, raising funds to help the Hornsbys pay their medical bills—these were not ideological endeavors. Indeed, there was an innocence to them, perhaps. But it is an undeniable fact that for the ten months when Footloose enjoyed an active, viable existence, it had a profound impact on the members of their little community. During those ten months the members of Footloose experienced the true meaning—along with the pains, frustrations, and gratifications—of participating in a "community of memory."

The Anson Church of Christ had in many respects embodied the kind of private religious affiliation that turns into itself, ultimately separating a church from participation in its broader community. Its morality, reflecting twentieth-century Christianity as a whole perhaps (Bellah et al. 1985), had become personal, not social; private, not public; separating its members from the wider society. Doug Browning and P. B. Middlebrook had each in his own way grappled with the question of participation in one's community. Each had sought to relate his religious convictions to the larger world, extending these into a praxis that had an impact on the cultural, social, political, and economic structures of their community. Each had taken his church beyond the confines of its private observances into the world beyond, and in doing so they ran headlong into all of the psychological and social implications of encountering the Other.

The psychoanalytic contribution to our understanding of this problematic is its deep appreciation for the complexities of self-other engagement. The psychodynamics of boundary diffusion, the anxieties attendant to threats to our sense of separateness,

the importance of the Other in constituting a coherent sense of
self-identity, are factors at play in the turbulent world of difference—be it ethnic, social, cultural, economic, religious, or
some other form. Kristeva (1991) says the foreigner lives within
us. This is a statement that carries a distinctly psychoanalytic
sensibility, as is Kristeva's recipe for transcendence: "[the
foreigner] disappears when we all acknowledge ourselves as
foreigners, unamenable to bonds and communities." To invoke
such a notion is easy. To achieve it, across the gulf of the brute
facts that constitute the history of our ethnic antagonisms, or
the deep wounds that fester closer or farther from the surface,
is unspeakably hard. Such difficulties, however, do not invali-
date the truth of Kristeva's observation. Hers is a paradoxical
movement in which we are invited (entreated?) to participate:
community becomes possible only within the acknowledgement
of our separateness, our foreignness, just as true community is
undermined by the coercive requirement of a collective identity
governed by the exigencies of ideology, faith, clan, or ethnicity.
Such paradox is captured in the word itself: to be "apart" or to
be "a part"—the roots of our difference and of our solidarity rest
in the same moment.

REPRISE

On December 6, 1987, the *Abilene Reporter News* ran an article
"Dead End for Dancing." Mercy Torres's son, Peter, president
of the Anson High School student body, and another student
council officer were pictured, glum-faced with books in hand,
standing in front of the school. The students had petitioned the
school Board of Trustees to permit school-sponsored dances.
After a closed meeting (legally only permitted to discuss per-
sonnel matters, lawsuits, and real estate purchases) the board
had met in open session, where one of the trustees entered a
motion to allow school-sponsored dances. The board then rejected the trustee's motion by a 4-3 vote. One of the board members was Mercy's husband, Salvador. He was clearly incensed

by the trustees' vote: "There is no legitimate reason why we can't have dances for the children," he said. "We don't have much to offer in this area for social events. . . . I'm for anything that will give them good, healthy entertainment under supervision." His words were hauntingly familiar. It seemed like a verbatim replay of the debates in the city council chambers earlier that spring.

The board members voting against the dancing motion claimed to be motivated by concerns that dances might cause wear and tear to school buildings. At least this was the tack that the chairman of the Board of Trustees took in public. "A gym floor is not made for dancing," he had said. But the trustees also challenged the student council representatives, suggesting that they did not reflect the wishes of the majority of students at the high school. "We're not trying to deprive our students of anything," said the Board chairman, "but we haven't heard from more than five people out of our 2,500 residents," and he couldn't see "the connection between dances and the education of students."

While for months now it had been legal for people in Anson to sponsor a dance, the teenagers whose parents had huddled together at Bea's café almost a year earlier in January of 1987 still could only go to a renegade prom. Gym floors and philosophical debates regarding educational and non-educational activities in the schools aside, a cold, hard fact loomed over the deliberations of the Board of Trustees: the majority of the board continued to consist of members from the Anson Church of Christ and the fundamentalist Baptist churches in town.

A year after the Footloose Club's Victory Dance, in the fall of 1988, Anson's dance fight seemed almost a vague memory to Paul Davidson, who had been the group's vice-president. We sat on his living room couch as he watched his children. Although it was a brisk fall day, his two sons, one still in diapers, ran in and out of the house barefoot and not warmly dressed, but apparently none the worse for wear. The small, two-bedroom, wood-frame house desperately needed paint. In front, whatever

grass there had been was now worn to the roots, the ground
beaten to a smooth surface, presumably under the feet of the
children. A rusting washing machine sat off to one side in the
front yard.

An unframed painting done by Davidson some years ago hung
on one wall. On another wall hung the plumed cow skull that
had been the logo of Davidson's band, Bittercreek. Our interview was punctuated by the kids' repeated arguments that required their father's mediation. Davidson seemed distracted by
his current plight. He had no job. His band, which had been a
source of supplementary income, had not been working much
either. Yet Davidson seemed subtly proud of his house-husband
lifestyle with its implicit critique of the mainstream establishment. Davidson, wearing Levis and a V-necked sweater, appeared thinner than when I'd met him a year earlier.

After a short stint at a local community college, Paul Davidson
had gone to work in the oil fields, a major source of employment
for rural Texas youth during the oil boom of the late 1970s and
early 1980s. There, despite his long hair, he had proven himself in the macho world of the oil fields. With the collapse of the
oil market in the mid 1980s, Davidson and his wife, Becky,
moved to Anson, her home town, where Davidson landed the
job as assistant editor for *The Western Observer*. His responsi-
bilities were diverse. Davidson wrote stories and covered local
news events, while also serving as office manager, bill-payer,
and general handyman for the newspaper. As a reporter, Davidson, an outsider, became rather well known in town. It helped
that he'd married a local girl, of course. But the fact that he
played the electric guitar in a country western band, coupled
with his longish hair, did not help integrate him into the community. In addition, although raised in the Church of Christ,
Davidson did not attend any local church. He was somewhat
cynical toward organized religion.

Davidson had been unemployed for over a year, since losing
his position as assistant editor at the culmination of the dance

fight. Though he clearly felt that his prominent involvement with the Footloose organization had played a major role in his firing, he stopped short of directly accusing the newspaper's owner, Jerry Wallace, of firing him for that reason.

Now Paul Davidson seemed a bit listless. No job. No cause. It was as if he were waiting for some inspiration to give him a reason to move on. The year had taken a toll on him. "I'm going to stay home with the children the whole year," Davidson said. "My wife's making a lot more than I could if I could get a job, so. . . ." More than anything Davidson seemed to be worn out.

By the fall of 1988, there was a notable flatness to the Footloose Club members' feelings about the events that had transpired. Perhaps it was not clear to them what had really happened. They had apparently won their struggle with the city council. That the city ordinance had been changed was irrefutable. The actual meaning of that victory, however, was unclear. What had they won? The right to dance? Or a more fundamental change in the way their community worked and lived together? Were the youth of Anson better off for their struggle? Was there a change in the way the people of Anson managed their lives?

Eighteen months after the dance fight, as I interviewed Footloose members, for the most part I found just fragments of those old ideals that had originally spurred the group. Footloose appeared to be dead in body and spirit. Davidson gave me a synopsis of what had become of most of the Footloose leadership: "Jane Sandoval moved to Abilene. She was looking for a little prestige out of this and got the opposite. She was snubbed. She changed churches after the city council meeting and started going to the Methodist Church. Donna and Lonnie Carens changed to the Methodist Church, too. Mercy's big thing now is restoring the Opera House." Later, as we sat at her breakfast table, Donna Carens proudly showed me her tickets to the Mason-Dixon concert, the victory celebration that had been Footloose's moment of glory. The tickets were pretty much all that she had left from those days.

Donna reflected on the events that had transpired that year.

> To me it was not about dancing. If I believed that dancing
> was immoral I think I would have still felt that the deci-
> sion should be mine and not the city's. You can't legislate
> morality. I have a very strong faith and a strong belief. But
> the Constitution guarantees the separation of church and
> state and that's necessary for me to have my freedom of
> worship. That wasn't the point for everybody involved. A
> lot of people were interested in dances for their children.
> To me, that was a minor thing. I wanted to go to city hall
> and say, "We don't have this right." And it took several ses-
> sions and a lot of argument and a lot of people hurt on both
> sides.

Jane Andruss, one of Footloose's founding members, was now
totally removed from Footloose and its struggles: "My personal
life has changed a great deal," she told me as we sat in her living room, having just viewed a videotape of Abilene's TV news
coverage of the infamous council meeting. "I don't have the time
to devote to Footloose now. Then I was single and not dating
anyone and had time. Now I'm dating a man and we're busy. . . .
I would have liked to have seen them push the school board to
let us have dances on school property. That's what needed to be
done. We stopped short of that."

Davidson summed it up: "It's over. There were lots of hard
feelings, lots of people had problems with it, and lots of people
felt it was time to end it."

The note of defeat was unmistakable in the reflections of this
once-vibrant group of Anson citizens. "Through the whole thing,"
Davidson said, "there was a lot of fear. We weren't fighting
dancing, we were fighting some sort of fear." It was fear linked
to those primordial, tribal instincts that make change and
difference so threatening. Perhaps fear had won after all. After
the "victory" party at Pioneer Hall, Footloose's efforts to hold
additional dances there had been completely thwarted. The

farmer who had made his barn available to Footloose was no longer willing to do so. The board of the Cowboys' Christmas Ball Association was not interested in renting the Pioneer Hall to Footloose for reasons that were not clear. "Nobody will rent space to us," Davidson said with a sense of frustration. "After the victory dance, that fear set in again."

The year had been a heady time for Footloose. They had accomplished a great deal, and most important of all, they had led an unprecedented successful challenge against city hall. Or so it had seemed. Now, almost all the Footloose members questioned what had really been gained. Their victory seemed to have evaporated. Footloose itself had fallen into disarray. The baton was passed on to new officers who lacked the leadership and influence of a Mercy Torres. Members' interest dwindled. Perhaps, like Paul Davidson, they had just grown tired.

Davidson was the unofficial Footloose "historian," and his array of Footloose materials was in shambles. He was unsure if he still had his clippings in order. The collection was stored in a cluttered cardboard box, an ignominious ending to the little group that, like David against Goliath, had risen so bravely to face the Anson Church of Christ and other representatives of a local power elite. "To be honest, I'm not sure there *is* a Footloose anymore," Davidson said ruefully.

The struggle that Footloose sparked within the community, that had galvanized it, represented a loss of innocence for Anson. For years, the little West Texas town had been gradually changing. Social and economic structures were being reshaped by forces beyond the control of the local populace. Like some kind of diagnostic dye, the conflict over dancing had made visible what was once obscure and imperceptible. The tissues that held this town together, that *constituted* this town, were different from those of just twenty or twenty-five years ago. Most citizens, especially those white families who had been here for many generations, did not fully recognize how *really* different the community had become. Footloose and its actions changed that.

The conflict between the old and the new in Anson was summarized most succinctly by Jane Sandoval's comments to a reporter: "Most of the ones who were really working at fighting the dancing ordinance were new people in town. We weren't people who had been raised here. We weren't concerned about stepping on the toes of a friend of great grandmother's, because we didn't have those ties. Our ties were in other communities. So we were free to do what we felt was the right thing to do."

Back in his living room, Paul Davidson drew heavily on his cigarette and slouched on the tattered couch with an air of satisfaction. "I've still got three copies of that *Texas Monthly* [that featured him]. It's great! Like Andy Warhol's fifteen minutes of fame. That's my fifteen minutes of fame! I like the photograph from the *Dallas Morning News* best, because he let me keep my sunglasses on!" That familiar wry, impish smile broke across his face again. Perhaps, for Paul Davidson, the struggle had not been entirely in vain.

MELTING POT OR ETHNIC PRIDE?

America once prided itself as the world's melting pot. In the rest of the world people were locked into static roles limited by class, race, or religion, but in America, so the belief went, immigrants could shed those yokes for boundless opportunities. Prior to the '60s, a good number of white Americans could describe their ethnicity as the "Heinz 57 variety"—a way of playfully celebrating the fact that they were the products of such extensive interbreeding that their ancestry was virtually untraceable. The very designation "American" evoked an individual whose essence was a kind of genetic amalgam, whose prior ethnic history was thoroughly blended. If on other continents purity of lineage was revered, America seemed to delight in its success at transcending such notions. This mindset descended from the populist spirit that reigned in the colonies prior to the American Revolution.

The 1960s brought to light the limits of this collective myth, revealing that the "Heinz 57 variety" in reality referred to a certain pool of assimilative possibilities. For example, most of the descendants of African slaves remained absolutely marginalized—deeply in the shadows at the historical moment when the American Dream seemed to reach its pinnacle. Other people "of color" similarly grew restive in the face of what seemed an unattainable aim: a life of social and economic parity with those whose ancestry was primarily derived from Eastern or Western Europe. The consensual myth that America was the world's ethnic melting pot started to show cracks.

America faces a daunting task: how to fashion a society with sufficient consensus to reasonably accommodate ethnic, religious, and economic differences. These differences have deep roots intermingled into an immensely dense and complex web of psychological and sociological elements. Nevertheless, it is such a consensus that provides us with a common basis with which to live together. In *Democracy in America*, de Tocqueville (1969) outlined a formula for the key contributory elements that made democracy viable: family life, political participation, and religious life. It is these elements, de Tocqueville suggested, that link individuals within communities to the wider society.

In contemporary America, diversity has become the watchword in part because we have become, in fact, so diverse. There are three primary constituents of this new diversity: the historical white majority, Americans once on society's margins who now insist on full inclusion, and the new immigrants, who bring with them a great variety of languages and cultures. Today's America is increasingly fragmented. While imparting a spirit of respect and tolerance for difference, the contemporary vision of American pluralism, as a guiding philosophy for the nation, also invites a retreat from true engagement with the Other. At heart, pluralism is a centrifugal rather than a centripetal force. The integrationist vision of Martin Luther King Jr. has been replaced by the separatist vision of the young Malcolm X. Not withstanding the gains of blacks in the South, Americans live more segregated lives today than ever (*New York Times*, July 31, 1994). The same article quotes a black woman who reveals the paradox of the current situation: "We [blacks in the pre-civil rights south who lived in their own communities] were in a cocoon bathed in a warm fluid, where we were expected to excel . . . and then something called desegregation punctured it. We went from our own land to being tourists in someone else's. It never did come together, and I think it's on the verge of falling apart altogether now."

There may be less trust, and greater enmity between blacks and whites now than at any point since the early 1960s when the civil rights movement forced the question of race relations into the open. Tribalisms are resurging rather than receding. In the present-day South, according to Peter Applebome, "For every Malcolm X cap worn by a black, there's a T-shirt worn by a white with the Confederate battle flag and the slogan 'You Wear Your X, I'll Wear Mine'" (*New York Times*, August 3, 1994).

In *Habits of the Heart*, Bellah and colleagues (1985) note that the vitality of a culture, by which they mean the vitality of its symbols, ideals, and ways of feeling, "is always an argument about the meaning of the destiny its members share. Cultures are dramatic conversations about things that matter to their participants. . . ." In contemporary America that argument is unquestionably alive. It is by turns pointed, acrimonious, and heated, but it is alive. This suggests that the much-maligned notion of the American Dream still has considerable play in our lives, notwithstanding the challenges that face us as a society. Our fate as a people lies in this conversation happening all over America as the issue of ethnicity permeates the consciousness of the nation.

Powerful psychological forces complicate the attainment of these goals. Among our earliest organizing experiences of infancy, just as we begin to have consciousness of a reality beyond the psychological enclosure of the maternal holding environment, is the discovery of "the stranger," the Other. It is a discovery that to a greater or lesser extent stirs anxiety and fear in every human infant (Mahler et al. 1975, Spitz 1965). The social universe of human beings becomes dichotomous. It also becomes increasingly or more consciously and explicitly cultural, mediated by the infinite cultural signifiers with which parents wrap a child's life. Thus, people come to know that there are those who are part of me, and those who are not me. Every child, and later every adult, bifurcates the social world into good and bad, ally and enemy (Volkan 1988).

What we consider good and sustaining we try to bring into closer proximity to ourselves. What we consider bad and anxiety provoking we try to keep out. When that badness is a part of ourselves, it creates tension and anxiety that threaten our inner equilibrium. Such experienced inner badness, therefore, is projected onto others, creating the basis for the universal, normal paranoid processes that govern all human groupings (Bion 1959). In times of stress or uncertainty, such normal paranoid processes become pathologically exacerbated because we feel increasingly vulnerable. Splitting as a defensive mechanism becomes more entrenched and pervasive, and the Other is more readily dehumanized and viewed as a container of all badness including greed, sexuality, and aggression. In this context, the real transgressions and injustices experienced by a people (individually and collectively) become harder to set aside. On the contrary, they are given new life in the psychologies of those who have lived them. The world of allies becomes more tightly held and desperately sought. The world of enemies is experienced as more alien and more threatening than ever.

Martin Luther King Jr. speaks to our need for allies. The young Malcolm X speaks to our need for enemies. King speaks to the inclusive, incorporative, assimilative impulse. The young Malcolm X speaks to the differentiating, separating, individuating impulse. Both are basic, irreducible elements of human psychology: a complementary series that may be as essential for human social life as it is associated with complications and problems in living with one another. Neither impulse can be dismissed or exorcised. The challenge is how to temper them so that our painful and divisive histories can be tolerated within a shared, collective identity.

A RURAL ROMEO AND JULIET

The wedding was registered in the Jones County records office in the cold, sparse way in which bureaucratic machinery reduces personal realities to their lowest common denominator. It gave the dates of birth of Ramiro Perez Jr. (May 20, 1968) and Stephanie L. Lollar (May 3, 1970). They had been married on May 16, 1988, less than two weeks after Stephanie's eighteenth birthday, that arbitrary social divide at which individuals suddenly become adults and are no longer subject to the dictates of their parents. Leon Sharp, the preacher at the Anson Church of Christ, had married them.

The marriage of Ramiro and Stephanie had especially stirred up Anson's gossip mill. By local standards the Lollars were a prominent and relatively wealthy family. Steve Lollar, Stephanie's father, owned a successful welding business in town; he was also county commissioner and deacon at the Church of Christ. In yet another battle in the ongoing internecine war at the church, Lollar had recently feuded with Earl McCaleb. The confrontation culminated in McCaleb's stepping down from the eldership.

The Lollars had been in Anson for generations. They were among the pillars of the community. Ramiro's father, on the other hand, was an oil pump inspector, a descendant of generations of migrant farmers. Ramiro was Mexican-American and Stephanie was white. They came from two different spheres of the social universe, and this was troublesome to many of the townspeople.

"Used to be when people learned someone was getting married they'd ask if he was Church of Christ," one member of the church commented to me. The man paused to give full effect to his irony, "Now they ask if he's white."

Although such unions were on the rise and Stephanie was not the first white in Anson to marry a Mexican-American, most of the community was particularly perplexed by this marriage, mainly because Stephanie seemed to have it all. She was an attractive, petite brunette, a local "rich girl" with her own late-model car and fashionable clothes from the best shopping mall in Abilene. She was bright and had been accepted at Abilene Christian University for the coming fall semester, the school attended by the brightest children of Church of Christ families. The Lollars would be paying all of Stephanie's college expenses.

Ramiro, on the other hand, came from a relatively poor family who lived in a little cluster of homes on the outskirts of town known locally as Ramosville. He was a nice, handsome young man, whose family was honest and hardworking, but they lived in a completely different social niche from the Lollars.

The Lollars had panicked when Stephanie's involvement with Ramiro became increasingly serious. They tried everything to prevent her from seeing him; They tempted her with a new car. When that failed to produce the desired response, they threatened to take the car away. That didn't work either. The Lollars then sent her to stay with relatives. Despite all these efforts, nothing seemed to dilute Stephanie's determination to be with Ramiro. As soon as she turned 18, she went through with her plans to marry the boy from Ramosville.

Ramosville is three miles due west of Anson on a narrow road bordered by cotton fields. Toward the end of July, the cotton crop was knee-high and a deep emerald green. Two rows of cotton were planted, with three empty rows between, a pattern repeated over and over as directed by the U.S. Department of Agriculture, which had divined via some incomprehensible formula how much cotton could be sold, how much surplus could be absorbed, and how much they would pay farmers for the unplanted rows. The fields on the way to Ramosville were not planted in straight lines. They formed graceful, slowly arching curves of green. From the air they must have looked like those beautiful Peruvian land paintings that can only be fully appreciated from above.

"When you see a big white farm house on the right, you'll notice a little road coming in to your left. You can see their houses scattered all around up there," I was told by a patron at

Bea's café. The white house stood alone amid the open fields, stately. It couldn't be missed. A narrow dirt utility road started there and seemed to drift into the infinity of the fields beyond. The farmer had eight or ten empty cotton trailers sitting there in a cluster. Some clumps of cotton that had been snagged in the wire siding of the trailers had managed to hold on and avoid being sucked up by the giant vacuums that drew the cotton into the cavernous entrails of the cotton gin. The clumps swayed triumphantly in the wind. Nearby, the various contraptions that farmers hitch onto their big tractors to plant, weed, spray, strip, and reap rested haphazardly like so many abandoned toys. They represented an investment of hundreds of thousands of dollars.

Ramosville. For two or three years I had heard about it. It had a certain mystique in Anson. The little colony had been started by a Mexican-American whose family kept building homes around each other in a cluster.

I turned off the main road and proceeded a short distance to a small, wood-frame house. Two metal poles about twenty-five feet high held up a large rectangular sign that read "Los Perez." Only Ramiro Perez, Sr., the father of the recent groom, was at home. His wife had taken the grandchildren into Abilene to see a movie. Mr Perez was outside working on the chassis of a 1959 Chevrolet pickup that he was restoring. The metal frame, with four tires and a steering column, was all there was to the pickup. He sat next to a bucket of sand and a blasting machine he was using to remove the old paint and rust from the chassis. Sand was everywhere, including in his hair.

Perez extended his hand. He was a short, robust, dark-haired man in his mid-fifties. His grip was firm and rough as he looked me in the eye with a bit of reserve. He started talking about his work on the pickup. He was painting the chassis to protect it from rust, having already put in new brake drums and brake lines. He spoke mostly in Spanish, punctuating his speech here and there with words derived from English: "la *trocka*," "es un *fifty-nine Chevy*," "nos fuimos en la *pickup*."

As we talked, Perez brightened somewhat. He opened the door to the large garage where the rest of the old pickup was stored in pieces—doors, windows, splash guards, and fenders. The parts had been sanded and sprayed with primer. He showed me where the door had been severely dented, but now was perfectly smooth. All of the original paint had been removed. The speedometer and odometer were housed in a handsome v-shaped display—the odometer read 90,000 plus miles. The place was a veritable body shop. I thought it was a '56 Chevrolet, but Ramiro quickly corrected me, *"No, es cinquenta-y-nueve"* (No, it's a fifty-nine). *"Mire nomás,"* he said, *"va a quedar muy bien"* (It's going to turn out real nice). Behind the pickup's cab was a 1965 Ford Mustang, completely restored. It looked brand new. "I've been offered over five grand for it," Perez said, "but I'm not selling it."

We stepped back out into the July morning. It was clear, dry, almost fresh. We walked over to his 1990 pickup truck, which, Ramiro informed me, was equipped with an overdrive. The pickup was furnished by Permian Oil, a large company with production in over twenty states. He worked as an inspector for oil pumps and covered a vast area, sometimes ranging as far as 250 miles from home. Each pump required a yearly inspection, and any needed repairs were made by Ramiro as well. The bed of the pickup was crammed with equipment and tools.

"Before Ramiro and *la* Stephanie got married," he told me, "my in-laws avoided me. I think he'd see my green truck coming. You could see it for miles." He laughed and went on. "Sometimes he'd turn and head the other way. Now it's not like that. He's polite. We treat each other with courtesy. Not more, but not less either."

Ramiro opened the glove compartment and took out a parts catalogue for vintage Chevrolet cars. *"Mire,"* he said, "every part I need for my pickup I can get here, but it's expensive." A pair of 1959 hubcaps, small ones, cost $144. He had tried to salvage as much as possible from the original. Fifty-nine pickups were rare in junk yards, but Perez looked whenever he had the opportunity. "Since I drive all over the state," he said, "I never know what I might find."

"This is how I spend my time," Ramiro said. "I love to work on these things. At least it's doing something constructive. When I get home from work, or on the weekends, or just whenever I'm in the mood, I get a lot of enjoyment out of this."

I asked Ramiro about his son's marriage to Stephanie. He replied that he had been worried when they started going out. Stephanie was not the first *bolilla* that young Ramiro had dated, and always the relationships had ended in problems. The *bolillos* didn't want their daughters going out with *Mexicanos*. That was their business. At first, he had tried to tell him to marry a Mexican girl, but when his son persevered, Perez backed him all the way.

Perez was born in Mercedes, Texas, in the Rio Grande Valley. In English, the town's name is pronounced like the expensive German car. In Spanish, the word has a softer, more religious meaning derived from the word "merced," or "mercy." The Perez family followed the crops out of the valley as migrant workers until he was 11 or 12 years old, when he came to stay in Anson for two years. He remembers those early days vividly and with some bitterness. "In the Valley, Mexicans were treated like everybody else, but up here it was different. It was *real* different."

Perez told how restaurants in town, like Bea's café, made him go to the back door to place an order and made him eat out back as well. He recalled the soda fountain where one could order drinks or sandwiches but could not eat them there. In the movie house, only white people could sit downstairs; Mexicans and blacks sat up in the balcony. This was only twenty-five years ago. He had not forgotten.

"I don't shop down there much," he said. "If I need something, I go to Abilene." Despite the fact that Bea's café had not had a "Whites Only" sign for years, Perez would not set foot in it. The memories were still fresh. (I remembered Jack Hornsby's statement: "There's not a Spanish person in this town that won't holler at me . . . but they do not trade with me.")

"Pásele pa' dentro," (come inside) he said. He wanted to show me photographs of his family. The house was clean and orderly

with the walls virtually unadorned. A wooden shelf behind the living room couch held a variety of family photographs. In addition to Ramiro Jr., Perez and his wife had another son and a daughter, both also married. The photographs in the living room included several of Ramiro, Jr. and Stephanie's daughter, Lana Jill, a beautiful 18-month-old toddler, sitting up straight in a smart white dress with royal blue stripes. She had an engaging smile. I thought she resembled Stephanie. But before I could utter the thought, Ramiro noted how she really did not look like a *bolilla* with her big brown eyes and brown hair. *"Parece una Mexicanita, mire nomas,"* he said, using the affectionate diminutive form. He was a proud grandfather who felt quite warmly toward his little granddaughter.

This child forged a link between two different cultures, two different world views, now permanently joined by virtue of her being. It required no effort on her part. Her mere existence created an undeniable fact that members of her two families had to assimilate into their respective lives.

After their wedding, Stephanie and Ramiro had moved to Snyder, Texas, where he was employed as a prison correctional officer. Recently, they had moved back to Anson and he now commuted the sixty miles to Snyder, sharing rides with another correctional officer who also lived in Anson. Stephanie was employed at Doug Browning's video store. Stephanie and Ramiro now had a newborn, Daniel, who was eighteen months younger than Lana Jill.

When the Footloose Club had organized its challenge against the city fathers Stephanie had been relatively disinterested. "I could understand both sides," Stephanie commented. "With the religious background I was raised with, I could understand the opposition to dancing, but I could also understand my friends, because it was a stupid law." Stephanie had attended the victory party at the old Pioneer Hall despite the fact that her father was a deacon at the Church of Christ.

Her religious convictions were not the primary force behind her relative disinterest in the dancing controversy. It was her

sweet adolescent rapture. The only thing she could think about
was being with Ramiro, and the feeling was mutual.

Tragically, if inevitably, the problem was that their love could
not exist exclusively within the confines of their time together.
It existed within a community directly involved in their choices,
whether they wanted it that way or not. The reaction of the
Lollar and Perez families was just the beginning. Everyone in
Anson had something to say about this relationship. Their relationship had broken a taboo.

Stephanie remembered, "It wasn't just my parents, it was
everybody else. There were rumors going around. We just wanted
to be together. We wanted people to leave us alone. . . . Even
one of my friends said later that when Laurie [Hornsby] shot
herself, 'Everything that Stephanie is doing to her parents is
just as bad as what Laurie did to hers.'"

Despite their strong opposition, after the marriage took place,
the Lollars worked to accept the unacceptable. "My dad and
mom, as soon as we got married, were real nice to Ramiro,"
Stephanie recalled. "They were trying to make life easier, I
suppose. At first I didn't want to go to my parents' house," she
continued. "There was too much tension. It was awkward. But
they got to know Ramiro and he got to know them, and, don't
get me wrong, it's not as though either side will ever forget. . . ."
Stephanie's voice trailed off. She was incapable of downplaying
the full repercussions of that turbulent time in their lives. After
a moment, she continued. "Yesterday Ramiro worked with my
dad all day. And when they go on vacation, they leave him the
car keys and the keys to the house. If anything, they take his
side of things."

As she reflected on their marriage, Stephanie felt it had met
the test of time. "People wouldn't have given you a dime for our
marriage," Stephanie recalled. "People would say 'give them six
months, six months and it'll all be over.'"

Toward the end of our interview, as I remembered all the
versions I'd heard about their courtship and marriage, I asked
her the obvious question. Here was a young white girl who had

social status, a new car, admission to Abilene Christian University. What were her thoughts, I wondered, as she looked back.

"Everybody thought I had the world at my feet, but I didn't feel like I did, because what I wanted was Ramiro," Stephanie reflected. "I loved the new car, but it wasn't worth it to me. . . ." Stephanie's only regret, shared by Ramiro, was that they had not gone on to get a higher education. When living in Snyder each had enrolled in some college courses at the local community college, but with two young children, their educational plans were on long-term hold.

Finally, this marriage represented a personal confrontation with the changes in Anson and similar towns not only in the Southwest but throughout America. The roots of this event ran deep and wrapped themselves around social structures that were a way of life in this community and others like it. The changes in Anson became immediate and real in this Anglo-Mexican union.

THE EXILES AT THE TRUBY CHURCH OF CHRIST

The Truby Church of Christ is a small, white structure that sits back about thirty yards from the road linking Anson with the little town of Truby and its 600 or so inhabitants. A peeling black-and-white sign lists the hours for services and invites passersby to come worship. There is a beauty to the church, a sort of pastoral purity to it, as it stands in contrast to the lush green fields behind and around it. The congregation at Truby was primarily comprised of expatriate members of the Anson church. It is here that P. B. Middlebrook had come to preach and also the church the Brownings had joined.

On the Sunday after Easter in the spring of 1991, there was a sprinkling of cars in the parking lot. Inside, the church seemed even smaller—a single room not much bigger than the average suburban living room. The church reflected the austere aesthetics of Church of Christ worship that could be traced to Zwingli's brand of sixteenth-century Protestantism. The wooden walls

and ceiling were painted white and were without decoration
except for delicate translucent curtains that framed the windows
along the side walls. A dusty basket of artificial red geraniums
graced a table off to the side of the pulpit. They were clearly
an oversight rather than an attempt to decorate the church—
someone had forgotten to put them away.

Doug Browning stood at the door with P. B. Middlebrook,
shaking hands with the arriving worshipers. It was a bright,
clear day, with a light wind blowing out of the east. Promptly
at eleven o'clock, the doors were closed and Browning walked
to the front of the church.

"There are some new faces here today and we'd like to welcome you to the Truby Church of Christ," Browning said, referring to my photographer and me. He asked if anyone had any
announcements. Two people were named who were ill and
not present, one apparently dying of cancer. Middlebrook announced that he had received a call last night from George
Brown, a Navajo Indian, who had just learned that his sister,
27 years old, had also been diagnosed with cancer—probably
inoperable.

"The Navajo have names just like us," Middlebrook said. "Of
course they also have Indian names. George has asked us to
remember his sister and keep her in our prayers in hope that
God will be able to help her recover." The call from George
Brown reflected Middlebrook's impact on some of those to whom
he had ministered while on the Indian reservation. They may
not have been "true" Christians to some of the elders at the
Anson Church of Christ, but they were real people to Middlebrook. Years after his missionary work he still received phone
calls from Española, New Mexico, and Moctezuma Creek, Utah,
from people whose lives he had touched, wanting him to marry
their children, or bury their parents, or counsel them in times
of difficulty. In short, Middlebrook still played a role in defining moments in peoples' lives. If some of the elders had reservations about the authenticity of Middlebrook's Christian work
in New Mexico and Utah, the calls and letters constituted in-

controvertible evidence that something genuine had happened there, whether or not one chose to call it Christian.

Middlebrook was about to sit down when he suddenly remembered a woman sitting in the back pew. "I'm sorry," Middlebrook said after a moment's pause, "I almost forgot Catrina and her daughter who just lost her baby last night. She's at the Anson hospital recovering. Please keep her in your prayers too." Another of Catrina's daughters is the young woman whose wedding I had attended, a wedding officiated by Middlebrook at the "Peanuts" building in Anson. He sat down next to his wife, Dorothy. His mother, nearly 90 years old, was also at church that morning, as were his daughter, son-in-law, and several grandchildren. The Middlebrook clan accounted for a notable subset of the congregation.

The church felt diminutive and cozy inside, with only seven rows of pews on each side of the center aisle. It was mysteriously serene, very different from the sense of the unfathomable that one gets in the great cathedrals and ornate chapels. The church reflected its members in its absolute lack of pretense. The light shining through the windows took on an evanescent, ethereal quality, accentuating the simple beauty of the church's interior. Along the back wall, a hat rack bore three or four fine Stetsons, along with a number of more modest straw western hats and gimme caps. Only Middlebrook and the preacher, Brother Kenny Crow, wore ties. (Middlebrook had retired from preaching a few months earlier.)

Doug Browning, now standing at the pulpit, spoke casually, colloquially, to the assembled. There was no barrier of formality between him and the congregation. There was no effort to invoke the power and authority of the divine, which is what I reflexively expected. The informality was as disarming as it was refreshing. A sign behind Browning noted the number of people in attendance (71) on Easter Sunday. The money collected to-date for the year, also noted on the same sign, was $1,872.13.

The members of the Truby Church of Christ had decided not to have elders or deacons. There were no education committees, or membership committees, or missionary work committees, or any other type of formal church structure for that matter. The exiles from the Anson church still felt the sting of the power struggles and influence that had characterized the church hierarchy there. Here things were different. When necessary, a meeting was held before or after church services to decide what pressing issues required a response from the congregation. The money they had accumulated went primarily to help fellow church members in need. The decision to give, and the amount to be given, were communal decisions.

The song books in the pews were worn from years of use: the pages were bent smooth and felt brittle to the touch. Mine was missing the satin page marker. They were hand-me-downs, as were the church pews, donated by a wealthier Abilene church that had been renovated and that had purchased new song books. The pews had replaced the plain wooden benches, which for years had provided the seating at the Truby Church of Christ. Before the two ceiling fans were installed, and before the new pews arrived, worshipers' perspiration made them stick to the benches during summer services. "You wouldn't wear your good clothes out there," one church member noted.

Doug Browning pulled out a chewing gum wrapper on which he had written the numbers of the songs the congregation would be singing that morning. He announced a number in the songbook and, following a slight pause, launched into the first song. The Church of Christ belief that the human voice is the only musical instrument worthy of the Lord's house has resulted in a rich tradition of vocal music. Accordingly, all thirty or so voices sang *a capella,* with men's and women's voices periodically diverging to sing different harmonic or contrapuntal lines.

As the singing continued, I found myself experiencing an intense, peculiar inner force. The power of the music was regressive, enveloping. I felt my rational faculties dissolving in a strange emotional vortex as the small congregation sang on. It was primarily the music, but it was also the setting, the lack of pretense, the hopefulness, the simple curtains fluttering in the breeze, lost in the plain whiteness of the church. It took all of my force of will to muscle down the impulse to leave the church in what would have been an act of self-preservation.

Fortunately, there were only three songs. Those initial moments of the service became an experience I find perplexing to this day. My skepticism was momentarily shaken. Like an anthropologist on the verge of being swept away by some primitive rite, I felt rescued by the silence. The spell was broken and the service moved ahead to its next phase.

Middlebrook and a local rancher named J. L. Beasley served communion. Juanita Beasley, the rancher's wife, had been president of the Cowboys Christmas Ball Association for years. Doug Browning announced for the visitors' benefit that the Church of Christ believes that anyone may participate in the communion service who feels so moved and whose conscience is sufficiently clear. A silver-colored aluminum tray was passed around containing two or three large portions of unleavened bread from which each person could break a piece. This was followed by a different tray holding thimble-sized plastic glasses of grape juice. After the offering basket was passed, Browning led in another song. Finally it was time for the sermon.

Brother Kenny stepped up to the pulpit. He seemed a bit nervous. He was in his late twenties, wearing a light blue tie that matched his eyes perfectly, with a fishing rod tie clip. Brother Kenny apologized for the possibility that what he was going to say might offend some people. He had prepared his sermon without knowledge of some of the breaking news. He was referring to the woman who had just lost her grandchild. He recalled working last summer in his father's pathology lab, looking at diseased flesh and healthy flesh under a microscope. He had a strange fascination with death, he said. He remembered seeing a cadaver in the morgue and it reminded him of the many times he had been asked, in his Baptist youth, "Are you ready? If you were to die today would you be ready?"

Using a strategy that betrayed the extent to which pop psychology has infiltrated every nook and cranny of contemporary

American culture, substituting prefabricated, conjured experience for the spontaneous and organic, Brother Kenny asked the
congregation to close their eyes and recall their earliest memories, then gradually brought them to the present. What were
the regrets? What did they wish they hadn't done? What would
they like to take back? Then he instructed the congregation to
open their eyes again.

"If you were to die today, would you be ready?" he asked.

The congregation was silent except for several babies who
fussed. Brother Kenny asked the congregation to close their eyes
and said:

> Now imagine you are a bull rider at the rodeo. You sit down
> on that big bull in his chute, tie yourself to him with the
> leather straps. In that small space you can feel the heat of
> the animal and its power. Then suddenly you're out of the
> chute, you're flailing wildly trying to hold on as long as
> possible, and you are able to do it until the bell rings and
> you jump off of that wild raging bull, and you start head-
> ing back toward the fence when all of a sudden everything
> goes black.

After a moment's pause Brother Kenny instructed everyone
to open their eyes.

"That's a true story," he said. Apparently a famous rodeo bull
rider had died in just this manner. "He rode bulls right here in
our very own Joe C. Long Arena. He was a world-class bull rider.
It had been a great ride. He'd scored nine-something and he
must have felt great. Then, suddenly, the bull turned and charged
and killed him. It's a true story."

Brother Kenny paused for effect. "Are you ready if your time
comes? Are you ready to die today?" He asked this in earnest, not
figuratively. Then he closed with a prayer, asking God to look
after all those who were present and to help us live good lives.

Browning led a closing song, after which he smiled his distinctive, wry smile and simply said, "That's it. Ya'll can go home

now. Please join us back here at 6 P.M. if you can make it for our evening service."

Middlebrook and Browning, well-known members of the Anson Church of Christ, had been expelled. They had both been missionaries, one working local "foreign" territory, the other farther removed geographically. Both had entered that danger-ous terrain where the "we" and the "not-we" come into contact—a treacherous area of experience where one's basic psychologi-cal/cultural moorings easily become threatened. The existence of the Other poses challenges. The Other must either be brought into the self, or severed from it. As Browning put it one day at the Hatahoe, "If we didn't change them, the day would come when they would change us."

Like all missionaries, Middlebrook and Browning endeavored to change the Other. In the process they themselves were changed. Middlebrook's inner torment, and the arguments with his fellow elders as to who had changed the most, made this abundantly clear. The potential alteration of the self via "con-tamination" with the Other elicits anxiety and is therefore often avoided. Like Bartolomé de Las Casas before them, the price of engaging the Other had been costly in personal and social ways for Middlebrook and Browning.

I will confess that leaving the Truby Church of Christ that morning I experienced utopian thoughts. The church seemed to represent a triumph of the human spirit. The expatriates from the Anson church had not fallen into a hopeless despair. Rather, they had regrouped in this modest church in an effort to carry on. The congregation seemed a cohesive little cluster of human-ity, turning within itself to find strength and succor.

THE DREAM OF COMMUNITY

On a wintry December evening in 1990, the road into Anson from Abilene was desolate. The little white Baptist church by the roadside looked serene, almost lonely. Its bright red neon sign still announced the same simple message: "Jesus Saves."

There was something contradictory about the incandescent brilliance of the red neon and the plain understatement of the church itself. Perhaps the aesthetic intent was to suggest that only a spiritual link to Jesus can make one truly alive. But the conflicts within the little town of Anson, Texas showed just how complex and difficult is the human struggle to live the good life. The lights of Anson seemed brighter than usual in the crisp winter darkness. The entire town was nestled like a cluster of sparkling diamonds surrounded by the West Texas plains. For a moment, all the tensions and conflicts that characterize human lives seemed to have vanished. From the vantage of that little rise in the "Big Country" plain, those sparkling lights could not be separated into Church of Christ lights, Methodist lights, Mexican lights, black lights, white lights, rich lights or poor lights. They simply stood together in a natural coherence, a natural grace. It seemed momentarily that this was what everyone in Anson wanted, what everyone everywhere wanted: the elusive human dream of community.

Anson's streets were nearly deserted. Behind the Church of Christ, in a corner of the parking lot, a special garage was in mid-construction to house the church's expensive new bus, now used to ferry retirees into Abilene's mall rather than poor minority kids to church. Down the street, at Bea's café, a light was on in the kitchen, but the café was empty. At the softball field, near Anson's junior high school, a young couple sat in a shiny, black pickup truck listening to Randy Travis sing "On the Other Hand"—a song about a man caught between the temptations of infidelity and marital commitment. The couple giggled and laughed and flirted with one another, oblivious to the world beyond the cab of the pickup truck.

At the Jones County Courthouse, the statue of Anson Jones, the last president of the Republic of Texas, faced south toward Abilene. It is rumored that following the Civil War, many of the state buildings in Texas were built facing South as a final act of defiance against the victorious North. A pickup drove by with three teenagers in the cab and another four in the back. The four huddled in back had only denim jackets to protect them from the cold.

Anson seemed lost in time. But time, for better or for worse, was catching up. The new highway brought the shopping malls of Abilene closer. The local video store carried all the latest movies. In the comfort of one's own living room, sitting in front of the television, one could just as well be in Pittsburgh, or Chicago, or Los Angeles as in West Texas. Like the rest of West Texas, Anson was rapidly being enveloped by the great homogenization process that was stripping the last vestiges of distinctiveness from America's regional character. According to Tom Isbell, the newly elected city council member whose defection from the fundamentalists at their final meeting with the city council had been pivotal to Footloose's victory, it was probably only a matter of time before a bypass was built on U. S. Highway 277, which would reduce to a trickle any business Anson got from the north-south traffic linking Abilene to communities like Stamford, Haskell, and ultimately Wichita Falls, to the north. Isbell was now the president of the Anson Chamber of Commerce. It was speculated that there might be some employment generated by the bypass; perhaps a motel might be built there. No doubt the major twenty-four-hour, one-stop convenience chains would build out on the bypass, and it was rumored that a "fancy" restaurant might be built there as well. But such vague promises were not reassuring to Tom Isbell or Anson's other residents. They knew that in all likelihood the bypass, if approved, spelled doom for the community. Local businesses were only barely holding on now. Few thought they could survive such a development. The news of the bypass plans only darkened the bleak picture of Anson's situation. Cotton prices were strongly subsidized, and there were perennial congressional debates about reducing or dismantling these subsidies all together. This would open up American markets to less expensive cotton grown abroad.

Anson was braced for the worst. There were other developments that left the citizenry feeling concerned about its future. The fall of 1990 ushered in one dismal news item after another.

At a recent school-board trustees' meeting, a group of white parents had voiced concern that the high school had become a dangerous place because of a new threat: youth gangs whose members were mostly Mexican-American. The parents said that their children were afraid to stay for after-school activities such as band and football because of the physical threats that they had received or witnessed.

"As surely as some parents abuse their children through harassment and physical abuse, our schools—you, the school board and administration—are turning your heads away from the abuse of our children," one parent told the trustees, according to *The Western Observer*. The parents suggested that gang members had beaten several students, had committed date-rape, were generally violent, and were responsible for the increasing amount of graffiti seen around town.

A week later, *The Western Observer* reported that George White's 1978 Ford LTD had been stolen and driven through southern Jones County, ripping down fences, running over mail boxes, and tearing down traffic signs. The car had ended up in a cotton field, its torn-up grille full of cotton leaves and bolls. Muddy footprints indicated that the culprits had run up and down over the car causing severe dents. In addition, the car's headliner was cut out, seats were ripped, the glove compartment stomped through, and obscenities had been scratched into the automobile's paint. Mr. White's only means of transportation was a total loss. It had been a senseless, destructive joy ride.

As if things were not bad enough, the December 13, 1990 issue of *The Western Observer* ran the following headline: "No Christmas Dinner from Jack and Bea." The year before they had served nearly six hundred meals.

The custom had come to an end because in late summer of 1990, just before school was about to begin, vandals committed a senseless break-in. Everyone in town knew that Jack and Bea never locked the doors to the café. The public was invited to come in and fix a pot of coffee, or anything else for that matter, any time of the day or night, whether the Hornsbys were there or not. What Jack Hornsby found when he went to work that morning was a nightmare. Every cup, plate, and saucer had been thrown against the north wall of the dining room and broken. Every table was turned over, some were broken, one was thrown through a plate glass window facing Commercial Street. The Hornsby's large walk-in refrigerator was open and the contents emptied onto the floor. All of the food was ruined. The cash register, Bea's usual battle station, had been thrown to the floor and broken. At least twenty dollars in change and bills were scattered over the floor, indicating that money had not been the object of the break-in.

Sometime later that morning, a young man presented himself at the Anson Hospital Emergency Room. He had suffered severe lacerations while participating in the vandalism the night before. A police investigation revealed that three boys were involved. One was the son of one of Jack Hornsby's best fishing buddies. Sheer pleasure in destroying someone's property was the apparent motive, although there were unconfirmed reports that the youths had been on drugs. By one estimate, the wanton destruction cost the Hornsbys nearly $10,000. This year, they could not afford to give Anson their Christmas gift.

Together these events could have had the town on the ropes. Fortunately, there were also some hopeful developments. That same summer, a small manufacturing firm, Fashion Dynamics, had decided to make Anson its home. It was the first bright economic news since Anson had learned that the state of Texas was considering building a new prison in the county. Anson had made a strong bid for the prison but was eventually edged out by Abilene. Fashion Dynamics hired eight locals to work in their plant, which they set up in a building just north of the county courthouse on Commercial Street where once a thriving John Deere tractor dealership had been housed. Fashion Dynamics eventually hoped to hire thirty to forty employees making quality western dusters, a garment that looks like an overcoat, of the sort that cowboys used to wear. The fall 1990 University of Texas football team poster featured the players wearing their

western dusters and cowboy hats and looking very tough. Perhaps the dusters would launch a new wave of Texas chic.

Another bright spot on the horizon was that Western Texas
College, a two-year college based in Snyder, was trying to set
up a satellite campus in town. Their first effort in the summer
of 1990 had failed. Not enough students had enrolled. In the fall,
however, they had offered English 101 and American History,
in addition to two courses in criminal justice, which, according
to local publicity, would help students obtain jobs in the prison
now under construction between Anson and Abilene. More than
anything, the town spirit remained strangely optimistic. The
Tigers, Anson's high school football team, had just won the dis-
trict championship. Things couldn't be all that bad.

But the resilience of Anson's residents was perhaps best reflected in their response to the vandalism at Bea's café. Within
an hour of the discovery of the break-in, at least twenty people
had come down to help Jack and Bea. They brought cups and
dishes from their own homes and plywood to board up the
broken plate-glass window. They swept and cleaned and
mopped. Someone lent Jack money to go down to Anson's only
remaining grocery store and buy enough produce and meat to
put a menu together for the day. Within four hours, Jack and
Bea were back in business, ready for the lunch crowd.

Time had changed Anson. When twenty-five years ago, few non-
white families lived in town, now one-third of Anson's residents
were Mexican-American or African-American. Weddings like that
of Stephanie Lollar to Ramiro Perez were common, much to the
consternation of many in the white community. All Mercy Torres's
children had married whites. On the other hand, Jack and Bea
Hornsby's marriage was simply a given reality in Anson; no one
seemed to think much about it. Y. Z. Jimenez, the only Mexican-
American farmer in the county, had married a white woman after the death of his first wife from cancer. The examples were
countless. Life in Anson, like the rest of America, was changing.

The exception was Anson's African-American population. The
few blacks in Anson were poorer, as a whole, than everyone else

in town. They were as marginalized as ever. I found no black clerks in the stores, no blacks on the police force, no black cheerleaders or class presidents. The handful of blacks living in Anson seemed almost invisible—a familiar feeling within that community.

Without being fully cognizant of it, the Anson Church of Christ had been engaged in a battle with a world it could not understand, much less accommodate. The changes included every major aspect of their lives. Cotton farming was now viewed by some as a glorified welfare program, as the government propped up the prices and told farmers how much they could plant and when to plant it. While this theoretically ensured a livelihood for the farmer, most farmers were relieved if they could make ends meet. As was happening all over rural America, farmers were being squeezed out, their lands bought up by larger and larger conglomerates. Few farmers saw any future in a way of life that for generations had sustained their families and their community. For this reason, fewer still wanted their children to follow in their footsteps.

One afternoon Dave Reves, the retired sheriff, had taken me to the "Anson Club" where Anson's white men, most of them elderly, played dominoes every afternoon. The domino hall was as good an index as any that things would never be the same again.

The domino hall had once been a hub of activity in Anson. Local politics, opinions about American agricultural policy, the effects of current weather conditions on the cotton crop, as well as noteworthy gossip, all received extensive play between domino hands. While these topics were still discussed, the Anson Club had lost its sense of vibrancy. Not many weighty decisions were made in this little building anymore. The game of dominoes had become less and less a medium through which these vital discussions took place, and increasingly an end in itself.

Dave Reves beckoned me over to the wall opposite the soda machine. A board hung on it that Reves identified as the membership roster. It contained some fifty or sixty names, but at least half of them had been crossed out. Most of these had died, but a few had moved to retirement homes or to live near their

Domino players at the Anson Club Domino Hall. Photo: Nancy Scanlan.

grown children. There were no Mexican-American names on the roster and I assumed none were African-American. Thus, the roster represented a kind of unobtrusive measure, an artifact from a prior era in which Anson's ethnic divisions were much more firmly drawn.

"There's just a few of us left now," Reves lamented, "and there are hardly any young people. Most of *them* don't seem that interested in dominoes."

I could see that it was true just looking at the two tables of domino players across the room from us, as they slapped their dominos down and voiced their excitement at a good scoring run. Most of them were retired, wearing their gimme hats from local cotton gins or tractor dealerships, boots, and blue jeans or overalls. There probably wasn't a domino player under 65 years of age in the place. Reves said that dues were only three dollars a month, but they were afraid that it might become necessary to increase them. The Anson Club's insurance premiums had skyrocketed for some unknown reason.

A past way of life was evaporating from consciousness. Reves was not mourning the loss of the south's Jim Crow laws and the racist reality they had enforced. Reves was mourning the loss of his friends. But it was more than that. He was mourning the loss of a way of life. He was mourning the death of the familiar.

Immense social change, of the sort the United States has experienced in the last three decades, defies simplistic formulations. Economic, political, and social elements clearly play important roles in how such change affects us. However, whatever the relative admixture of these elements, they come to reside, ultimately, in the psychological, where they are represented as subjective realities and where they are responded to in accord with these. Social change always reconfigures individual lives. As I drove out of Anson, past Bea's café and the Anson Church of Christ and the Hatahoe, headed south toward Abilene, I thought of the people I had met in Anson. In urban America, the anonymous character of city life can shield us from seeing how individuals grapple with social realities. In Anson, these realities were inescapable, brutal, a fact that made each and every person in this small community a more direct participant. This circumstance brought the issues into relief, but did not change their primary features. In urban America, there was more room for self-deception and insulation than there was here in rural Texas, where everyone, for better or for worse, had to come to grips with the immediacy of these issues.

Back in Austin, I renewed my subscription to *The Western Observer,* combing its pages for news of people I knew. I read the letters to the editor, the obituaries, the "Activity Center News" column, and stories about the winners of the 4-H competitions, the crop reports, and the fate of the Anson High School Tigers. I found it reassuring that life just seemed to go on out there in West Texas.

From my study at home in Austin, looking out at the bougainvilleas on the back patio, I reflected on my experiences in Anson. One of Dave Reves's favorite adages kept coming back to me: "Time changes everything and everybody, except downright honesty." I had heard it at least a hundred times as the ex-sheriff and I traversed the dusty roads of Jones County. The essential truth of this adage, whatever its origin, had increasingly impressed me over the years. It spoke to the inevitability of change. Perhaps it also spoke to a universal ambivalence regarding change, even good change. But it also spoke to an ultimate faith in human character: faith that regardless of the conflicts and hatreds and resentments with which human history is perennially wrapped, essential hope remains.

Change was everywhere in Anson. Virtually every facet of that community had been altered in just a few decades—its economy, its demography, its place within the broader social landscape of America. Yet, certain transcendent truths prevailed. I felt them in the interviews as I listened to them in my study. I saw them in the faces and landscapes in my many photographs of Anson and Jones County. Like people everywhere, fate, history, and human nature itself had orchestrated the divisions that defined the lives of the people of Anson—a people groping for common ground in a complex world.

References

Arce, C. H., Murquin, E., and Parker Frisbie, W. (1987). Phenotype and life changes of Chicanos. *Hispanic Journal of Behavioral Sciences* 9:19–32.

Allport, G. (1954) *The Nature of Prejudice.* Cambridge, MA: Addison-Wesley.

"A sweetness tempers the south's bitter past." *New York Times* July 31, 1994.

Bellah, R. N., Madsen, R., Sullivan, W. M., et al. (1985). *Habits of the Heart: Individualism and Commitment in American Life.* New York: Harper & Row.

Bion, W. R. (1959). *Experiences in Groups and Other Papers.* New York: Basic Books.

Blos, P. (1968). *The Adolescent Passage.* New York: International Universities Press.

Bollas, C. (1987). *The Shadow of the Object.* London: Free Association.

Borges, J. L. (1954). *Historia Universal de la Infamia.* Buenos Aires: Emecé Editores, S. A.

Braddock, I., Crain, R., and McParkland, J. (1984). A long-term view of school desegregation: some recent studies of graduates as adults. *Phi Delta Kappan* 66:259–264.

Brion, M. (1929). *Bartolomé de Las Casas: Father of the Indians.* New York: E. P. Dutton.

Cardenas, J. (1977). School desegregation in metropolitan areas: Choices and perspectives: a national conference, March 15–16. National Institute of Education. Washington, DC: U.S. Government Printing Office.

Castillo, B. D. del (1980). *Historia de la Conquista de Nueva España.* Mexico City: Porrúa.

Chused, J. F. (1991). The evocative power of enactments. *Journal of the American Psychoanalytic Association* 39: 615–640.

Coles, R. (1964). *Children of Crisis: A Study of Courage and Fear.* Boston: Little, Brown.

——— (1977). *Eskimos. Chicanos, Indians: Volume IV of Children in Crisis.* Boston: Little, Brown.

Conference Report (1977). *Desegregation and education concerns of the Hispanic community.* Washington, DC: National Institute of Education.

Crain, R., and Strauss, J. (1985). *School Desegregation and Black Occupational Attainments: Results from Long-Term Experiment.* Baltimore: Johns Hopkins University, Center for Social Organization of Schools.

Davidson, M. J., and Cooper, C. L. (1992). *Shattering the Glass Ceiling: The Woman Manager.* London: Paul Chapman.

de Tocqueville, A. (1969). *Democracy in America,* trans. G. Lawrence, ed. J. P. Mayer. New York: Doubleday, Anchor.

Dole, A. A. (1995). Why not drop race as a term? *American Psychologist* 50:40.

Feagin, J. R. (1978). *Racial and Ethnic Relations.* Englewood, NJ: Prentice-Hall.

Fehrenback, T. R. (1968). *Lone Star: A History of Texas and the Texans.* New York: Collier Books.

Fornari, F. (1966). *The Psychoanalysis of War.* Trans, A. Pfeifer. Bloomington: Indiana University Press, 1975.

Freud S. (1923). The ego and the superego. *Standard Edition* 19.

——— (1926). Address to the society of B'nai B'rith. *Standard Edition* 20.

Gaiter, L. (1994). The revolt of the black bourgeoisie. *New York Times Magazine,* June 26.

Geertz, C. (1973). *The Interpretation of Cultures*: New York: Basic Books.

Giovacchini, P. (1986). *Developmental Disorders*. Northvale, NJ: Jason Aronson.

Glass, J. M. (1985). *Delusion: Internal Dimensions of Political Life*. Chicago: University of Chicago Press.

Grinberg, L. (1977) *Introduction to the Work of Bion: Groups, Knowledge, Psychoses, Thought, Transformations, Psychoanalytic Practice*. New York: Jason Aronson.

Grinberg, L., and Grinberg, R. (1984). *Psychoanalytic Perspectives on Migration and Exile*. New Haven: Yale University Press.

Hanke, L. (1959). *Aristotle and the American Indians: A Study in Race Prejudice in the Modern World*. London: Hollis & Carter.

——— (1964). *The First Social Experiments in America: A Study of the Development of Spanish Indian Policy in the Sixteenth Century*. Gloucester, MA: P. Smith, Harvard Historical Monographs, 5.

——— (1965). *The Spanish Struggle for Justice in the Conquest of America*. Boston: Little, Brown.

Hartmann, H. (1939). *Ego Psychology and the Problems of Adaptation*. New York: International Universities Press.

Hochschild, J. L. (1984). *The New American Dilemma: Liberal Democracy and School Desegregation*. New Haven: Yale University Press.

Horowitz, D. L. (1985). *Ethnic Groups in Conflict*. Berkeley: University of California Press.

Ireland, P. R. (1994). *The Policy Challenge of Ethnic Diversity: Immigrant Politics in France and Switzerland*. Cambridge: Harvard University Press.

Isaacs, J. R. (1975). *Idols of the Tribe: Group Identity and Political Change*. New York: Harper & Row.

Jhally, S., and Lewis, J. (1992). *Enlightened Racism: The Cosby Show, Audiences, and the Myth of the American Dream*. Boulder, CO.: University of Colorado Press.

Kernberg, O. (1975) *Borderline Conditions and Pathological Narcissism*. New York: Jason Aronson.

————— (1976). *Object Relations Theory and Clinical Psycho-analysis*. New York: Jason Aronson.

————— (1980). *Internal World and External Reality: Object Relations Theory Applied*. New York: Jason Aronson.

Kohut, H. (1971). *The Analysis of the Self*. New York: International Universities Press.

————— (1977). *The Restoration of the Self*. New York: International Universities Press.

Kraft, C. H. (1963). Christian conversion or cultural conversion? *Practical Anthropology* 10:179–186.

Kristeva, J. (1991). *Strangers to Ourselves*. New York: Columbia University Press.

Kubie, L. E. (1965). The ontogeny of racial prejudice. *The Journal of Nervous and Mental Disorders* 141 :265–273.

Limón, J. E. (1994). *Dancing with the Devil: Society and Cultural Poetics in Mexican-American South Texas*. Madison, WI: University of Wisconsin Press.

Locke, A. R. (1992). *Race Contacts and Interracial Relations: Lectures on the Theory and Practice of Race*. Washington, DC: Howard University Press.

Mahler, M. S., Pine, F., and Bergman, A. (1975). *Psychological Birth of the Human Infant: Symbiosis and Individuation*. New York: Basic Books.

McLaughlin, J. T. (1991). Clinical and theoretical aspects of enactment. *Journal of the American Psychoanalytic Association* 39: 595–614.

Modell, A. H. (1968). *Object Love and Reality: An Introduction to a Psychoanalytic Theory of Object Relations*. New York: International Universities Press.

————— (1976). The "holding environment" and the therapeutic action of psychoanalysis. *Journal of the American Psychoanalytic Association* 24: 285–307.

————— (1991). A confusion of tongues, or, whose reality is it? *Psychoanalytic Quarterly* 60: 227–244.

Montejano, D. (1987). *Anglos and Mexicans in the Making of Texas. 1836–1986*. Austin: University of Texas Press.

Nida, E. A. (1965). Culture and church growth. *Practical Anthropology* 12:22–37.

Oliver, M. (1994). Politics in black and white: race and power in Los Angeles. *Contemporary Sociology*, July, 23(4): 481.

Pao, P. (1965). The role of hatred in the ego. *Psychoanalytic Quarterly* 34:257–264.

Paz, O. (1950). *El Laberinto de la Soledad*. Mexico: Fondo de Cultura Economica.

Pinderhughes, C. A. (1970). The universal resolution of ambivalence by paranoia with an example in black and white. *American Journal of Psychotherapy* 24:597–610.

——— (1979). Differential bonding: toward a theory of psychophysiological theory of stereotyping. *American Journal of Psychiatry* 136:33–37.

Pinderhughes, E. (1989). *Understanding Race. Ethnicity, and Power: The Key to Efficacy in Clinical Practice*. New York: Free Press.

Pine, F. (1990). *Drive, Ego, Object, and Self: A Synthesis for Clinical Work*. New York: Basic Books.

Quintana, S. M. (1994). A model of ethnic perspective-taking ability applied to Mexican-American children and youth. *International Journal of Intercultural Relations* 18(4): 419–448.

Relethford, J. H., Stern, M. P., Gaskell, S. P., and Hazuda, H. P. (1983). Social class, admixture and skin color variation in Mexican-Americans and Anglo-Americans living in San Antonio, Texas. *American Journal of Physical Anthropology* 61: 97–102.

Rist, R. C. (1978). *The Invisible Children: School Integration in American Society*. Cambridge: Harvard University Press.

Roberts, S. (1993). *Who We Are: A Portrait of America*. New York: Times Books.

Rodriguez, R. (1992). *Days of Obligation: An Argument with My Mexican Father*. New York: Penguin Books.

Russell, C. H. (1990). *The Carrot and the Stick for School Desegregation Policy: Magnet Schools or Forced Busing?* Philadelphia: Temple University Press.

St. John, N. H. (1981). The effects of school desegregation on children: a new look at the research evidence. In *Race and Schooling in the City,* A. Yarmolinsky, L. Liebman, and C. S. Shelling, eds. Cambridge: Harvard University Press.

Scott, R. (1981). *Education and Ethnicity: the US Experiment in School Integration.* Washington, D.C.: The Council for Social and Economic Studies. *Journal of Social, Political and Economic Studies Monograph Series* 17: 347–378.

Shils, E. (1957). Primordial, personal, sacred, and civil ties. *British Journal of Sociology* 8: 130–145.

Spitz, R. A. (1965). *The First Year of Life: A Psychoanalytic Study of Normal and Deviant Development of Object Relations.* New York: International Universities Press.

Stanfield, J. H. (1982). Urban public school desegregation: the reproduction of normative white domination. *The Journal of Negro Education* 51: 90–100.

Telles, E. E., and Murguia, E. (1990). Phenotypic discrimination and income differences among Mexican Americans. *Social Science Quarterly* 71: 682–696.

Tractenberg, M. (1989). Circumcision, crucifixion, and anti-Semitism: the antithetical character of ideologics and their symbols which contain crossed lines. *International Review of Psycho-Analysis* 16:459–471.

Volkan, V. D. (1986). The narcissism of minor differences in the psychological gap between opposing nations. *Psychoanalytic Inquiry* 6:175–191.

——— (1988). *The Need to Have Enemies and Allies: From Clinical Practice to International Relationships.* Northvale, NJ: Jason Aronson.

Winnicott, D. W. (1953). Transitional objects and transitional phenomena. *International Journal of Psycho-Analysis* 34: 899–97.

X, Malcolm (1965). *The Autobiography of Malcolm X.* With the assistance of Alex Haley. New York: Ballantine Books.

Yee, A. H., Fairchild, H. H., Weizmann, F., and Wyatt, G. E. (1993). Addressing psychology's problems with race. *American Psychologist* 48: 1132–1140.

Index